Praise for *The Ecological Hoofprint*

'In *The Ecological Hoofprint* Weis puts meat at the centre of global problems like climate change, poverty, workers' rights, and speciesism. Anyone seeking a just and sustainable world needs to consider his compelling argument that radical change must start by combating the meatification of the human diet.'

Peter Singer, Princeton University, author of Animal Liberation

'Tony Weis has a mind that spans a multitude of disciplines, from philosophy to international political economy, from ecology to biology. In *The Ecological Hoofprint*, he brings these considerable skills to craft a concise, readable, and important reading of today's meatified world. It's an analysis that couldn't be more timely nor more urgent.'

Raj Patel, author of Stuffed and Starved: The Hidden Battle for the World Food System

'With the metaphor of the ecological hoofprint Tony Weis sounds a clear warning about the perils of the rising global consumption of meat. The powerful message of this book is that ascending the animal protein ladder is a formula for deepening social inequalities and compounding ecological risk. With compelling detail the author demonstrates that meatification is an inefficient and potentially catastrophic use of planetary resources. This didactic book provides an unforgettable perspective on the illusion of identifying animal protein consumption with modern progress.'

Philip McMichael, Cornell University, author of Development and Social Change: A Global Perspective

'With Tony Weis's powerful insights, we see that humanity's sudden, catastrophic shift to meat-centric farming and eating – killing us and our planet – is neither inevitable nor progress. We learn we have real choice. Packed with startling facts and framed in a compelling narrative, *The Ecological Hoofprint* is a mighty motivator. Bravo!'

Frances Moore Lappé, author of Diet for a Small Planet *and co-founder of The Small Planet Institute*

'Weis delivers a penetrating and systematic structural analysis of the global industrial feeds-livestock complex that reveals the extent to which Earth's resources are subsumed to the logic of cheap meat production. Insightful, accessible, compelling, this is a must read for scholars and students of the food system.'

Colin Sage, University College Cork, author of Environment and Food

'Weis provides an intellectually compelling argument against the industrial farming of livestock. While recognizing that increasing meat consumption is often viewed favorably – as evidence of the globalization of the Western diet – he carefully details the costs for human health, the environment, and industrially reared animals. Weis calls for an urgent reappraisal of factory farming as a first step in reducing the ecological hoofprint on planet meat. It's a great book!'

Geoffrey Lawrence, professor of sociology and leader of the Food Security Program, Global Change Institute, University of Queensland

'A must read if you want to understand the scale, inefficiency, and wide-ranging impact of the rapid "meatification" of diets since the mid-twentieth century. The number of slaughtered animals, Tony Weis notes, has rocketed from 8 billion to 64 billion in fifty years. The dynamic driving this ecologically damaging change, he rightly argues, is an industrial grain-oilseed-livestock complex driven by the demands of capitalism to seek new means of increasing returns, which involves totally reorganizing nature.'

Geoff Tansey, co-editor of The Future Control of Food *and member and trustee of The Food Ethics Council*

About the author

Tony Weis is an associate professor of geography at the University of Western Ontario, with research broadly located in the field of political ecology. He is the author of *The Global Food Economy: The Battle for the Future of Farming* (Zed Books, 2007), and numerous articles and book chapters on environmental and development issues regarding agriculture.

THE ECOLOGICAL HOOFPRINT

THE GLOBAL BURDEN OF INDUSTRIAL LIVESTOCK

Tony Weis

Zed Books
LONDON | NEW YORK

The Ecological Hoofprint: the global burden of industrial livestock was first published in 2013 by Zed Books Ltd, 7 Cynthia Street, London N1 9JF, UK and Room 400, 175 Fifth Avenue, New York, NY 10010, USA

www.zedbooks.co.uk

Set in Monotype Plantin and FFKievit by Ewan Smith, London NW5
Index: ed.emery@thefreeuniversity.net
Cover design: www.alice-marwick.co.uk
Printed and bound by CPI Group (UK) Ltd, Croydon, CRO 4YY

Distributed in the USA exclusively by Palgrave Macmillan, a division of St Martin's Press, LLC, 175 Fifth Avenue, New York, NY 10010, USA

A catalogue record for this book is available from the British Library
Library of Congress Cataloging in Publication Data available

ISBN 978 1 78032 097 7 hb
ISBN 978 1 78032 096 0 pb

CONTENTS

FIGURES AND BOXES

Figures

Boxes

To Jenn, Marley, and Kevay,
for your abiding love and support

INTRODUCTION: MEATIFICATION AND WHY IT MATTERS

The vector of meatification

On a global scale, human diets are in the midst of a great transformation, which is wrapped up in the radical narrowing of agricultural production. One of the most fundamental aspects of this is the rising consumption of animal flesh and derivatives, principally from pigs, poultry, and cattle. The average person today eats almost twice as much meat as did the average person only two generations ago, along with many more eggs, in a world with more than twice as many people now as then. In 1961, just over three billion people ate an average of 23 kg of meat and 5 kg of eggs a year. By 2011, 7 billion people ate 43 kg of meat and 10 kg of eggs a year. This translates to a *quadrupling* of world meat production in a mere half-century, from 71 to 297 million tonnes, and an even greater rise in world egg production, from 15 to 69 million tonnes. World milk production more than doubled, roughly in line with human population growth, with the average person consuming 104 kg in 2010.[1]

Industrial livestock production is the driving force behind the rapid growth in meat and egg consumption, in what are variously referred to as Intensive or Industrial Livestock Operations (ILOs), Concentrated Animal Feeding Operations (CAFOs), or factory farms and feedlots. This transformation permeates everyday life in a way that is both intimate, in the bodily encounter with food, and overwhelmingly unconscious. Rapid growth is expected to continue in the coming decades. By 2050, the Food and Agriculture Organization (FAO) of the United Nations projects that global meat production will rise to 52 kg per person in a world with 9.3 billion people, which amounts to 484 million tonnes (see Figure 0.1). Put another way, if the current course continues, there will be about one third more people and two-thirds more meat produced in four decades than there is today.[2]

This broad picture contains huge disparities. Although increasing per capita meat consumption is occurring almost everywhere, people in rich countries consume vastly more meat than do most people in

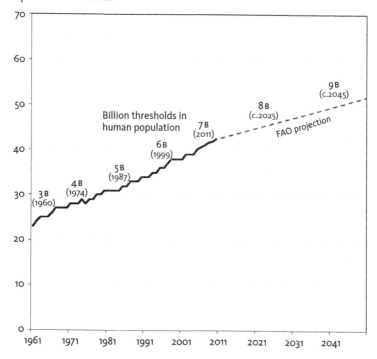

0.1 Global per capita meat consumption (kg/person) (*sources*: FAOSTATS 2013 and UNFPA 2011)

the global South. To take one simple example, between 2001 and 2010, an average American consumed roughly eight times more meat than someone in Africa and over twenty times more meat than someone in South Asia.[3] At the same time, global-scale inequalities tend to be mirrored in class disparities within poor countries, while the biggest consumption increases are occurring in the world's fastest-growing economies – and the upper and middle classes within them – with China and Brazil in the vanguard. China, for instance, now produces and consumes roughly half of the world's total pig meat.[4]

When the lens moves from volume increases to individual animals consumed, the pace of growth becomes even more staggering. In a mere half-century, from 1961 to 2010, the global population of slaughtered animals leapt from roughly 8 to 64 billion, which will double again to 120 billion by 2050 if current rates of growth continue. The stunning rise in the number of individual animals slaughtered reflects the absolute growth in the volume of meat production and consumption, the quickening turnover time for livestock in industrial systems, and the increasing shift towards poultry birds, which have smaller bodies and are more efficient – or better, *less inefficient* – at converting feed to food than larger animals. The FAO projects that poultry consumption will increase by 2.3 times between 2010 and 2050, in comparison to an increase of between 1.4 and 1.8 times with other livestock.[5]

This general trajectory has been termed the 'livestock revolution' in one frequently cited report.[6] It is also often described in terms of a 'nutritional transition' towards improved diets, with the rising consumption of animal protein portrayed as a more or less inevitable aspiration, part of humans' omnivorous nature, that gets materialized as individuals and societies become wealthier and there are increasing quantities of meat in the marketplace. This imagery might seem plain enough, as per capita meat consumption has clearly marched in step with rising affluence, but it is not nearly as simple as this. The framing of massive inequalities in consumption through the lens of a universal nutritional transition harkens to development theories about the transition to modernity, in which societies of high mass consumption such as the USA are presented as the summit that can be reached and should be aspired to by all countries.[7] Such transitional narratives have a naturalizing effect, because if different parts of the world are seen to be located at different stages along the same course, with all moving towards an improved condition, it can serve to legitimize the course itself and make large inequalities seem less troubling.

Layered onto this is an insistence by prominent actors that further yield enhancement is the key to solving present and future world food problems, which is sometimes described in terms of closing global 'yield gaps,' especially in poor 'under-yielding' countries. Yield-centric narratives are also linked to an insistence that world food production must double by mid-century if it is to meet future demand.[8] But the scale of chronic hunger (nearly one billion people) and malnourishment today, and expected population growth (more than two billion), still do not come close to adding up to a doubling scenario, which must also be understood to contain an uncritical expectation that meat consumption will continue climbing rapidly. These assumptions – there *will* be more meat consumed, total food production *must* double – are influential starting points for contemporary debates about agricultural futures. They are also extremely dubious and dangerous ones.

Rather than a nutritional transition, I prefer to mark the increasing and highly uneven global consumption of meat with more evocative terminology: as the *'meatification'* of diets.[9] First, this seeks to call attention to the pace and scale of change. For most of the 10,000-year history of agriculture, meat, eggs, and dairy were consumed periodically and in relatively small volumes, and it was not until the industrialization of livestock production that they began to shift from the periphery to the center of human diets on a world scale. Secondly, the notion of meatification seeks to dispel the imagery of a course that is natural, inevitable, or benign. Great volumes of industrial grains and oilseeds are being inefficiently cycled through soaring populations of concentrated animals, with much usable nutrition lost in the metabolic processes of animals before getting converted to meat, eggs, and dairy. The ensuing production is then highly skewed toward wealthier consumers when, as indicated, one in seven people on earth are hungry or malnourished and many more in varying states of food insecurity. Globally, livestock consume around one third of all grains and a much larger share of all oilseeds, and flows of crops through livestock are much higher in industrialized countries than in poor ones. The aim of this book is to provide a new way of understanding the momentousness of this trajectory, its multidimensional impacts, and the urgency of confronting it.

Rising attention

This aim should not imply that this book is stepping into a vacuum. On the contrary, there has been a great deal of important work examining the nature and impacts of industrial livestock. Three of the key foundations were Ruth Harrison's pioneering assessment of the early stages of industrializing livestock, Frances Moore Lappé's seminal argument about the global injustice of cycling rising volumes of grain through livestock in a world of widespread hunger, and Peter Singer's moral-philosophical case against speciesism, which included a searing indictment of the treatment of animals in factory farms.[10] These were followed by a number of other pivotal contributions that helped establish the major lines of critical analysis on industrial livestock,[11] which can be broadly seen to focus on:

- human health (e.g. chronic diseases, food safety risks);
- environmental impacts (e.g. climate change, water use and pollution, biodiversity loss);

- the decline of family farms, rural life, and small towns;
- hazardous, insecure, and poorly paid labour; and,
- the suffering of farm animals.

The growing significance of these problems is reflected in the proliferation of both scholarly and more popularly oriented literature. There has also been increasing attention to the trajectory of livestock production within key UN organizations, most notably the landmark FAO report *Livestock's Long Shadow*.[12] The essential message of this report – the 'long shadow' – was that livestock production commands extensive amounts of land, water, and resources and entails a heavy pollution load, which loom over most major environmental problems, including making one of the greatest contributions to climate change of any economic sector. The contribution of livestock to climate change was further underlined when the chairman of the Intergovernmental Panel on Climate Change (IPCC) stated that reducing meat consumption could have a significant role in cutting greenhouse gas (GHG) emissions.[13]

Concerns about industrial livestock are beginning to penetrate mainstream environmental thought and activism, a reflection of which can be seen in a selection of headlines in popular green magazines and the corporate news media. A recent spate of critical documentary films is another significant part of the rising attention to the negative impacts of industrial livestock, as are compelling visual-informational resources on the internet (Box o.1).

Yet while awareness of the impacts of industrial livestock production is surely growing, it should not be exaggerated. When the environmental impacts of industrial livestock are discussed, too often responses are framed in limited ways, centered mainly on individual ethics but without connection to other struggles. Such emphases can serve to diminish the interconnectedness of problems and the magnitude of the whole, and divert attention away from the system of production. But the far bigger matter remains the continuing unconsciousness with which immense volumes of pork, ham, bacon, pepperoni, hotdogs, sausages, hamburgers, steak, beef, ribs, shawarma, souvlaki, kofta, chicken balls, nuggets, wings, breasts, eggs, milk, cheese, and miscellaneous flesh, derivatives, and by-products are consumed. The clearest indication of the limits of awareness and concern lies in the fact that meatification on a world scale shows

> **Box 0.1 Rising attention: selected examples from media, film, and the internet**
>
> Popular 'green' magazines:
>
> 'Meat: the slavery of our time.' *E Magazine* (July/August 2008)
>
> 'Meat: now, it's not personal! But like it or not, meat-eating is becoming a problem for everyone on the planet.' *World-Watch Magazine* (July/August 2004)
>
> 'Meat factories: hellish hog plants, lakes of sewage, and lifeless waterways.' *Sierra* (January/February1999)
>
> Corporate news media:
>
> 'Save the planet: stop eating meat.' *Maclean's* (30 March 2010)
>
> 'Gut check: here's the meat of the problem.' *Washington Post* (29 July 2009)
>
> 'The cow is a climate bomb.' *Der Spiegel* (27 August 2008)
>
> 'Rethinking the meat guzzler.' *New York Times* (27 January 2008)
>
> 'Pollution on the hoof.' *Los Angeles Times* (15 October 2007)
>
> Documentaries with a major focus on industrial livestock production:
>
> *Forks over Knives* (2011)
> *Death on a Factory Farm* (2009)
> *Peaceable Kingdom: The Journey Home* (2009)
> *Pig Business* (2009)
> *Earthlings* (2005)

no signs of slowing while, as emphasized, the expectation that there will be continuing growth is a major part of calls for the doubling of world food production. The FAO, an agency that simultaneously influences dominant narratives about world agriculture and is an important barometer of them, exemplifies this momentum: though it reports on the 'long shadow' cast by livestock and warns that approaching a doubling of production would 'place a considerable

The Emotional World of Farm Animals (2004)
A Cow at My Table (1998)

Documentaries focusing on industrial agriculture, containing substantial critiques of some aspect of industrial livestock production:

Farmageddon: The Unseen War on American Family Farms
(2010)
Food Inc. (2009)
King Corn (2007)
Our Daily Bread (2005)

Internet animations and other resources:

Animal Visuals (www.animalvisuals.org)
The Meatrix (www.themeatrix.com)
Mad Sausage (www.madsausage.com)
Farm to Fridge (www.meatvideo.com)
CAFO (www.cafothebook.org)
Meat (www.meat.org)
HumaneMyth (www.humanemyth.org)
United Poultry Concerns (www.upc-online.org)
The True Cost of Food (www.truecostoffood.org)
Compassion in World Farming (www.ciwf.org.uk)
A Cage is a Cage: The Human Farming Association (www.
hfa.org)
Food and Water Watch (www.factoryfarmmap.org)
Physicians Committee for Responsible Medicine (www.pcrm.
org)
Academy of Nutrition and Dietetics (www.eatright.org)

burden on already strained natural resources,'[14] it gives little indication that this course can or should be challenged in a major way, instead focusing much more on things like improved management, regulations, and monitoring, and more technological innovation, from facility design to enhancing the ratio at which feed is converted into flesh, eggs, and dairy.

The industrial grain-oilseed-livestock complex and the ecological hoofprint

To appreciate the vector of meatification, the strength of its momentum, and the impacts of industrial livestock production, they need to be set within the dynamics of the *industrial grain-oilseed-livestock complex*. The industrial grain-oilseed-livestock complex is the dominant system of agriculture across the temperate world, and is spreading to significant parts of the tropics. Its landscapes can be likened to islands of concentrated livestock within seas of grain and oilseed monocultures, with soaring populations of a few livestock species reared in high densities, disarticulated from the surrounding fields. These islands of concentrated livestock and seas of monocultures are then rearticulated by heavy flows of crops such as corn/maize, barley, sorghum, soybeans, and rapeseed/canola cycling through animals. This disarticulation and rearticulation is mediated by an array of technologies, inputs, and large corporations, and marked by the loss of large volumes of usable nutrition.

Revolutionary increases in yield and output per farmer have been fundamental to this system, which underpins world food security and has reconfigured diets in very uneven ways. On one hand, productivity increases have stoked the lopsided meatification of diets discussed earlier; on the other, they have sown a severe dependence upon cheap grain imports in many poor countries. This has also simultaneously placed intense competitive pressures on small farm livelihoods, from the world's agro-industrial heartlands to impoverished, highly agrarian, and food import-dependent regions.[15] But high productivity and low prices belie deep instabilities, or what I have described as a series of *chronic biophysical contradictions*.[16] This implies that the biological and physical foundations of agriculture are being rapidly undermined by industrial productivity, which is in turn overridden in ways that hinge on the unsustainable use of non-renewable resources, particularly fossil energy, and generate tremendous emissions and wastes. It also means that the logic of efficiency which determines the price of cheap food – and has had an important role in shaping patterns of world food security – amounts to a giant illusion. However, this illusion is now starting to crack amid intensifying and converging problems of biodiversity loss, soil degradation, diminishing freshwater availability, declines in key non-renewable resources, and climate change. In other words, chronic biophysical contradictions are now accelerating. As this occurs, previously cheap industrial foods are bound to become more expensive, with the greatest vulnerability centered in the world's Low Income Food Import Dependent Countries (LIFDCs). Further, many LIFDCs are located in the semi-arid tropics, where climate change is projected to affect agriculture first and worst.

Today, much critical attention given to global food imbalances is focused on the stark disparities associated with the industrial agrofuel boom and the new land grabs. Industrial agrofuels are demanding rising shares of agricultural land and crop production, with dubious energetic budgets (i.e. there is limited energy returned relative to the energy invested in production), and there is an obvious regressivity to the growing competition between people with cars and people struggling to secure enough food. Agrofuels also factor in the land grabbing unfolding across the South, especially in Africa, in which varying combinations of transnational corporations, finance capital, sovereign wealth funds, and state investment agencies are conspiring with local elites and corrupt governments to grab large tracts of land for both productive and speculative uses.[17] Yet as important as the agrofuel boom is, it should not detract from the inequity and ecological impacts of industrial livestock production, which constitutes an older, bigger, and similarly regressive pull on world grain and oilseed harvests.

The increasing scale and industrialization of livestock production and the inherent feed conversion inefficiencies have a magnifying effect on the land area, water, energy, and other resources that must be devoted to grain and oilseed monocultures, and to the pollutants and GHG emissions ensuing from them. Added to this are the water, energy, and other inputs going into factory farms and feedlots, and the effluence pouring out of them. This means that the uneven meatification of diets is not only a *reflection* of global inequality but also a major factor *exacerbating* it, foremost through climate change.

Outline and arguments

Chapter 1 sets the context for assessing the environmental problems posed by the growth of industrial livestock production, and for why it is an underappreciated and very important aspect of global inequality. It starts by considering the decline of self-organizing ecosystems, the biodiversity crisis, and climate change, followed by influential narratives given to explain them that fixate on human population growth pressing up against asocial biophysical limits. These narratives continue to feature prominently in mainstream environmental movements, and are important to consider given how this book calls attention to a different 'population bomb' than the much more familiar one. This discussion also helps to highlight some of the major cross-currents and blind spots that prevail within the messy terrain of environmentalism, before pointing toward the need to center political economy in any understanding of environmental change and degradation – in line with the field of political ecology. A basic implication of this, which guides the approach in later chapters, is that it is important to consider the systemic imperatives which shape how resources get defined and how nature gets organized in the quest for incessant economic growth. Next, the landmark concept of the ecological footprint is marked as a valuable lens through which to frame environmental injustice, and to highlight the unequal responsibility for the impoverishment of the biosphere and for climate change. As a calculation, the ecological footprint seeks to approximate the resource budgets and pollution loads contained in production and consumption and then translate this into a measure of the ecological and atmospheric space needed to sustain them, which then folds into a valuable pedagogical tool. In complex modern societies where human interactions with ecosystems are overwhelmingly mediated through commodities and markets, the footprint can provide a valuable starting point into the nexus of social inequality and environmental problems, which is the connotation I hope to maintain in playing off the footprint metaphor and transposing hooves onto feet (the price of which is the semantic imprecision of using *hoof* to mark a framework that embraces not only ungulate farm mammals like pigs and cattle but also poultry birds, which represent by far the greatest number of animals and the fastest-growing dimension of industrial livestock by volume). Agriculture's ecological footprint is next drawn in broad contours, and from there the hoofprint is introduced as a framework for understanding the nature and impacts of industrial livestock production.

Chapter 2 establishes the big picture of an unequally meaty planet, examining the scale, growth, and inequality of meat consumption and production on a world scale. It starts by reviewing the historic shift of animal flesh and derivatives from the periphery to the center of human diets, and some of the key ideas that have accompanied this transition. A central argument is that narratives about universal nutrition transitions not only *correspond to* linear theories of development, as suggested earlier; they have been *embedded in* them, from European imperialism to China's current race up the 'animal protein ladder.' In other words, the meatification of diets has been a significant promise of modernization and treated as a visible marker of development. This discussion also briefly considers some of the major health and nutrition debates surrounding this dietary change, from the claims of protein superiority to the proliferation of chronic health problems linked to the Western diet, which helps to understand why it has been so celebrated – but also exaggerated – as a matter of human progress. The chapter concludes by exploring the highly imbalanced growth of world grain, oilseed, and livestock production and the tremendous disparities in food consumption it is entwined with. Here, attention is given to the deep and increasingly precarious dependence on cheap grain imports that exists in many poor countries, where the risks of rising world food prices and market shocks are compounding problems of widespread malnutrition, at the same time as the race to consume more animal protein continues in fast-industrializing countries. Taken together, the uneven meatification of diets and the imbalanced geography of the industrial grain-oilseed-livestock complex provide a basis for appreciating the lopsided burden of the ecological hoofprint, which gets developed in the following chapter.

Chapter 3 develops a systematic approach for understanding the industrial grain-oilseed-livestock complex, which is necessary to unravel the scope of its wide-ranging environmental burden. In the process, it aims to demystify the celebrated efficiency of industrial agriculture, which pivots on narrow metrics (tremendous productivity per worker and high yields of plants and animals) while concealing many un- and undervalued costs. The basic approach starts by considering the pressures driving the mechanization, standardization, and biological simplification of agricultural production, and how these generate or exacerbate a range of biophysical instabilities which are then overridden by an assortment of inputs, that in turn entail a range of resource demands. For heuristic purposes, systemic instabilities and overrides are examined at two basic levels: first, focusing on industrial grain and oilseed monocultures, and next at sites of industrial livestock production, which are intertwined through the large volumes of grains and oilseeds flowing inefficiently through animals. This means that the resource budgets and pollution loads associated with industrial livestock production are simultaneously *spatially diffuse* (in magnifying monoculture production) and *highly concentrated* (at factory farms and feedlots), and these must be added together to arrive at a full sense of the ecological hoofprint. Indeed, a central motivation in using the hoofprint metaphor is to highlight how sites of industrial livestock production dominate landscapes, command resources, and wreak environmental damage far beyond their immediate locations. The islands of concentrated livestock cannot be understood outside the seas of grains and oilseeds.

Chapter 4 starts by adding up the burden of industrial livestock production following the systemic framework developed in Chapter 3: first, focusing on the impacts on land, water, the atmosphere, and public health; and next, considering how the scale and nature of violence in this system represents a revolution in the way humans relate to other species, which then reverberates in especially dangerous and dehumanizing work. When we see the ecological hoofprint as a whole, it helps to make it clear why the continuing meatification of diets and expansion of industrial livestock production bear so heavily on the world's environment and development challenges, and threaten the very biophysical basis of agriculture. Although there is a powerful momentum behind this trajectory, from the corporate complexes directing it to consumer desires and narratives about diet and development, it is far from inevitable. In this spirit, the book concludes with a case for why the deindustrialization of livestock and the demeatification of diets are central to the hope of a more sustainable, just, and humane world, and why these problems cannot be reduced solely to a matter of dietary choice.

1 | CONTEXTUALIZING THE HOOFPRINT: GLOBAL ENVIRONMENTAL CHANGE AND INEQUALITY

Agriculture and the creeping simplification of ecosystems

For over 99 percent of the last 2 million years, 'our ancestors lived off the land in small, mobile groups.'[1] During this time, all energy was ultimately derived from the sun, converted by photosynthesis along with carbon dioxide (CO_2), nutrients, and water into usable biochemical forms. Humans harvested only a minuscule part of the total biomass contained in ecosystems through gathering, hunting, and fishing, and did little to impact the structure, self-organization, and process of succession toward climax communities, which are richest in species diversity and almost always have the highest net primary production (NPP) in any given bioregion.[2] Yet as part of nature and evolution, humans have always had some impact on the ecosystems and animal populations around them, and many gatherer-hunter societies were in fact agents of ecological change on a considerable scale. Some intermittently arrested succession through fire, modifying their environments in order to increase the abundance of key prey species, and there is much evidence that hunting pressures were implicated in significant extirpations and even in extinctions of large mammals before the rise of agriculture.[3]

Agriculture arose roughly ten thousand years ago and its expansion was the dominant force of ecological change over most of the Holocene, the relatively warm and stable geological epoch from the end of the last ice age that began around twelve thousand years ago. Agriculture revolutionized how humans obtained biomass and nutrients from the environment, gave rise to new class and gender hierarchies, and established new inter-species relations through the course of domestication. In a biophysical sense, the essence of the agricultural revolution was that humans began to direct photosynthetic activity (and not just appropriate its products) by reorganizing plants, animals, and physical materials within ecosystems and managing their interactions, in order to increase the volume of more proximate and easily accessible nutrition, energy, fibre, and other resources. This also entails a degree of intervention in the earth's biogeochemical cycles: the movement of elements or molecules through living organisms, the atmosphere, water bodies, the earth's crust, and the crucial interface between the crust and the living world, the soil. In particular, as Vandana Shiva emphasizes, agriculture might be understood, in part, as organizing cycles of 'living carbon.'[4]

Permanently arresting the process of natural succession toward climax communities also entails a reduction in the photosynthetic activity within a given area, and hence the biomass available to most other animals.[5] Thus, over millennia the slow but steady march of agriculture meant that human societies were displacing more diverse and biologically productive self-organizing ecosystems, and the space for non-domesticated species was inching slowly downward. But apart from the long-distance dispersions of domesticated plants and animals, which radiated from a small number of key hearths, agricultural societies were predominantly oriented within bioregions, bound by limits of technology, surpluses, storage, and usable biomass.

So long as the movement of goods was based on animal and human labor and biomass was the primary source of fuel, a heavy *friction of distance* prevailed. Put simply, most goods could not move very far, especially if they were bulky or perishable, and until very recently only a small number of agricultural products were ever traded across significant distances, and what was traded was not depended on for sustenance but rather had value for flavoring, preservation, or medicinal functions. Wind and water did enable some movement and grinding power, but it was not until around the fifteenth century that wind power began to be harnessed in a way that significantly reduced the friction of distance. The heavy friction of distance also conditioned agricultural practices for most of agrarian history, with the exceptions of the episodic introductions of new crops and livestock and the fact that some old agricultural societies did manage to draw irrigation across significant distances.

Agriculture poses a number of endemic biophysical challenges, such as preventing soil degradation, containing undesirable species (or 'pests,' the definition of which varies), and coping with weather and moisture variability, especially prolonged periods of dryness. The heavy friction of distance meant that solutions had to be largely place-based; that is, reliant on nearby resources and rooted in local ecological knowledge and innovation. The challenge of sustaining long-term soil health is among the most fundamental and underappreciated imperatives facing any civilization. Frequently dismissed as mere 'dirt,' soil is better understood as a thin and fragile 'living skin of the earth,' a dynamic combination of diverse organisms from microorganisms (e.g. bacteria, protozoa, fungi) to invertebrates (e.g. worms, insects), chemical elements (e.g. carbon, nitrogen, phosphorus, and potassium) and molecules, and larger physical materials undergoing interactive biological and chemical processes. As David Montgomery puts it: 'soil is our most underappreciated, least valued, and yet essential natural resource ... the whole biological enterprise of life outside the oceans depends on the nutrients soil produces and retains. These circulate through the ecosystem, moving from soil to plants and animals, and then back again into the soil.'[6] Appreciating soil as a living organ highlights how soil fundamentally underpins all terrestrial ecosystems and all human economies, and how it can reproduce and grow but can also become unhealthy and even die, as in desertification. Soil tends to build up slowly under conditions of natural succession, and when land is converted to agriculture soil tends to be lost faster than it forms – though this is not inevitable.

In order for agriculture to endure, then, farmers had to develop a range of localized practices to reduce erosion and enhance the biological activity, diversity, and recycling of organic matter within soils. Key practices included such things as: returning organic wastes and nutrients close to where they were withdrawn; designing intercropping patterns to limit soil erosion; terracing steeply sloping land; rotating crops; and establishing complementary roles for small livestock populations. With livestock, this meant things like grazing on fallowed land and small pastures, scavenging crop stubble and wastes around households, and depositing organic material through manure to fields. Sustaining healthy soils was also an important basis for containing 'pest' species and retaining moisture, goals achievement of which could be further enhanced by planting multiple crops in mutually beneficial combinations, or intercropping. Another key to successful farming was to understand relations between pests and their predators, and find ways of maintaining adequate populations of the latter. In sum, while agriculture inevitably simplifies ecosystems and arrests succession, durable farming landscapes nevertheless had to be premised on functional diversity, and had to approximate relatively 'closed-loop' cycles of organic and inorganic materials and the key elements they contain.[7]

This should not, however, imply an image of perfect equilibrium. First, agro-ecological knowledge was never static, and gradually advanced over time. Processes of learning, experimenting, accruing knowledge, and teaching were always guided by the goal of making improvements, starting with the selection of seeds and the breeding of animals. Secondly, short-term vulnerabilities could be reduced but were never eliminated, nor could this loop ever be entirely closed, particularly with respect to soil. The relationship between rates of soil loss and soil formation has thus been a crucial one historically; when managed effectively, societies could be stable over long periods, but when soils were severely depleted this had a powerful and recurring role in the decline of civilizations.[8] So while many lessons and much applied knowledge about functional diversity can be taken from non-industrial agricultural systems, which can have great value moving forward toward sustainable futures, this is not something that should be romanticized either.

From creeping to careening: the accelerating pace and scale of ecological change

The friction of distance started to lessen following the rise of capitalism, as expansion into new resource frontiers both motivated and materially bolstered great innovations in transportation technologies and infrastructures. Advances in nautical engineering first began to reshape world agriculture by dramatically expanding the long-distance dispersions of plants and animals, most notably in the Columbian Exchange between 'Old' and 'New' Worlds. As will be discussed further in the following chapter, livestock were at the vanguard of ecological change across large areas of the Americas and Australasia, expanding quickly in both intentional and unintentional ways, along with the more deliberate establishment of crops like wheat, barley, oats, sugar, and coffee, while crops like maize, potatoes, tomatoes, cocoa, and tobacco moved from the New World to the Old.[9] These transformations became tied, over time, to the increasing movement of tropical commodities from parts of the Americas, Africa, and Asia and temperate grain and livestock products from places such as North America, the southern cone of South America, Australasia, and the Indian Punjab. The expansion of European commodity frontiers into new landscapes involved sweeping dislocations of indigenous peoples, slavery and other forms of forced labor, and greatly accelerated the pace of deforestation, especially from the eighteenth century onwards.[10] It also left behind enduring inequalities in land distribution.

The friction of distance began to lessen more dramatically after the onset of the Industrial Revolution and the rise of coal and steam power in the nineteenth century and oil and the internal combustion engine in the twentieth century; what is sometimes referred to as the compression of time and space. As noted, the reliance on locally produced biomass for fuel was central to the heavy friction of distance that prevailed through most of human history, and this had also imposed limits on the productivity of human and animal labor. The mining of coal, oil, and natural gas – ancient biomass that had accumulated and compacted into dense bundles of energy over a long geologic period – exploded these limits. Suddenly centuries of biological productivity could be tapped. This shift from renewable to ancient stores of biomass for fuel, or from 'living' to 'dead' carbon,[11] provided much of the energetic basis of global economic integration, as well as fundamentally altering the carbon cycle. Fossil-fuel-powered steamships and trains, and later transport trucks and airplanes, enhanced the scale at which new resource frontiers could be accessed, and fossil-fuel-powered machines, factories, and electrical utilities enabled tremendous increases in output per worker. These great advances in transportation and labor productivity were entwined with the rising scale and specialization of production and, in turn, staggering transformations of the world's forests, wetlands, and grasslands. Well over half of the world's arable land was plowed and converted to agricultural uses after 1860.[12]

The UN *Millennium Ecosystem Assessment* was the most detailed and authoritative review of the state of the biosphere ever undertaken, drawing on the work of over 1,300 scientists, and it concluded that 'the structure and functioning of the world's ecosystems changed more rapidly in the second half of the twentieth century than at any time in human history.'[13] The magnitude of this change is sometimes expressed in terms of the rising *human appropriation of net primary production* (HANPP), which relates to both the volume of biological materials consumed, directly and indirectly, and the fact that land use changes have almost always tended to decrease total photosynthetic activity. Infinitesimal for almost all of the history of our species, humans now appropriate between 24 and 40 percent of the total NPP occurring over the earth's land surface. This in turn implies a massive reduction in the biomass available to other species and in food webs more broadly.[14]

At the center of this is deforestation, particularly the sharp decline in old-growth or climax forests, what esteemed ecologist E. O. Wilson calls 'one of the most profound and rapid environmental changes in the history of the planet.'[15] Tropical rainforests are the world's greatest storehouses of biodiversity, and not long ago comprised 12 percent of the earth's land surface. Over millennia, rainforests were home to both hunting and gathering and swidden agriculture (clearing small patches of forests for short periods), which at low densities had small impacts. But nearly *half* the world's rainforests have been cleared for permanent uses in a mere century, most of this in the past half-century, and if current rates of deforestation continue a large share of what remains today will be destroyed in only two or three more decades. Further, because a significant amount of the rain that falls in the tropics comes from the forests themselves, as they shrink there are great risks that declining transpiration will lead to powerful feedbacks of reduced cloud cover, lower rainfall levels, heightened temperatures and aridity, worse fires, and accelerated erosion, which are magnified by climate change. The Amazon is by far the world's largest tropical rainforest, and if recent rates of clearance and desiccation continue, roughly half of the remaining Amazonian forest could be lost in the coming decades, causing large declines in regional rainfall. Experts warn that this amounts to a fast-approaching 'point of no return' that might be as near as a decade away, beyond which the momentum of positive feedbacks greatly reduces conservation prospects.[16]

The clearing of old-growth forests is a major driver of climate change, destabilizing the carbon flux between the biosphere and the atmosphere in two basic ways. First, there is a short-term burst of CO_2 and methane released into the atmosphere as forests are cleared. Secondly, subsequent land uses, predominantly agriculture and pasture, then sequester much less carbon in organic matter. Further, large-scale clearance reduces transpiration, moisture, and cloud cover, and in turn solar reflectivity. Thus, while estimates vary as to the precise share of GHG emissions attributable to deforestation since the beginning of the Industrial Revolution, it has indisputably been a major force in climate change.[17]

Agricultural expansion has also been the principal cause of declining fertility in the world's drylands, about 10 percent of which are considered to have been 'degraded' as a result of reduced vegetative cover, erosion by wind and water, compaction, and the effects of excessive irrigation such as salinization, waterlogging, and nutrient leaching.[18] The most extreme form of dryland degradation is desertification, and though there are debates over definition, measurements, and data, it is generally recognized that severe damage to soil fertility in arid regions tends to be irreversible on the time scales of human civilizations, and that Africa and Asia are most susceptible to desertification at present.[19] Though natural grasslands have much lower primary productivity than do forests, desertification also contributes to climate change, as carbon is released from vegetation and soils and sequestration capacity declines, as well as negatively impacting the quality of habitats for other species.

Another momentous change, particularly over the past half-century, has been the alteration of freshwater and oceanic ecosystems. There are now more than 45,000 large dams in the world, the great majority of which have been built after 1950, and more than three-quarters of the world's flowing water is altered to some degree by human engineering.[20] Overfishing has inflicted staggering losses to higher trophic levels across the world's oceans, and all of the world's open ocean fisheries peaked before the end of the twentieth century. In addition to fleets moving farther and farther offshore, aquaculture production has soared. Between 1980 and 2000, the volume of fish, crustaceans, and molluscs produced in intensive aquaculture systems increased by a factor of 7, rising from 5 to 36 million tonnes, and aquaculture now accounts for nearly half of the world's total fish consumption. This raises a range of environmental problems, including the sourcing of feedstock (which pulls on resources elsewhere, with links to industrial agriculture), increasing disease risks, and the quickening destruction of coastal ecosystems such as mangroves.[21]

The destruction of diversity

These careening ecological transformations obviously mean that there are fewer, smaller, and more fragmented areas where processes of natural succession are unfolding, and where a large degree of self-organization prevails, placing more and more stress on other species. The stresses of habitat loss and fragmentation are exacerbated by the persistence and bioaccumulation of toxic chemicals, the excessive loading of elements like nitrogen and phosphorus in aquatic ecosystems, and climate change. With climate change, new temperature and moisture extremes will place physiological strain on many plants and animals, at a pace that is far quicker than some can adapt to or can migrate. Further, adaptive and migratory responses (mainly pole-ward or up in elevation) will be widely constrained by the extent of fragmentation within human-dominated landscapes. In other words, some species may not be able to find suitable new habitats, and others may not be able to reach them as they change, dynamics which are further complicated by shifting distributions of pests and disease vectors.[22]

The *Millennium Ecosystem Assessment* determined that two-thirds of the earth's ecosystems are now 'at risk' of destruction, which is linked to its projection that more than 12 percent of all birds, 25 percent of all mammals, and 32 percent of all fish will be pushed to extinction over the coming century, on the present course. These projections closely mirror the great global register of endangerment, the IUCN *Red List*, which indicates that between 13 and 14 percent of all birds, 21 to 36 percent of all mammals, and 30 to 56 percent of all amphibians are threatened with extinction if current trends continue.[23] Taken together, this amounts to an extinction spasm among the most rapid and far reaching in the 3.5-billion-year history of organic evolution. E. O. Wilson likens this to 'a final struggle with the rest of life.'[24]

This 'struggle with the rest of life' appears most powerfully through the decline of large animals, or 'charismatic mega-fauna,' many of which now survive on a knife's edge. For example, there are only 1,000–2,000 giant pandas, 4,000–6,600 snow leopards, 2,600 Indian rhinos, and 3,000 tigers living in suitable habitats after precipitous declines over the past century or so. Of our closest evolutionary kin, the non-human great apes, only about half a million now live in natural conditions outside of zoos and laboratories, including 29,000–50,000 bonobos, 52,000–76,000 orang-utans, 173,000–300,000 chimpanzees, and probably well under 100,000 gorillas – part of a broader primate extinction crisis.[25] The decline of other animal species should also be understood in their extirpation and confinement to smaller and smaller patches of their past range, even if they are not on the edge of extinction.

Major global conservation organizations such as the IUCN, Conservation International, the Nature Conservancy, and the Worldwide

Fund for Nature have long prioritized the protection of large mammals as a moral imperative in itself, a symbolic representation of something bigger (e.g. pandas as icons and 'ambassadors' of biodiversity), and as a practical target for protecting natural areas from human domination (and often from human occupation altogether). The moral case taps into the awe and emotive connection that many people feel toward other large mammals, reflected in different forms of veneration in various cultural traditions. The practical case relates to the position of mammals at or near the top of trophic webs, which means that their viability is often seen as a crucial indicator of overall ecosystem health, especially where the presence or absence of that particular species fundamentally alters ecosystem dynamics. This function is denoted by the term *keystone species*. The conception of *umbrella species* reflects the use of a species' range to set a conservation objective, implying that if the 'umbrella' (i.e. a protected area) is big enough to sustain viable populations of large mammals with large ranges it will benefit an array of other species and ecosystem processes operating below this scale. Though debates about umbrella species in conservation biology are far more complex than this, suffice to say here that threatened populations of large mammals have often had influential roles in conservation prioritization and planning. In the face of fast-shrinking populations and habitats, these convictions have locked conservationists into a desperate race to protect natural patches of land as parks and protected areas within ever more biologically simplified and fragmented landscapes, as well as to find ways of enhancing connectivity and corridors between core habitats.[26]

Although attention to threatened and endangered animals can help to make the destruction of biodiversity less abstract, and challenge people to think critically about inter-species relations and responsibilities, one risk is that it can lead to a misconception that the perils of an ecologically simplified world are being *imposed* but not *faced* by human societies. Among other things, this can distract from the fact that the relentless simplification of diverse ecologies has important human dimensions, at the foreground of which is the ongoing dispossession and assault on surviving indigenous cultures. As Wade Davis argues, the impoverishment of the biosphere is utterly connected to the impoverishment of the *ethnosphere*, or the loss of cultural diversity on a world scale.[27]

It is also important to problematize the boundless faith held by industrial societies that ecological complexity can be incessantly over-ridden and that stability in simplified environments can always be engineered, which is a major focus in Chapter 3. Increasingly, the functional role of biodiversity is being depicted in terms of essential 'ecological services.'[28] This means giving attention to the underappreci-ated ways that biophysical processes make regions habitable and pro-ductive for humans, through such things as pollination, soil formation, water and biogeochemical cycles, and the existing and potential uses of diverse species in realms like agriculture and pharmaceuticals. The vital role of bees in pollinating a large share of the world's flowering plants and many key crops is a simple illustration of this deep yet often disregarded interdependence, especially amid mounting concerns about the widespread decline of bee populations and the uncertainty over what is driving 'colony collapse syndrome.'[29] Climate change is further magnifying the functional case for biodiversity conservation, as species-rich ecosystems are needed both to mitigate the extent of warming and to widen the scope of adaptive possibilities.

The wide recognition of the need to conserve biodiversity can be seen in such things as the UN Convention on Biological Diversity (with 193 signatories, excluding the USA) and the UN's 'International Year of Biodiversity' (2010) and 'Decade on Biodiversity' (2011–20), though there is good reason to question the depth of the multilateral responses that have accompanied this understanding.

Into the Anthropocene: risks and regressivity

The great sweep of earth history has seen long periods of both major cooling and warming, from ice ages to tropical conditions at the poles. However, the entire history of agriculture has occurred within the Holocene, an epoch of relative climatic stability. This means that while agricultural societies have always faced some climatic variability, they have never faced changes of the magnitude that are projected, and have begun to unfold.

Over the course of the Holocene, paleoclimate records have deter-mined that the concentrations of CO_2 in the atmosphere varied only slightly, ranging between roughly 260 and 280 parts per million (ppm). Atmospheric CO_2 concentrations began to increase with the rising combustion of 'dead carbon' since the Industrial Revolution, along with the increasing release of the living carbon stored in ecosystems, especially from old-growth forests, and once released an average

CO_2 molecule circulates in the atmosphere for about one hundred years. In 1970, atmospheric CO_2 concentrations passed 325 ppm, and since the late 1970s have increased steadily by almost 2 ppm per year, nearing 400 ppm in 2013.[30] Fossil energy has been and remains central in this. In 2008, fossil energy accounted for over four-fifths of the world's total primary energy consumption, the aggregation of all of the energy used in production, transportation, and household consumption, with 33 percent from oil, 27 percent from coal, and 21 percent from natural gas. Oil is not only the single largest source of total primary energy consumption, but it provides virtually all of the liquid fuel that powers modern transportation systems, making it the principal energetic basis of time-space compression.[31]

The enhanced heat-trapping capacity associated with higher CO_2 concentrations is augmented by rising emissions and atmospheric concentrations of other heat-trapping gases, especially methane and nitrous oxide. On average, methane persists in the atmosphere for roughly ten to fifteen years, and nitrous oxide for more than a hundred years, with nitrous oxide also the leading ozone-depleting emission.[32] The fact that such dramatic changes to the chemistry of the atmosphere would drive planetary warming has been well established for decades, and so far average world temperatures have increased by at least 0.6°C above pre-industrial levels.[33] However, the complexity of biophysical processes, interactions, and feedbacks, along with open questions about future emissions and land-use changes, means that climate science involves a large range of variables, relies heavily on computer modelling, and is laden with inevitable uncertainties, which have long been spun by those seeking to deny climate change.

From the 1990s onwards, rising attacks on climate science – many funded by oil, coal, and related industries – sought to deny changes, downplay risks, exempt human causation, and essentially advocate complacency, with aggressive public relations campaigning modelled on the tobacco industry's denial of health concerns. For a significant period of time, this campaign seriously distorted the mounting confidence within expert communities, the nature of debates in the peer-reviewed scientific literature, and the scale of risks posed, and managed to have considerable purchase in politics and the media. Yet while inaction persists, the grounds for discussions have at least shifted considerably. Climate change denial is now mostly confined to the blogosphere, while governments around the world and most of the corporate media accept the overwhelming consensus in the peer-reviewed scientific literature that climate change is occurring, and that the arc of current and projected warming falls outside of any natural variability and is attributable to human-induced or anthropogenic 'forcings.' As Tim Flannery puts it, 'all but the most ignorant, biased, and sceptical now admit this truth.'[34]

This consensus stems from the proliferation of scientific research, the convergence of findings from a wide spectrum of sub-fields, and the fact that as time passes climate models (some of which stretch back well over a decade) have increasingly been tested against an array of empirical evidence. Frighteningly, most of the changes that are being recorded surpass the upper-end projections from earlier models, including temperature increases and declines in Arctic sea ice, the Greenland and West Antarctic ice sheets, and mid-latitude glaciers. Worse yet, there are powerful feedbacks at play with these changes, with declining Arctic sea ice among the most far reaching: as floating ice sheets thin, fracture, and then slip from land into the sea the rate of their decline potentially increases, with melting land-based ice tied to the prospect of rising sea levels. Warming is greatest at the poles, and less ice means less albedo, less solar radiation reflected, and more thermal absorption in the water, which will not only intensify warming but will compromise thermohaline currents 'pumped' by cold, dense salty water in the Arctic and in turn the 'conveyor belt' of deep-ocean circulation – a major control on the global climate system. The warming of Arctic lands similarly means less energy is reflected and more is absorbed, with thawing permafrost promising to release significant volumes of carbon and methane.

The destabilization of the carbon cycle is also driving major changes in ocean chemistry. The world's oceans are vast carbon sinks, and the biggest way that CO_2 gets absorbed out of the atmosphere. Thus, as atmospheric CO_2 concentrations have risen so too has the amount of CO_2 absorbed by oceans: roughly one quarter of the pulse of CO_2 stemming from fossil fuels ends up in the oceans. The pH of oceans had been relatively stable for millions of years, although there is evidence that it has become badly imbalanced, with catastrophic effects, over even longer periods of earth history, and there is now significant evidence that oceans are becoming more acidic. This poses great risks to oceanic life, starting with the algae at the basis of trophic webs and the ocean's function as a carbon sink. While the long-term implications of acidification are obviously dire for all marine ecosystems, the most immediate threat is to the world's coral reefs, the 'rainforests of the sea' in terms of species diversity. Since 1980, over one fifth of the world's coral reefs have been destroyed and another fifth have been degraded, and experts worry the remainder will be lost within a century owing to climate change.[35]

The earth is already committed to a significant amount of warming irrespective of GHG emission reductions. This stems from a range of factors, including the persistence of GHGs in the atmosphere, the extent of ecosystem degradation and reduced carbon sequestration capacity, various positive feedbacks, and the thermal lag of the oceans. Oceans heat up slowly owing to their great thermal mass, so there is a time lag in the impact of atmospheric warming on oceans, meaning that the rise in global average temperatures so far has not yet had its full impact on global ocean temperatures. This also relates very powerfully to sea-level rise, since water expands as it warms.

At minimum, global average temperatures are expected to rise 1 to 2°C above pre-industrial averages, with recent research suggesting that it may already be too late to keep the increase below 2°C. The magnitude of this committed warming, along with the changes in atmospheric and ocean chemistry that have occurred, are far beyond the variability found within the Holocene – *before* even addressing unknowable variables such as future emissions levels. In other words, the earth is being pushed into a new, unchartered geologic epoch, one that is increasingly being marked by scientists as the *Anthropocene* in order to highlight its basis in human-induced climate forcings.

Scientific pleas to reduce emissions and stabilize GHG concentrations now resound in the desperate terms of 'final wake-up calls,' given how quickly the window for containing change within ostensibly 'safe' thresholds is seen to be closing. The most common target for safe levels of warming is no more than 2°C above pre-industrial average temperatures, which is widely seen to require reducing atmospheric CO_2 concentrations to 350 ppm, to the extent that well-known US environmentalist Bill McKibben used this to frame an important initiative fighting for action on climate change: 350.org. In the words of the executive secretary of the UN Framework Convention on Climate Change (UNFCCC), 'what is at stake here is none other than the long-term, sustainable future of humanity ... We know the milestones science has set. We know by when and by how much

GHG emissions must drop to have a chance of avoiding the worst impacts of climate change, devastating for the most vulnerable and the poorest around the world. Time is not on our side.'[36] To help widen popular consciousness about the change already unfolding, 350.org has developed a participatory pedagogical tool to show connections between patterns of extreme weather events around the world and the projections of climate science (www.climatedots.org).

However, some scientists have railed against the 2°C target as being far from safe, far higher than what the scientific understanding compels, and very likely to entail catastrophic outcomes for many parts of the world, in particular for the semi-arid tropics, low-lying mega-deltas, and small islands. The matter of safe thresholds also ties directly to the risks of soon passing 'tipping points,' beyond which the weight of positive feedbacks and the degree of non-linear changes push the climate system past a 'point of no return,' when an irreversible momentum toward catastrophic changes ensues. This catastrophic course would entail such things as: the permanent loss of Arctic sea ice and changes in ocean circulation; the melting of ice shelves and extensive coastal flooding; severe heat waves and droughts; massive declines in freshwater availability; the collapse of many ecosystems and agricultural areas; and the lethal acidification of oceans.

While no country is immune to climate change, particularly if key thresholds are passed, intensifying risks are highly uneven on a world scale for at least the short to medium term, a point that gets developed further below.

An insatiable species? The 'population bomb' and biophysical limits to growth

The most pervasive explanation for both biodiversity loss and climate change is simply that there are too many people in a world of limited resources. For instance, in writing about the 'revenge of Gaia,' and the potential for a vicious spiral of positive climatic feedbacks, famed systems theorist James Lovelock states that 'the root of our problems with the environment comes from a lack of constraint on the growth of population.' To explain the forces driving the loss of biodiversity, E. O. Wilson points to the HIPPO framework in conservation biology (Habitat destruction; Invasive species; Pollution; Population; Overharvesting), and argues that 'the prime mover ... around the world is the second P – too many people consuming too much of the land and sea space and the resources they contain.' Such views can also be seen in the United Nations Environment Programme (UNEP), whose executive director recently stated that 'the human population is now so large that the amount of resources needed to sustain it exceeds what is available at current consumption patterns.'[37] Framed in this way, population control becomes the world's most fundamental environmental imperative. As advocates sometimes pose it: what pressing environmental problem could not be more easily resolved if there were fewer people on earth? (Box 1.1 gives some notable examples of population advocacy).

The basis for these claims might seem straightforward enough. While there were fewer than half a billion people at the dawn of European imperialism and about one billion around the start of the Industrial Revolution in 1800, there are now more than seven billion, and over the past decade almost eighty million more people have been added every year (see Figure 1.1). The UN Population Fund projects that the world population will pass 8 billion around 2025 and 9 billion around 2045, before plateauing somewhere between 9 and 10 billion. Almost all future growth is expected to occur in the global South, and most of it in cities. This translates into a dramatic decline in arable land per capita on a world scale, which fell by more than half in a mere half-century, from over 0.4 ha/person in 1961 to 0.2 ha/person in 2010, despite the immense conversion of land to agriculture that occurred over this time.

Box 1.1 Population advocacy: selected examples

Population Institute (www.populationinstitute.org)
Global Population Speakout (www.populationspeakout.org)
Population Action International (www.populationaction.org)
Population Media Center (www.populationmedia.org)
Population Matters for a Sustainable Future (www.population
matters.org)
Population Council (www.popcouncil.org)
Population Reference Bureau (www.prb.org)
Global Population and the Environment (Sierra Club) (www.
sierraclub.org/population)

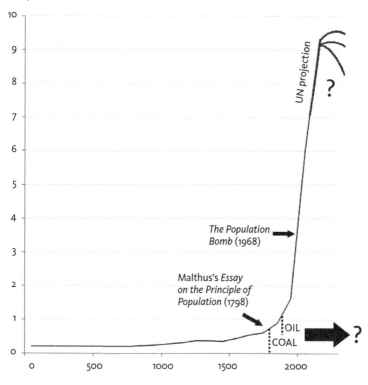

1.1 Human population, 0–2050 CE (billions)

Yet however plain this might seem – more people competing for a certain bundle of resources – it can obscure a great deal to locate population at the center of environmental problems, a narrative that Angus and Butler call 'populationism.'[38] To appreciate this, it helps to follow the intellectual lineage of populationism back to Thomas Malthus's 1798 *Essay on the Principle of Population*, in which he argued that human population growth was bound to outstrip the growth in food supply, dressing this as a law of nature. In contrast with how he is often portrayed, Malthus had no concern for the environment, or even 'overpopulation,' and was aiming at a very different target: to naturalize poverty and inequality in human societies by locating them in the irrepressible reproduction and moral failure of the poor. Excessive reproduction, he argued, served to endlessly entrap the poor in conditions of hunger, starvation, and disease, which amounted to self-correcting biological checks on growth. From this claim that social problems and scarcity pivoted on reproduction, he then attacked efforts at social improvement such as improved wages, as they would lead only to more births and more forceful checks in the end. In blaming poverty on biology, and the poor themselves, Malthusian theory (and its inflections in Social Darwinism in the nineteenth century) provided an appealing ideological weapon for British and other European elites amid the convulsions of enclosures, depeasant-ization, proletarianization, and early industrialization at home, and the slavery, slave trading, forced labour, dispossession, enclosures, onerous taxation, and imbalanced trade relations in the colonies. To critics, Malthus was a crass class apologist, and 'no other work was more hated by the English working class, nor so strongly criticized by Marx and Engels.'[39]

The explosive population growth that followed Malthus's time flew utterly in the face of his theory. In little more than a century, the world's population doubled from 1 to 2 billion people, as the Industrial Revolution literally and figuratively gained steam, and as important public health improvements curbed death rates – in con-trast to the inevitable checks Malthus believed would constrain such growth. It then doubled again, from 2 to 4 billion, in just over half a century. Yet during this next doubling, Malthus reemerged with a new twist, as population growth became positioned as a primary cause of environmental degradation. The rise of Neo-Malthusianism within environmentalism in the 1960s was marked by Kenneth Boulding's insistence that human societies had to solve the 'population trap' with strong efforts to control population, Garrett Hardin's population-ist depiction of the 'tragedy of the commons,' and Paul Ehrlich's 'population bomb,' which warned of humanity 'breed[ing] itself into oblivion.'[40]

In this sort of biological imagery, humans were seen to be con-stantly expanding beyond the carrying capacity of ecosystems, yet were adaptive enough to colonize ever more ecological niches, permitting unsustainable growth while undermining the long-term health of life support systems. The image of an insatiable humanity devour-ing resources was often evoked through metaphors such as plagues, locusts, and cancer, spreading dangerously within a 'Spaceship Earth' or a 'lifeboat.' The fixation at a generalized species level is captured well in the attempt by a famous Canadian environmentalist to analyze humans as 'rogue primates,' aiming less at 'what we do, or even what we think,' and instead on 'what we *are*. The human animal as an evolved biological phenomenon. The animal with something askew.'[41]

The population narrative gained further momentum with the *Limits to Growth – Club of Rome Report*, to this day the best-selling environmental book ever published. *Limits to Growth* was based on empirical evidence of an array of sharp growth trends (exponential 'J-curves') in things like population, urbanization, fossil energy, metal ores, and some forms of pollution, and elaborate models of their trajectories and interactions. Like Boulding, Hardin, and Ehrlich, *Limits to Growth* emphasized the biophysical finiteness of the earth's carrying capacity, and the fact that while limits might be breached and displaced for a time, rising populations and consumption levels, declining resources, and deteriorating environmental conditions were likely to lead to 'a rather sudden and uncontrollable decline in both population and industrial capacity' in less than 100 years. While signaling the importance of innovations in resource efficiency, the authors tried to shoot down the faith that 'technological breakthroughs' could 'go on raising physical ceilings indefinitely,' and warned that technology could not resolve – but could divert attention from – 'the essential problem, which is exponential growth in a finite and complex system.' They also took aim at the notion that economic growth was needed to reduce poverty, noting how, on the contrary, it tended to be entwined with rising inequality. Still, in spite of this recognition, the absence of political economy was glaring, as the 'need for fundamental change' was located 'in the values of society,' while population growth was described as 'the greatest possible impediment to more equal distribution of the world's resources.'[42]

In addition to climate change, today biophysical limits to growth are also commonly presented in terms of the peaking supply of many key non-renewable resources, dubbed 'peak everything' by Richard Heinberg. The notion of a resource 'peak' implies that when the total past consumption of a resource is added to remaining global reserves, the halfway point is either near or has already been crossed. This also generally signals the fact that the most accessible and hence lowest-cost reserves have been discovered and are declining, and that remaining reserves will be increasingly difficult, costly, and energy intensive to extract and refine. Thus, while we may still be on a rising J-curve of annual consumption, it is on borrowed time, as the second half of the resource supply is bound to be used up a lot faster than the first – as well as being more energy intensive, expensive, and polluting. This concern is fixed most of all on fossil energy, especially conventional oil reserves.[43]

As emphasized earlier, transformations in productivity, trade, transportation, and household activities have been utterly intertwined with the increasing consumption of fossil energy, with oil being the most important source of energy on a world scale given both its volume and its role as the lifeblood of global transportation systems. There are abundant indications that conventional oil reserves are shrinking fast, as production and exploration move toward riskier sites (e.g. the poles, deeper and farther offshore) and toward 'unconventional' sources like shale formations, with the rapid rise of hydraulic fracturing ('fracking') techniques, and bitumen-based tar sands. Fracking involves the high-pressure injection of large volumes of water/chemical/sand mixtures to fracture underground shale formations and release trapped oil and natural gas, and it has moved from an experimental process to large pockets of production to widespread global surveys at warp speed despite the enormous uncertainties and risks, especially those stemming from the large quantities of toxic and difficult-to-contain waste water.[44]

In 2010, the International Energy Agency (IEA) projected three basic scenarios for world primary energy demand, with its mid-range 'New Policies Scenario' anticipating 36 percent growth from 2008 to 2035 and a 24 percent increase in total fossil energy consumption, rising from 9,970 to 12,344 million tonnes of oil equivalent (Mtoe). It is very notable that this scenario assumes some improved policies from the present, but fewer than what are deemed to be sufficient to keep atmospheric GHG concentrations below 450 ppm – still far above 'safe' targets. Even more worrying for climate change is that the rise of fracking techniques has led the International Energy Agency to upwardly revise its estimates of oil and gas reserves in recent years. This broad picture is made worse still by coal, which remains the leading source of power in energy grids in many countries (including the USA, China, India, and Australia), is the worst fossil fuel in terms of CO_2 emissions as well as other forms of air pollution, and constitutes the great majority of the world's remaining non-renewable energy supply, with the greatest reserves held by the largest consuming nations.[45]

Given the centrality of fossil energy to the global economy, and especially the world's food supply, some environmentalists tie the spectacular pulse of fossil energy since 1800 to the surge in human population from 1 to 7 billion, with the implication that a world population of 7 (or 9+) billion will not be viable when this energy runs out. In other words, fossil energy is seen to have inflated a population 'bubble.' While the challenges associated with increasingly expensive fossil energy extraction might seem greatest in advanced industrial societies, most of the world's poorest countries are highly vulnerable to these rising costs. At the forefront of this, as should become clear in subsequent chapters, is the dependence upon cheap industrial food surpluses and their embedded fossil energy.

An insatiable economic order? Contesting environmentalisms

As David Pepper puts it, 'within the environmental movement there is a host of ideologies and cross-currents, and there are many classifications ... which overlap and produce confusion.'[46] One of the starkest illustrations of this lies in the fact that many of the world's largest environmental organizations – which constitute what might be broadly described as 'mainstream' environmentalism – receive core funding from some of the world's largest and most polluting transnational corporations (TNCs), and draw largely from relatively wealthy constituencies.[47]

Populationist environmentalism has largely pointed at the global South, where almost all population growth is occurring. At its best, the aim of reducing fertility has drawn encouraging attention to the need to advance gender equity and women's and girls' rights in the process of demographic transition, a perspective which can establish some connections between environmental and human development goals (though, as discussed below, calls for population control have come in more virulent forms as well). The focus on human population growth has also folded directly onto the crisis management approach to biodiversity conservation noted earlier. From this vantage, environmentalism centers on urgent, defensive battles to protect imperiled wildlife and fragments of wilderness before the 'human tidal wave' washes over everything,[48] with parks and protected areas treated as the cornerstone of conservation and the primary containers of biodiversity on a world scale. Beyond the defense of 'wild' species and areas, mainstream environmentalism has tended to channel concerns about resource scarcity and limits to growth toward things like individual consumer choices, ethical self-restraint ('voluntary simplicity'), re-cycling, and enhanced energy efficiency.

In spite of the limits of these horizons, mainstream environmental-ism has also faced continuous attack from the right. Julian Simon famously led this charge, arguing that there were no fixed limits to economic growth, and that human ingenuity (the 'ultimate resource') was infinitely capable of resolving all problems of resource scarcity, ecological disruption, and pollution in the march toward ever-rising material wealth with ever more people. In the process, he heaped scorn on environmentalists as irrational, fear-mongering, and anti-modern 'Chicken Littles,' locked in self-serving campaigns.[49] Simon's political influence stretched into his role as a presidential advisor to Ronald Reagan, whose administration marked the ascendance of neoliberalism and aggressively rolled back environmental regulations as a core part of its ideological agenda. He also helped establish a field of anti-environmental writing that fuses a nihilistic or exceptionally selective position toward scholarly environmental science with repeated calls for free markets and corporate self-regulation and, to the extent that biophysical limits are acknowledged, a messianic faith that they can be overridden by technology. Though much of this writing emanates from corporate-funded think tanks, it frequently masquerades as though exposing the hegemony of scientific 'opinion' from an unbiased, moral, and iconoclastic stance. Complementing these attacks has been the rise of an industry of positive spin known as corporate greenwash.[50]

Extreme technological optimism can be seen to have infused the highly ambiguous concept of 'sustainable development,' which evolved through a series of UN conferences and culminated in the schizo-phrenic *World Commission on Environment and Development*, known more commonly as the Brundtland Report. The Brundtland Report identified many of the same population and resource concerns as did *Limits to Growth*, and called for controls on population growth, major expansions in protected areas (establishing the oft-cited target for nations to set aside 12 percent of their land as protected areas), and more efficient resource use. It also highlighted some significant dynamics of global inequality, such as expanding corporate power, commodity dependence in poor countries, and uneven terms of trade, and yet culminated in a call for more global market integration, more leadership in sustainability from TNCs, and more economic growth, in order to be able to 'afford' environmental protection. Ultimately, the core failures of development were rebranded as solutions, with the world's most powerful nations and corporations tasked with guiding the way toward green growth, enhanced techno-efficiency, and more careful environmental and resource management.[51]

A main priority in this managerial perspective has been to try to translate conservation into the metrics of capitalism in order to correct what are portrayed as market failures. This means putting prices on ecological services (and stocks of 'natural capital') relative to their vast and mostly unaccounted economic contributions, and putting costs on the vast and mostly unaccounted impacts of things like biodiversity loss, the proliferation of toxins, and GHG emissions. To its champions, assigning economic values to things like forests, wetlands, plant and animal species, pollution, and GHG emissions is the most efficient and practical way to urgently reorient decision-making, and the complexities of this task are at the core of the sub-disciplines of environmental and ecological economics – thinking which now infuses a range of organizations from the World Bank, to UNEP, to many development agencies and environmental NGOs. In this framework, Wolfgang Sachs suggests, the essence of the environmental 'question now becomes: which of nature's "services" are to what extent indispensable for further development? Or the other way around: which "services" of nature are dispensable or can be substituted by, for example, new materials or genetic engineering? In other words, nature turns into a variable, albeit a critical one, in sustaining development.'[52]

For critics on the left, much of what falls under the broad banner of environmentalism is exceptionally narrow and misdirected, with the focus on population growth a longstanding lightning rod. Much as Marx attacked Malthus for attempting to naturalize poverty, exonerate the privileged, and cast blame on the poor, radical environmentalists have condemned attempts to turn Malthus from crass class apologist into someone with something to say about ecology, and treat population growth as the driving force in degradation. Clear echoes of this apologia can be heard in projections of environmental blame onto the poor and ignorant masses, which came through especially loudly in Garrett Hardin's infamous 'lifeboat ethics' that was explicitly linked to a 'case against helping the poor.'[53] Such perspectives continue to reverberate within some forms of environmentalism in different ways, including in reactionary calls for things like stricter immigration control in wealthy countries, authoritarian contraceptive measures, and the removal of foreign assistance to low-income countries. This projection of responsibility onto the global South is summed up well in E. O. Wilson's claim that: 'The environmental fate of the world lies ultimately in *their* hands. *They* now account for virtually all global population growth, and *their* drive toward higher per capita consumption will be relentless' (emphasis added).[54]

As well as focusing on a distant *other*, populationist environmentalism also frequently slides into generalized misanthropy, as in the plague-like imagery of the human species noted earlier, which is sometimes accompanied by casting blame on big, all-encompassing things like the human species or the rise of civilization.[55] Focusing at the level of fertility and the human species in the abstract can 'derail serious social critique,' as 'problems of property ownership, economic exploitation, class rule, racial prejudice, gender oppression, nationalism, civil wars between competing repressive rulers, imperialism – all are biologized out of existence.'[56] Rather than the persistence of high fertility rates being a *cause* of poverty and degradation, critics counter, these are better understood as a *symptom* or an *effect* of things like class, patriarchy, and other inequalities, and the dependence of the poor upon children for such things as labor and old-age security. Similar criticisms have been leveled at limits to growth or 'peak' resource narratives, if they are narrowly focused on material scarcity and carrying capacity without attention to the systematic imperatives governing how resources are defined, produced, and distributed.

To some, part of the blinders of mainstream environmentalism stem from a philosophical dualism in which, on one side, humans are seen to be above and outside nature (yet biologically programmed to expand), and on the other side pure or 'wild' nature is venerated beyond human presence and use. This dualism goes hand in hand with the fact that the dramatic expansion of protected areas in the global South has involved a widespread failure to recognize the land inequalities that surround conservation priorities, and led to the displacement of indigenous and local populations from traditional lands or to restrictions in customary access to resources and subsistence activities. The spiral of exclusion and antagonism has sometimes fostered a siege mentality, to an extent that it has come to be characterized as 'fortress' or 'coercive conservation,' administered through fences, fines, and even guns.[57]

Radicals have also criticized market-centric environmentalism whereby individuals 'vote' with their money and various ecosystem services are priced and traded. At its worst, excessive focus on consumer behavior can be a chimera for real economic democracy, and flow into movement-deflating preoccupations such as people feeling complacent with their 'green' consumerism or moralizing about consumption decisions that are not green enough. Wariness about pricing ecosystem services stems from a position that these sorts of calculations are not only impossible but that this process, even if it adds up to trillions of dollars, can lead down a slippery slope where ever more things are turned into commodities and subject to the competitive pressures of markets.

For radical environmentalists, it is not that concerns like improved access to birth control, better technologies, the protection of endangered species, conscious consumption, self-restraint, and finding ways to properly value sustainable production are unimportant. Rather it is that they are too often seen in fragmented ways, while leaving aside the elephant in the room: the fundamental incompatibility of a finite biosphere with a system based not on meeting human needs but rather on a distinctive set of economic compulsions geared toward incessant growth. At the center of this is the fact that those who control the means of production systematically appropriate the surplus value generated by workers while being locked in a constant competition to pursue profit, make and sell ever more commodities, and accumulate ever more capital – or else lose out.

In this competition, it is paramount for the owners of capital to find ways of increasing the productivity of labor, given the role of labor in creating surplus value, which in turn spurs tremendous technological dynamism. This can also be seen as an inbuilt pressure to displace labor with technology. There is, very simply, what Murray Bookchin calls a 'grow or die' character to the system, from the owners of capital to the economy as a whole, all of which is set within extremely short-term time horizons. One plain indication of this can be seen in the common target of 3 percent annualized growth needed for an economy to be 'healthy,' which translates into a doubling time of a mere twenty-five years.

The systemic nature of environmental problems is increasingly being interpreted through the reinvigoration of Marx's argument that capitalism established a 'metabolic rift between city and country, human beings and the earth' which, as John Bellamy Foster puts it, 'has now been heightened beyond anything he could have imagined.'[58] Drawing from the pioneering soil science of Justus von Liebig (1803–73), who discovered how the depletion of key elements like nitrogen and phosphorus set limits on soil fertility, and how historic cycles were being ruptured, Marx insisted that the imperatives of capitalist production were bound to exploit soils in addition to workers. Foster has been at the forefront of elaborating this into a more generalized framework through which to understand how a mounting array of biophysical contradictions must be overridden *in situ*, as by importing fertilizers, and by *shifting* resource demands and ecological burdens across ever wider spaces, as from Europe to its colonies in the past, or in the push farther into the earth's crust and in the destabilization of the atmosphere today. The ultimate result of these rifts, shifts, and overrides is never resolution, but bigger and riskier problems, while new technological innovation tends to heighten rather than abate demand for resources.

For Jason Moore, however, it is insufficient to see the metabolic rift as repeated chains of negative outcomes and responses, then ever more problematic outcomes and more challenging responses. This, he argues, accedes to the society–nature binary inherited from Descartes (discussed in Chapter 2), where human civilization appears as an external force acting upon the environment and is driven to expand as ecosystems are degraded and resources depleted, when the essential problem is, in Moore's terms, *ontologically prior* to this: in the *socio-ecological constitution* of capitalist relations. Instead of a society–nature binary, he urges us to see the 'accumulation of capital and the production of nature in a dialectical unity.'[59] To have the commodity form generalized and insatiable capital accumulation as the dominant motive force in a civilization is to lock in the unremitting appropriation and simplification of ecosystems and ensure that the diversity of the world will be progressively converted into exchangeable parts. As such, expansion appears less as a release valve and more as part of a pounding appetite. Another important dimension of this argument is that 'ecological surpluses' extracted from commodity frontiers have, from the very beginnings of capitalism, had an essential role in its historical development, providing cheap food, energy, raw materials, food, and labor – what Moore calls the 'Four Cheaps' – which have fired productivity revolutions time and again. That is, the appropriation of crops, livestock, soils, fossil fuels, forests, minerals, and human toil from new frontiers, at low costs (though with much violence) and high returns, has always subsidized the great leaps that have been made in commodity production, in particular by deflating the system-wide costs of labor and inflating the productivity per worker, 'the decisive metric of competitive fitness in historical capitalism.'[60] More simply, taking things in a big way has always helped to enable the making of things in new ways.

Appreciating these recurrent cycles of plunder and productivity gains also provides a helpful way into endemic systemic crises, including the current and possibly terminal one, with the very strong probability that large-scale frontiers are now largely closed and the 'Four Cheaps' are bound to become more costly. Ultimately, Moore makes a compelling case that capitalism should be seen not only as a social or an economic system but as a *world-ecology*:

> Capitalism, in this perspective, does not *have* an ecological regime. It *is* an ecological regime – signifying those relatively durable patterns of class structure, technological innovation and the development of productive forces, organizational forms and governance (formal and informal) that have sustained and propelled successive phases of world accumulation since the long 16th century [1492–1640].[61]

From individuals to corporations, decisions and activities might appear as if alienated from nature, but Moore insists that quite the converse is true. Over time capitalist civilization has entangled the totality of people's lives in ever wider, more complex, and, though less immediate, in many respects even more intimate relations with the rest of life than in any prior epoch. Industrial livestock is, I will argue, a very important dimension of this.

So while the notion of the Anthropocene is an evocative indicator of the magnitude of environmental change, to the extent that it risks advancing the species-level imagery of humans as a plague-like force of nature, Moore insists that it would be better to call the new epoch in earth history the '*Capitalocene*.'[62]

Ecological and atmospheric footprints: foregrounding inequality

The ecological footprint is both a broad, empirical measure and a tool for education and advocacy. As a measure, the ecological footprint seeks to estimate the area required (in agriculture, pasture, forests, etc.) to produce goods and absorb wastes at a given level of consumption, thereby illustrating how societies depend upon distant and mostly invisible ecosystems for resources and as sinks. In the words of its co-creators, Wackernagel and Rees, the footprint is a 'snapshot of economy–land relationships at a particular point in time,' and its strong educational punch is that it can 'communicate simply and graphically the general nature and magnitude of the biophysical "connectedness" between humankind and the ecosphere.'[63] This built on and extended some of the core concerns of the *Limits to Growth*, as well as William Catton's *Overshoot*, which made similar species-level claims about human populations consuming beyond carrying capacities: deceptively in the short term, ruinously in the long term.[64] It was also expressly presented as a challenge to the discipline of economics, for its blindness to the earth's biophysical infrastructure and basic laws of physics, and to the hollowness of popular notions of sustainable development, as in *The Brundtland Report*, that vests too much faith in human ingenuity and technological efficiency gains as the means to boundless economic growth.

In contrast, the ecological footprint portrays the world economy as 'a complex "dissipative structure" embedded within the ecosphere,' where production degrades energy, matter, and the regenerative capacity of ecosystems.[65] Boundless growth then becomes a deceptive lodestar: ecological limits might be silently traversed, burdens displaced, and costs externalized for a time, but not forever. Because the ecological footprint involves some inevitable oversimplifications and the focus on productive and assimilative capacity does not account for the space needed by other species, Wackernagel and Rees conceded that it could be fairly criticized for being too human centered and narrowly functional, and for erring too far on the side of underestimation.

Still, the footprint provides a valuable proxy of total ecological demand, which on a world scale was estimated to have grown by over 70 percent between 1961 and 1999, reaching 120 percent of the regenerative capacity of the biosphere by the turn of the twenty-first century. One of the most valuable contributions of the ecological footprint is its comparative lens, as it can be approached and compared across different scales, from individuals to countries. It gives a highly uneven picture, with the average person in a rich country occupying much more ecologically productive land than the average person in a low-income country. For instance, in 1999 the per capita footprint of the average US citizen was estimated to be more than four times above the unsustainable world average, which means that to project US consumption levels on a world scale – as per Rostow's famous ladder – would require 'phantom' planets' worth of resources and sinks.[66] Thus, while not grounded in a political economic critique, the ecological footprint was explicitly intended to draw global inequality to the heart of the story of environmentalism, showing how 'high material standards are maintained by a massive but unaccounted ecological deficit with the rest of the world,' and forcing 'over-consumers to face the otherwise hidden relationships and implicit trade-offs between their wealth and the poverty and human suffering that persists elsewhere.'[67]

The matter of population growth certainly does not disappear, but the fact that some people on earth are seen to be effectively 'larger' than others ensures that degradation cannot be washed away in an abstracted neo-Malthusian population bomb.[68] This also clearly implies an attack on theories of development which mythologize industrialized countries as the aspirational target, and can lead to bolder assessments of what sustainability entails. For instance, UNEP's *Global Environmental Outlook 2000* argued that 'a tenfold reduction in resource consumption in the industrialized countries is a necessary long-term target if adequate resources are to be released for the needs of developing countries,' while UNDP's *Human Development Report 1999* indicated clearly that 'the rich contribute more' to environmental problems, while 'the poor bear the brunt in loss of lives and risks to health from pollution and toxins – and in loss of lives from soil degradation, desertification, deforestation, and biodiversity loss.'[69] Important connections between the footprint as an empirical measure and the structural inequalities in the world economy have been further developed by a number of environmental sociologists, who draw attention to the fact that unequal exchange on a world scale (which critical development scholars have long focused on) grows much further when one considers the un- or under-accounted ecological burdens that are embedded in flows of resources. These sorts of analyses can in turn nourish concrete political demands, such as calls for debt cancellation for countries of the global South or, further, that 'ecological debt' is owed from North to South.[70]

The ecological footprint has also been adapted to concentrate on water demands and atmospheric loads. Water footprints help to illuminate the manifold and mostly invisible ways that water is used in complex modern societies, which is translated to the commodity level through the concept of 'virtual' (or 'embedded') water to account for the volume that went into production of a given product.[71]

Freshwater accounts for less than 3 percent of all water on earth, and a majority of this is either frozen (in glaciers and at the poles) or cycling in the atmosphere. While many people still perceive water to be a relatively boundless resource, especially in wealthy temperate countries, availability and consumption levels are exceptionally uneven around the world, and increasingly precarious in many places. UN-Water and the FAO project that 'by 2025, 1.8 billion people will be living in countries or regions with absolute water scarcity [<500 m³ per year per capita], and two-thirds of the world population could be under conditions of water stress.'[72]

Box 1.2 Footprint 'calculators': selected examples

Center for Sustainable Economy (www.myfootprint.org)

Global Footprint Network (www.footprintnetwork.org)

Water Footprint Network (www.waterfootprint.org)

Carbon Footprint of Nations (www.carbonfootprintofnations. com)

Climate Path (www.climatepath.org)

Carbon Independent (www.carbonindependent.org)

US EPA calculator (www.epa.gov/climatechange/ghg emissions/ind-calculator.html)

Nature Conservancy calculator (www.nature.org/greenliving/ carboncalculator/index.htm)

In spite of its potentially radical implications, it should be noted that the ecological footprint and its derivatives have also had considerable traction within mainstream environmentalism, where they have been pointed more at solutions like individual ethics, self-restraint, consumer choices, and carbon offsets. One reflection of this is that some of the popular footprint calculators listed here acknowledge support from a range of TNCs, including Coca-Cola, PepsiCo, Nestlé, and SNC-Lavalin.

Atmospheric footprints reveal wide global disparities in tonnes of CO_2 equivalent (t CO_2e) emitted per year, and are most accurate when adjusted for trade (i.e. not all of China's emissions belong to China, but are also effectively distributed through many countries through TNCs like Wal-Mart). This helps to make the unequal responsibility for climate change very clear. For instance, the average US citizen is responsible for roughly thirty times more t CO_2e per year than the average person in sub-Saharan Africa. With a mere 5 percent of world population, the USA and Canada together produce roughly one quarter of the world's total CO_2 emissions, while the 15 percent of humanity living in industrialized countries accounts for nearly half of the world's CO_2 emissions. Disparities in atmospheric footprints grow further when historic GHG emissions are taken into account, as their persistence in the atmosphere compels.[73]

The other side of the unequal responsibility for climate change is the unequal vulnerability to it. In tropical and semi-tropical regions, where many of the world's poorest countries are located, particularly acute threats are associated with changes such as: hotter average temperatures; more intense extreme weather events like heat waves, droughts, and tropical storms; more variable rainfall patterns; increased coastal vulnerability to flooding events and saltwater seepage with rising sea levels (threatening coastal groundwater, agricultural soils, and infrastructure and housing); and changes to the annual accretion and discharge from mid-latitude glaciers. The latter provide crucial stores of freshwater for more than a billion people inhabiting river basins beneath. In the short term, heavy seasonal melts threaten torrential seasonal runoffs (the risks of which have been seen very starkly in some disastrous floods in recent years, as in Pakistan in 2011 and India in 2013), and in the longer term the depletion of these freshwater stores threatens drinking and irrigation supplies.[74]

These changes loom heavily over agricultural production everywhere, but most ominously in the semi-arid tropics, which are home to more than one fifth of humanity and very high levels of agrarian livelihoods, poverty, and chronic hunger and malnourishment. Elevated heat will increase evaporation, reduce soil moisture, and heighten plant and animal stress. There is considerable scientific research indicating that significant warming will suppress yields in many major cereals, compounded by more variable rains and the reduced annual glacial discharge. Climatic shifts and less cold weather might also enhance conditions for the movement and reproduction of pests and pathogens, while more intense extreme weather events are likely to lead to increasing incidence of crop failure and livestock losses. In a submission to the UNFCCC in advance of the failed 2011 Cancún Ministerial Meeting, the FAO warned that slow-onset climate changes threaten to have 'potentially catastrophic effects on food production' across large areas of the global South, especially from the middle of the twenty-first century onwards.[75]

Further, environmental hazards tend to be greatly magnified by human inequalities. Research on famines and hazards has made it clear that what have often been viewed as 'natural disasters' should be understood within contexts of power, poverty, and unjust entitlements. One indication of the gaping differences in environmental vulnerabilities on a world scale can be seen in the fact that roughly one out of every nineteen citizens in developing countries was affected by climate-related disasters between 2000 and 2004, in contrast to only one in 1,500 in countries of the OECD. As environmental conditions become more extreme and erratic, the transmission of poverty to vulnerability to disaster is bound to grow. Related to this are fears that rising populations of environmental refugees could soar as populous areas of the semi-arid tropics and low-lying coastal regions become uninhabitable amid rising sea levels, disasters, warming, and water scarcity. The prospect of such displacement is now being described in terms of 'climate refugees,' which could number 200 million by 2050 according to the World Migration Organization. Sea-level rise threatens the very existence of some small island nation-states, and the process of relocation and evacuation planning has already begun for a few. This will also adversely affect many densely populated low-lying continental areas, such as the mega-delta regions in Asia and Africa. With this displacement also comes the potential for spiraling poverty, inequality, and violence, which powerful countries and corporations are bracing for in a variety of ways, such as tightened immigration policies and investments in security at a range of scales.[76]

In short, it is clear that climate change and the responses to it now overarch all prospects for human development, and that 'the problem of international equity is central.'[77] Response imperatives can be drawn along two basic lines: mitigation and adaptation, with mitigation setting the parameters for what adaptation is possible – either enabling or constraining possibilities across large areas. Climate change mitigation entails urgent efforts to avoid impending 'tipping points' and to lessen the scale of change by protecting and enhancing the capacity of ecosystems to take in GHGs out of the atmosphere and by drastically reducing annual GHG emissions. The need for GHG sequestration starts with the protection of primary forests, especially in the tropics, where carbon is absorbed most vigorously and stored in greatest volumes. To enhance sequestration capacity, there is a need to reduce the extent of biologically simplified landscapes and increase the land area given to self-organizing ecosystems. The nature of agriculture is central to any prospect of large-scale ecological restoration, and there are also great variations in the capacity for sequestration that can occur on farms, both of which are major reasons why the subject of this book is so important.

In setting emission reduction targets, Frank Ackerman argues that the precautionary principle should prevail in light of the scientific confidence about climate forcings and positive feedbacks, the magnitude of risks posed, and the worst-case scenarios that could ensue. This essentially means starting from the most cautious scientific interpretations of 'safe' thresholds for atmospheric GHG concentrations and average temperature increases, and then erring at the high end of the estimated emissions reductions needed to get there. Ackerman also provides a piercing criticism of the economic case for climate change inaction which, as outright denial has waned, has become a primary intellectual defense for failing to make aggressive mitigation efforts. One of the central arguments in the case for inaction is that it is too expensive, and that the associated costs could be better spent eradicating poverty. While it is patently absurd to pose mitigation versus assisting the poor as if it were a mutually exclusive choice being actively contemplated by industrialized countries, TNCs, and international financial institutions, beyond this lies the unanswered question of where the uplifted global poor would live if large areas of the tropics and semi-tropics become uninhabitable. Ackerman nevertheless treats the economic case for inaction seriously, on its own terms, and then summarily devastates it, showing how core concepts are both problematic and skewed with implausible and indefensible assumptions.[78]

The urgency of and responsibility for emission reductions is increasingly being framed in terms of demands for 'climate justice,' the broad rallying cry for a nascent movement (see Box 1.3). The precise articulation of climate justice varies, but in general it coheres around the recognition that highly unequal atmospheric footprints place a much heavier onus for immediate action on rich countries, and the wealthy within them, and that there is a need to discipline the activities of TNCs and finance capital. That is, justice demands finding policy mechanisms to ensure that those most responsible for climate change are forced to make faster and deeper reductions in per capita GHG emissions (beyond merely proportional cuts), along with making strong commitments to invest in climate change adaptation in the world's most vulnerable countries. George Monbiot presents a clear way of framing these demands. He insists that the precautionary end of academic climate science should be used to set a hard global annual GHG emissions cap, which would place it very far below the sorts of targets being discussed at UNFCCC meetings. Once a hard cap gets set, then the task turns to developing a system of rationing allowable emissions equitably on a world scale, which, for many rich countries, would translate to per capita emission reductions in the order of 80 percent or more from current levels.[79]

Climate change adaptation entails the need to adapt to the climatic changes the world is committed to, and is drawing increasing public and private investment, research, and planning. Adaptive responses range from physical infrastructure such as sea-defence systems to research on crop stress and resilience. Agricultural adaptation is especially challenging, given that a variety of changing physical

---

Box 1.3 Climate justice advocacy: selected examples

Climate Justice Now! (www.climate-justice-now.org)
Climate Justice Action (www.climate-justice-action.org)
Climate Justice: enforcing climate change law (www.
    climatelaw.org)
Climate Justice Collective (www.climatejusticecollective.org)
Durban Group for Climate Justice (www.durbanclimate
    justice.org)
Global Justice Ecology Project (www.globaljusticeecology.org/
    climate_justice.php)
Rising Tide (www.risingtide.org.uk)
Time for Climate Justice (www.climatejusticeonline.org)

conditions (e.g. temperatures, evaporation rates, rainfall patterns, watershed yields, etc.) affect a range of biological responses (e.g. crops, soil organisms, insects, disease, undesirable and invasive species, etc.), which themselves interact in complex ways. Again, global inequalities rear up in starkly uneven capacities for adaptation, as industrialized countries have by far the most financial, technical, institutional, and research capacities for assessing and responding to changes, while poor countries face the greatest risks with far more limited resources. Making matters worse is the fact that bilateral and multilateral support for adaptation initiatives across the global South has fallen far short of promises, wavering badly in the face of global economic instability, financial sector bailouts, and the dance between stimulus packages and austerity. Renowned anti-apartheid leader Desmond Tutu has warned that 'adaptation apartheid' threatens to become an important aspect of climate injustice. Taken together, it would be hard to exaggerate the regressive character of climate change; continuing inaction is very simply a 'prescription for a widening gap between the world's haves and have-nots.'[80]

The sense of 'inter-generational tyranny' described by ecologists in the context of the biodiversity crisis also rings out in the appeals of climate scientists, and Ackerman insists that one basic rallying cry for action on climate change is simply that 'your grandchildren's lives matter.'[81] Unfortunately, as yet global efforts at mitigation remain very depressing, with multilateral meetings stalemated by the combative inertia of rich countries while most national mitigation responses and promises resemble baby steps at a time when the scientific literature is screaming for huge and immediate leaps.

Agriculture's ecological footprint

Agriculture is by far the largest aspect of the ecological footprint on a world scale, and while many dynamics are interrelated, for clarity it helps to organize resource budgets and pollution loads at three basic levels, in terms of impacts on terrestrial environments, water, and the atmosphere.

Land Throughout the course of agrarian history, about half of the world's forests have been cleared for crop cultivation and grazing, along with widespread conversions of natural grasslands and wetlands. In general, agricultural societies have tended to use the best arable

land, with more fertile soils and lower gradients, for crop cultivation mixed with small populations of farm animals, while extensive
pastoralism has tended to spread across lower-quality arable land or
land that is not suited for crops. While some agricultural systems have
been more durable than others, and agriculture practices can serve to
enhance soils, in general the history of agriculture has been marked
by repeating cycles of land conversion, chronic soil degradation, and
more conversion. Agricultural expansion has had a central role in
the accelerating ecological transformations discussed earlier and in
confining other species to ever smaller and more fragmented habitats,
and agriculture's expansive command of land and water makes it
the world's 'largest threat to biodiversity and ecosystem function.'[82]

There are different ways to calculate the total land space given
to agriculture. The *Millennium Ecosystem Assessment* estimates that
cultivated systems cover one quarter of the earth's terrestrial surface,
which it defines as 'areas where at least 30 percent of the landscape
is in croplands, shifting cultivation, confined livestock production,
or freshwater aquaculture.'[83] *Livestock's Long Shadow* estimates that
roughly one tenth of the earth's ice-free land area is under cultivation and one quarter is in some form of meadow or pasture, while
a team of esteemed scientists put slightly more land area in crops
(12 percent) and slightly less in pasture (22 percent), based on an
assessment for the year 2000.[84] In either case, when the scale of feed
crops is added to pasture, livestock production emerges as 'by far the
single largest anthropogenic user of land' (see Figure 1.2).[85] A mere
ten crops dominate the world's arable land and generate about 75
percent of all plant-based calories consumed by humans, while the
'big three' livestock species – pigs, chicken, and cattle – account for
the vast majority of all meat, eggs, and dairy.

Total land for grazing	Pastures and rangelands degraded by overgrazing and erosion	Total land in feed crops
3.43 billion ha 26% of ice-free land surface	20% of total pasture and rangeland	471 million ha 33% of arable land

1.2 The magnitude of livestock production in global land use (*source*: Steinfeld et al. 2006: 271)

Nearly all good arable land with soils suitable for long-term cultivation or grazing is already in use, or has been paved over by cities,
roads, and infrastructure. With highly productive agricultural frontiers
largely closed and the conversion of arable land to urban and industrial
uses continuing, world cropland is projected to decline by 8 to 20
percent by mid-century owing to climate change and desertification.[86]
Should this occur, along with projected population growth, the amount
of arable land on a world scale could fall from roughly 0.2 ha/person
today to as little as 0.14 to 0.12 ha/person by mid-century, what
amounts to at least a threefold decline since 1960.

Where agricultural colonization still continues it is largely for
short-term gains, and often at momentous costs. As noted, the world's
most calamitous agricultural frontiers are in the tropics, where environmental impacts – in particular, damage to biodiversity, carbon
emissions, and diminished sequestration capacity – are made even
worse by the rapid erosion of thin soils. Cattle ranching has been
a leading force tearing into tropical rainforests since the 1960s, in
particular in Brazil and Central America, while industrial soybean
production emerged as another major factor in the deforestation
of the Brazilian Amazon since the 1990s. Another powerful recent
dynamic in tropical deforestation has been the expansion of industrial
oil palm plantations in Southeast Asia in order to produce agrofuels.[87]

While many areas of extensive pasture on productive grasslands
have been relatively stable over long periods, excessive stocking densities, overgrazing, and the continuing expansion of livestock onto
more marginal areas are a leading cause of dryland degradation and
desertification on a world scale.[88] Meanwhile, soil erosion greatly
exceeds soil formation on much of the world's cultivated lands, and
as soils are degraded a large resource budget is needed to keep land
in production – a crucial dynamic examined in Chapter 3. The FAO
estimates that erosion, salinization, and waterlogging destroy 75 billion tonnes of soil every year, which equates to the loss of almost 10
million ha of arable land, while another 20 million ha are abandoned
due to declining soil quality.[89]

Water Roughly half of the world's 45,000-plus large dams were con-
structed solely for irrigation, and the other half are 'multi-purpose,'
designed for varying combinations of irrigation, hydroelectricity, flood
control, and water supply. Global annual freshwater withdrawals for

agriculture grew by a factor of five in the twentieth century, from 500 km³ to over 2,500 km³, and the total area of irrigated land has more than doubled since 1950, primarily in Asia but also significantly in the USA and Europe. Agriculture accounts for over 70 percent of global freshwater withdrawals and most irrigation water is effectively consumed, meaning that much of what gets withdrawn is not returned to nearby waterways – a basic fact which urges us to think about the uneven degree to which water is embedded in different foods.[90] Further, the irrigation runoff returned to nearby waterways frequently bears considerable pollution loads, a subject that is developed further in Chapter 3.

World food security has come to hinge on the high productivity of irrigated agriculture, which comprises one fifth of all land in cultivation but produces two-fifths of all output, including three-fifths of all cereals. This 'irrigation miracle,' as it is sometimes called, makes agriculture the primary force in the dramatic declines in free-flowing waterways noted earlier, and the associated damage to fish, bird, and animal habitats within freshwater and riparian ecosystems.[91]

These underappreciated costs are dramatically illustrated in the USA, where an immense web of hydrological engineering has left only a small percentage of rivers and streams flowing naturally, one of the key factors behind the ongoing devastation of freshwater fish and amphibian populations. In Tim Flannery's estimation, 'the destruction of North America's waterways is arguably the greatest blow ever struck by the European Americans at the continent's biodiversity.'[92] Salmon are among the most striking examples of this loss, especially in the Pacific Northwest, where the once-mighty annual salmon returns that sustained indigenous cultures and mega-fauna are down to less than one *fourteenth* of historic levels. Meanwhile, having been 'driven to the verge of extinction across much of their range,' salmon are increasingly farmed in near-shore industrial enclosures.[93]

Even less widely appreciated is the fact that a significant amount of irrigated land and food production depends on the unsustainable pumping of groundwater. At the end of the twentieth century, between 150 and 200 km³ more groundwater was being pumped than was being recharged every year, with the drawdown or 'mining' of ancient aquifers (i.e. water supplies that are not recharged) a dwindling 'pillar' for some of the world's most productive breadbaskets, including the US High Plains, the North China Plain, and productive regions in

India and Mexico. The problems associated with overdrawing from rivers and lakes, falling water tables, and aquifers are bound to be magnified by climatic changes such as higher temperatures and aridity, declining seasonal runoff, and heightened evapotranspiration, which has led to mounting fears of a growing global crisis of freshwater scarcity – with agriculture front and centre.[94]

In spite of these costs and risks, it is important to recognize that irrigation-enhanced agricultural productivity could potentially reduce the scale of land in cultivation, and hence reserve more space for terrestrial ecosystems. However, as will be emphasized in Chapter 3, it is highly deceiving when such claims are used to justify further industrialization, especially when so much irrigated land is given to feed crops.

Atmosphere Agriculture makes one of the largest contributions to climate change of any human activity. At the center of this is the massive terrestrial footprint of pasture and cropland. When more biodiverse ecosystems are converted to agriculture, CO_2 is emitted from both the vegetation and soils in the short term, and there is a decline in the capacity of the land to sequester carbon over the long term.[95] While this has a clear historical dimension, part of the challenge of weighing agriculture's relative contribution to climate change lies in the question of how far back land conversions should be considered. That is, should the focus be solely on contemporary land conversions, implying that all past conversions to pasture and crops should be treated as more or less permanent? Do the impacts of land conversion on the carbon cycle stretch back to the approximate residence time of CO_2 in the atmosphere? Might this impact extend even further, with all extraneous land in pasture and cultivation weighed against its potential to sequester carbon?

The other major dimension of agriculture's atmospheric impact stems from the biophysical contradictions of the industrial grain-oil-seed-livestock complex, which Chapter 3 examines in detail. Mechanization and large-scale monocultures, factory farms, and feedlots generate or worsen problems of erosion, insects, weeds, and disease, and these problems are never resolved but instead get overridden by recurrent applications of fertilizers, insecticides, herbicides, fungicides, disinfectants, and pharmaceuticals. Fossil energy is vital at every turn, to an extent that agriculture now widely resembles 'the art of turning oil into food.'[96] The incredible productivity gains since the mid-twentieth century are therefore inextricably tied to this energy consumption and the ensuing CO_2 emissions, made worse by the fact that the industrial grain-oilseed-livestock complex is also a leading source of methane and nitrous oxide emissions.

In sum, agriculture is at the forefront of both mitigation and adaptation. This is clearly expressed by the UN Special Rapporteur on the right to food, Olivier De Schutter, who notes that from this point forward it is necessary 'that we think about climate change and agricultural development in combination.'[97] The urgent need for dramatic mitigation efforts challenges the industrial grain-oilseed-livestock complex at its foundations. Here, it is also crucial to recognize that the historic areal expansion of cultivated and pastureland is not an inevitable and fixed legacy. Rather, if agriculture's terrestrial footprint could somehow be shrunk, and more land ecologically restored, it would enhance the volume of biomass sequestering carbon.

Approaching the ecological hoofprint

The ecological *foot*print presents a call to understand consumption in terms of the bundles of land, water, resources, pollution, and GHG emissions embedded in production, and in turn the tremendous environmental dimensions of economic inequalities. The ecological *hoof*print seeks to connect and extend some of these basic concerns to a different and much bigger 'population bomb' than what environmentalists have long focused upon: that which is occurring within systems of industrial livestock production. While extensive rangelands are heavily implicated in major global environmental problems such as tropical deforestation and desertification, the soaring global production and consumption of animal flesh and derivatives are primarily rooted in intensive production, which commands roughly one third of all cultivated land in the world.

As Jeremy Rifkin put it, 'in all of the literature surrounding the issue of overpopulation, scant attention is paid to the fundamental shift in world agriculture ... from food grains to feed grains, a shift of monumental proportions whose impact has been felt at every level of human existence,' and which 'has had a more pronounced impact on the politics of land use and food distribution than any other single factor in modern times.'[98] Because so much usable nutrition is burned in animals' metabolic processes, cycling huge flows of grains and oilseeds through an expanding livestock population is an inherently inefficient way to use cultivated land – a key point that will be developed further in Chapters 2 and 3, starting from Francis Moore Lappé's seminal argumentation.

A primary goal of the ecological hoofprint as a concept and metaphor is to call attention to the large, wide-ranging, and highly uneven burden of industrial livestock production. To do this, it develops a political ecological framework for understanding the industrial grain-oilseed-livestock complex as a system *in motion*, and how its fundamental economic logic (or imperatives) gives shape to the social and ecological relations of production, including the associated instabilities and the ways they are overridden. The ultimate hope is, in the spirit of a radical pedagogy, that it might ultimately help 'to reveal or bring to light what would otherwise remain unseen – the hidden structures of meaning and power that shape our lives.'[99]

2 | THE UNEVEN GEOGRAPHY OF MEAT

Domestication and multifunctionality

Relatively small livestock populations were an important, complementary part of mixed farming systems for the large majority of agrarian history. As Carl Sauer put it, 'for the most part those who cultivated plants also kept animals.'[1] The world's major farm animals (cattle, pigs, sheep, goats, and chickens) were domesticated between 10,000 and 6,000 years ago, along an Asiatic arc stretching from Southeast Asia through the Indus Valley and the Middle East, and into Greece and the Balkans, with the Middle East being an especially key site of domestication and a dispersion corridor. The historic dispersion of domesticated animals, like that of crops, was one of the most powerful forces reshaping farming systems around the world.[2]

Farm animals have almost always had multifunctional roles. At the center of this has been the nutrition provided to humans, particularly protein, as animal protein provides highly usable packages of the essential amino acids which the human body must regularly take in.[3] It is very likely that the recognition of the nutritional value of milk and eggs was an important part of the origins of domestication. The fact that 'all the domestic herd animals are milked or have been thus used in the past' suggests that milking was 'both part of the process and purpose of their domestication,' while the use of poultry birds for meat was secondary to their role in laying eggs.[4] Protein tended to be a precious commodity in agricultural societies, and ruminants like cattle, sheep, and goats represented 'protein factories' in the sense that the rumen in their stomachs enables them to generate microbial protein from fiber and cellulose, and thus convert things with little or no food value to humans into things with much value, namely milk and meat.[5] This was especially true in areas where limited quality arable land and short growing seasons constrained the availability of plant protein. The uses of other bodily materials, foremost sheep wool and cattle skins, further augmented their utility. Agricultural societies were also able to nourish some animals such as poultry and pigs near households, producing nutritionally valuable eggs and flesh, in ways that largely complemented rather than competed with human supplies. For instance, small flocks of poultry could feed on various wastes, seeds, worms, and insects within a small radius, and small numbers of pigs regularly scavenged on a variety of farm and household organic wastes, such as crop residues, roots, and table scraps. In some cases, ruminants like cows were also fed heavily with farm and household wastes, reducing the arable land they occupied.

The role of farm animals concentrating energy and macro- and micro-nutrients for human diets was complemented by their role cycling energy and nutrients within farming landscapes and enhancing soil fertility.[6] While excessive animal densities could lead to damaging overgrazing and soil compaction, at modest densities farm animals provided valuable sources of fertilizer. Dried cow dung has also provided an invaluable source of fuel over millennia, particularly in the Indian subcontinent. As fertilizers, farm animal wastes contain concentrations of essential elements like nitrogen, phosphorus, and potassium, as well as organic matter, and much of this was historically dispersed across the land by the animals themselves. Where animal manure was concentrated in barns or other enclosures, it tended to be processed in ways (e.g. composting in straw bedding) where bio-oxidation reduced or eliminated potentially pathogenic microorganisms and left behind a safer and nutrient-rich fertilizer before it was applied to fields. The diversity of diets, ingestion of a range of microorganisms, ability to exercise, and exposure to the elements all helped animals maintain their general health and immune systems, and relatively low densities tended to mitigate disease risks.

The capacity to produce protein-dense foods from grasses and roughage allowed ruminants to be nourished on fallowed land, as rotations like grasses, alfalfa, and clover replenished soils, while at the same time nourishing soils with manure. The 'protein factory' capacity also enabled stocking in marginal arable regions and regions entirely unsuited to crops owing to soils, climate, or slope – hence the great role of pasture in converting land and permanently arresting succession over wide areas, given how so much land is not well suited for agriculture. In general pastoralism evolved out of agriculture, got practiced on its margins, and ultimately depended on agricultural communities to varying degrees. For instance, over millennia African land use was characterized by a basic moisture and soil continuum from sedentary farming in the highest-quality arable lands, to shifting cultivation and semi-pastoralism in lower-quality arable lands (with animals grazing and manuring fields left fallow for long periods), to extensive herding over dry grasslands following seasonal rains and vegetation, with trading relationships common between groups more focused on cultivation and others more focused on herding and animal husbandry (a number of herding cultures, such as the Maasai in East Africa, became exceptionally dependent upon their livestock for food). The fact that livestock could be moved around, made to forage on hardier plants during dry periods, and 'harvested' more selectively than crops was also a means to manage risk in the face of variable rainfall patterns.

Another primary function of large domesticated animals in agriculture has been as conscripted labor for plowing farmland and moving goods, drawn principally from cattle, horses, mules, donkeys, and water buffaloes. Cattle were first harnessed with the plow in Mesopotamia, and the productivity gains and surpluses that ensued gave rise to new classes (a key being the reduction of the time and human labor needed for food-getting), gendered divisions of labor and patriarchal cultures, conversions of common to private property, and ultimately powerful states with dominating rulers and dominated subjects. The increasing control over domesticated animals was thus an essential foundation for civilization and its emergent hierarchies. It was also a factor in slowly increasing human population growth, which began doubling every millennium following the oxen and plow, as plow-based agriculture gave rise to larger-scale (and much less diversified) systems. The importance of animal labor to human societies is not merely a historic relation. As many as 2 billion people in the global South still depend on the work of 300 million draft animals in a fundamental way, and the case remains today that 'in poor developing countries, for the bulk of their populations, donkey power is more ubiquitous, and more vital, than the internal combustion engine.'[7]

Yet while domesticated livestock were widely used in farming, supplementing diets, returning concentrated nutrients back to the soil, and providing labor, this was not always the case. In some instances agricultural innovation geared to simultaneously enhancing human nutrition and soil health was centered mainly or entirely on intercropping patterns involving things such as various beans, peas, and lentils. For instance, agriculture in the Americas involved very little livestock prior to Columbus yet supported some massive empires, as with the Aztec, Maya, and Inca. The famed *milpa* system of planting maize, beans, squash, and other crops together, which prevailed over much of Mesoamerica, provided a healthy combination of protein, fats, carbohydrates, and vitamins at the same time as the biophysical interrelationship of these plants helped to maintain healthy soils. This symbiosis was historically 'without an equal elsewhere,' as 'the corn plants grow tall and have first claim on sunlight and moisture. The beans climb up the corn stalks for their share of light; their roots support colonies of nitrogen-fixing bacteria. The squashes or pumpkins grow mainly prone on the ground and complete the ground cover.'[8]

Some regions of China also maintained agricultural systems with little or no livestock that were both nutritionally complete and eco-logically sustainable over very long periods, abetted by protein-dense and nitrogen-fixing soybeans and the recycling of human excreta (sometimes referred to as 'nightsoil' or humanure). The Tai Lake region of China is a notable example, though like most pre-industrial peasantries it should hardly be confused with a pre-industrial Eden, as 'what was ecologically efficient was hardship for the people; farmers worked to the limits of endurance and saw no opportunity for im-proving their situation.'[9]

The ambiguous contract

Human societies have tried to rationalize their relations with domesticated livestock in various ways. One recurring narrative is that animals have given some sort of tacit consent to the course of domestication, gaining enhanced feeding environments, sometimes shelter, and protection from predators in exchange for their labor, reproductive outputs, and slaughter and bodily consumption short of a full lifespan. Jonathan Safran Foer encapsulates the essence of this contractual narrative as conceivably told to animals: 'we'll protect you, arrange food for you, etc., and, in turn, your labor will be harnessed, your milk and eggs taken, and, at times, you will be killed and eaten,' which, he aptly notes, brought animals into 'a new kind of intimacy with humans – new kinds of care and new kinds of violence.'[10]

This inevitable violence makes the act of eating meat arguably one of the most basic acts and symbols that simultaneously reflects and reinforces human supremacy over other species. Still, the notion of a mutually beneficial contract certainly has some broad basis in the interdependence that grew over millennia, as thousands of years of selective breeding and husbandry massively expanded the spaces occupied by farm animals while making them less able to survive outside of the modified landscapes and protection afforded by humans. Sometimes this growth over space and in populations is given to indicate the benefits of domestication to animals, though the contractual imagery obviously manipulates animal consciousness and complicity, and simplifies an immensely more ambiguous story. For one, it fabricates the philosophical basis of early agriculture and herding, as domestication was not a swift and singular transition but the outcome of much experimentation and a long and fuzzy historical process of co-evolution. For another, humanity appears in an undifferentiated way, though domestication and the symbolism that attached to its consumption were historically tied to patriarchal and class hierarchies.[11]

Beyond this lies the tenuous relationship between protection and care on one hand and exploitation and killing on the other. Until very recently, these moral tensions and ambiguities of farm animal domestication were ever present in human societies, as livelihoods were overwhelmingly based on agriculture and most farmers and pastoralists would have known all of their animals as individual beings. This intimacy could still entail a wide spectrum of treatment, ranging from hard migrations, exhausting labor, and primitive systems of slaughter and confinement, to relatively comfortable and autonomous lives spent mostly rummaging about pastures or farm households. Nevertheless, abusive treatment was bounded at the very least by the strong self-interest of farmers and pastoralists in the health, nourishment, and long-term productivity of every animal, which might be seen to have set the minimal limits of farm animal welfare. This was partly because animal numbers were typically small and their multifunctional utility was so important, and partly because livestock were an important source of wealth that held a discernible exchange value, based on a range of use values, and could be moved and traded. As Jeremy Rifkin points out, 'the very word "cattle" comes from the same etymological root as the word "capital",' and from a very early stage 'cattle meant property.'[12]

At the maximal end of the spectrum of farm animal welfare, consideration from farmers and pastoralists has surely been widened by sincere feelings of affection, respect, and empathy, which have both infused and been shaped by different cultural and religious beliefs. One compelling illustration of this comes from anthropological research with the Ariaal herders of East Africa, for whom, as Wade Davis puts it, Zebu cattle 'are the fulcrum of life. When men meet on a trail, they ask first of the well-being of the herds, then of the families. Each animal has a mark and a name, a personality setting it apart. Cattle represent a man's wealth and status, and without herds, he cannot marry. But the bond is deeper, even spiritual, rooted in every intuition about the landscape and environment.'[13] India provides another example of this union of dependence and reverence, as cattle have had an age-old role providing labor, milk, and manure, and a sacred status in the Hindu religion – a functional-moral 'contract' encapsulated in Gandhi's famous depiction of cattle as a 'mother' to India.[14] India has the world's largest cattle population (over 210 million in 2010), and though their treatment may not always reflect this elevated status, in general human–cattle relations there are more symbiotic and less violent than most between humans and farm animals.

In sum, for most of agrarian history farm animal husbandry practices have been shaped by attitudes which place animals somewhere between *objects* of human self-interest and *subjects* of their own lives, with varying degrees of moral entitlements. The limits of technology have also tended to inhibit the extent of animal confinement, though not always, as Andrew Johnson emphasizes, as confined animal systems were found in places such as ancient Egypt and Rome.[15] The result was that farm animals generally retained some degree of spatial mobility, social interactivity, familial bonds, and independent decision-making in their lives, and experienced natural rhythms from day to night and season to season. When we recognize that farm animals have complex intellectual and emotional lives, it is possible to assume that many would have felt not only more secure in agricultural and pastoral landscapes but also, where they were reasonably well treated, an attachment to people that ran stronger than this.[16]

Livestock and changing views of nature in early modern Europe

Although livestock long held significant agricultural and nutritional functions, it is important to keep the scale in perspective: for the greater part of agrarian history, human diets centered on vegetable foods with animal flesh on the periphery, often limited to special celebrations and events, while milk and eggs tended to be consumed somewhat more frequently, though still far below contemporary levels.

Instead, carbohydrates like maize, rice, millet, and potatoes tended to be the center of the diet in most agricultural societies. Livestock densities were generally low, and where nutrient cycles in mixed farms and extensive pasture were effectively organized, long-term stability was possible – though excessive grazing and plowing by livestock was a major force in agricultural and ultimately civilizational decline, from the Fertile Crescent to Greece to the Roman Empire.[17]

In the older regions of domestication, cattle tended to be most valuable as labor, and secondarily for milk, and Europe was one of the first world regions where the production of beef became more important in cattle rearing. Over centuries, Europe became 'a region of meat-eaters,' much more so than anywhere else, devoting 'vast lands for pasturing animals' beyond the densely populated Mediterranean, with 'the riot of meat' established as 'a long-lasting feature on the tables of the rich' across the continent.[18] Very strong class connotations developed around 'meat, and especially beef' in England, as it was presumed by the nobility to be part of their 'greater strength and virility.'[19] Yet the scale of permanent and rotational pastures was such that meat did trickle down heavily from lord to peasant over centuries, especially in the wake of the Black Death (c. 1348–50), when Europe lost at least a fifth of its human population. This began to change, however, after the mid-sixteenth century, as meat moved back to the periphery of diets for the poor majority of Europeans for roughly the next three centuries. One illustration of this can be seen in the estimation that the average German consumed 100 kg of meat a year in the late Middle Ages, a level that would be very high on a world scale today, but only 20 kg a year by the early nineteenth century.[20]

Jason Moore argues that a deepening ecological crisis had a central role in the demise of the feudal order in Europe and its inability to continue generating the surpluses that sustained its particular configuration of class relations,[21] and the declining supply of meat to the poor majority might be seen as one manifestation of this. Moore's analysis of the transition from feudalism to capitalism also goes some way to explaining how capitalism emerged as a distinctive set of socio-ecological relations which have always been hard-wired for expansion. As discussed in Chapter 1, from the sixteenth century onwards the recurring plunder of large ecological surpluses on new commodity frontiers – bearing cheap food, energy, and raw materials with relatively little capital invested – was pivotal to revolutions in productivity, starting within Europe and soon extending far beyond. For instance, timber from Scandinavia and wheat from Poland bolstered the dynamism of the Dutch Republic, one of the early centers of capitalist development. In England the accelerating clearance of forests, drainage of wetlands, and enclosures of the commons went hand in hand with the rising production, before the plunder and productivity dialectic took on a much greater scale, first in Scotland and Ireland and later across the world with the rise of the British Empire and the Industrial Revolution.[22]

In spite of the strong disposition for beef in England, it was sheep rather than cattle and wool rather than meat which were most instrumental in the rise of agrarian capitalism there. The growing demand for wool from England's emerging commercial class gave a strong incentive for landlords and large tenants to increase the scale of their sheep flocks, which was met through both plunder and productivity. On one hand, growth in the scale of production occurred by appropriating more ecosystems, fencing off the commons, and displacing those uncompetitive peasants who could no longer afford higher rents in competitive land markets. On the other hand, this plunder was accompanied by concerted efforts to enhance yield and output per worker. In what became known as 'High Farming' in England, attention was given to understanding biophysical cycles between crops and livestock and the science of improving them, with rotational pastures and animals, in particular sheep flocks, understood to have a key role in fertilizing plowed lands. The notion of 'improvement' also came to frame the class project of agrarian change, and not only were great yield gains achieved but these were coupled with the long-term improvement of soil conditions. The result was a historically distinctive form of capitalist agriculture that, while highly unequal, was largely sustainable in a biophysical sense on farms themselves.[23]

The place of sheep in the rise of agrarian capitalism was reflected in Thomas More's (1478–1535) oft-cited reflection that 'sheep were eating men,' as peasants were being converted into a new class of landless workers. This dislocation and class formation was also implicated in the transformation of diets. Whereas English peasants had once consumed some variety of vegetables and dairy, and meat which they largely produced themselves, having relied on the commons for grazing livestock, the newly constituted working class at first came to depend heavily on a narrower diet of cheap food staples like bread and potatoes. Meanwhile, at the other end of the social order, new capitalist elites absorbed the old cultural associations about meat and power held by the nobility, and beef became a significant part of the bourgeois demonstration of class.[24]

It is also important to consider how changing socio-ecological relations were wrapped up in new ways of seeing and representing the world. In this, the ideas of Francis Bacon (1561–1626) and René Descartes (1596–1650) were especially influential, and it is telling that these ideas were forged in the two great early centers of capitalist dynamism, the Dutch Republic and England. Previously, much of the technological innovation in Europe had emerged from monastic orders, and the flowering of science and technology under capitalism was entwined with an extreme new faith in, or *religion of*, technology, which was also tied to 'an ideological elevation of mankind above nature.' To Bacon, 'man' was a 'mortal god,' not only entitled to dominate the earth but indeed called to conquer it, and reshape the despised wilderness or 'wastelands' to serve human needs. David Noble suggests that 'perhaps more than anyone else before or since, Bacon defined the Western project of modern technology' as a means to intensify the rightful conquest of 'man' over nature, a view that was also shaped by a fervent belief that the millennium was at hand. The sorts of representations of the world given by Bacon and Descartes were later part of the moral sanctioning of colonialism and the appropriation of vast 'wildernesses' (i.e. almost any non-European lands) abroad.[25]

Descartes similarly placed man and civilization both outside and above the rest of life, as the only species upon which God bestowed souls and consciousness, which was entwined with his separation of mind and body, spirit and matter, and in turn with a mechanistic depiction of animals and nature.[26] One of the clearest illustrations of this mechanism lies in Descartes' denigration of soul-less and unconscious animals as complex, instinctual *automata* ('beast machines') with an infamous analogy that a dog yelping in pain during vivisection was like the squeaking of an unoiled machine. To anyone with any empathy towards animals this surely sounds absurd, even psychotic, and this was true then as now, but the essential Cartesian dualism and mechanism have nevertheless had great traction in modernity.[27]

In the nineteenth century, evolutionary theory presented a fundamental challenge to Cartesian philosophy by radically repositioning humanity within a class of mammalian relatives. But the intellectual reverberations of evolutionary theory were extremely varied, and one influential narrative placed humanity as victor of an age-old biological competition, in a way partly reconciling the elevation of humanity over nature. From this view, as the pinnacle of evolution it is our competitive fitness which bestows the right to dominate the rest of life, a narrative which also spiraled into the racist morass of Social Darwinism.

Meat in empire and livestock on new frontiers

Over the course of European imperialism, livestock expanded through both intention and accident, and figured heavily in the dispossession, genocide, extraction of mineral wealth, and ecological change which ensued. In the 'New World,' animals like cattle, pigs, chickens, goats, sheep, horses, and donkeys tended to thrive in the vicinity of European settlements, and in many places pigs and cattle turned feral and pushed far beyond. This began on the islands of the Caribbean, where indigenous peoples had previously flourished through fishing and farming, as introduced livestock ran wild amid abundant vegetation, no large predators or competition, and no serious pest or disease risks. Though the Spanish quickly lost interest in the Caribbean and came to focus on the mainland, the livestock they unleashed made the islands useful as layover and supply stations for ships in Spain's convoy system moving back and forth across the Atlantic.[28]

On the mainland, livestock became essential to the Spanish mining economy, providing it with labor, meat, hides, and tallow. Livestock was also instrumental in the rise of a powerful class of landholding elites and in the extremely unequal distribution of agricultural land that has persisted to the present day. Starting with Hernán Cortés in central Mexico, Spanish colonizers appropriated huge areas from indigenous people for *haciendas*, which typically coupled extensive livestock ranching with some cultivation of Old World cereals, chiefly wheat. In colonial Brazil, the expansion of cattle also had an important role in facilitating the drive inland by the Portuguese. Moreover, as in the Caribbean, feral pigs and cattle became vigorous ecological invaders, sprawling autonomously across sizable areas from Mexico to Argentina, before their exploitation became increasingly coordinated over time. One great example of this was on the pampas, where wild cattle populations exploded and came to be hunted by *gauchos* into the eighteenth century, before being nomadically herded and eventually commercially ranched in conjunction with extensive grain farms.[29]

Plunder on an array of colonial frontiers nourished the productive dynamism of British capitalism, yielding such things as cheap labor, sugar, cotton, and wood. Livestock, especially cattle, was also intimately connected to the expansion of the British Empire in many parts of the world. As noted, unequal meat consumption was an important part of the demonstration of class in Britain, first for the nobility and later for emergent capitalist elites, and increasing meat consumption also became a strong aspiration of the working class. Beginning in the seventeenth century, rising demand for meat in England was partly met by taking and transforming large areas of Scotland and Ireland to effectively serve as English pasture, dispossessing many, with Ireland suffering spectacularly for this role. David Nally gives a penetrating account of how Britain incrementally transformed the Irish landscape and economy, seizing large areas of land for export-oriented estates, transforming systems of land tenure, and destroying self-provisioning small farms, craft industries, and traditional anti-scarcity systems over a long period before the Great Irish Famine of the 1840s, and then using the calamitous period of the Famine itself to intensify the expropriation and consolidation of land. Before and during the Famine – when roughly a million Irish died and another million migrated – large volumes of beef, pork, and other food were exported to England, and these exports grew further in the wake of this devastating depopulation.[30]

By drawing heavily from Irish and Scottish pastures, meat consumption in England dwarfed that of the rest of Europe well into the nineteenth century.[31] Still, for the English working class, bread was the most important food staple in the early Industrial Revolution and hence a pivotal *wage good*, which implies a central role in determining the price of labor. In other words, because food is an essential consumption item needed in the reproduction of working-class households, its cost weighs significantly on minimum wage levels. In 1846, the Corn Laws liberalized British trade in wheat, marking a turning point when its food security began to be increasingly tied to cheaper imports (as compared with agriculture in Europe), sourced from the great Europeanized grasslands of North America, southern South America, Australia, and New Zealand – an event that is widely given as a key indicator of the political ascendance of industrial over agrarian capital in Britain. The cheap food flowing from these frontiers helped to hold down the price of labor as the industrial working class grew, in line with Moore's insistence that the incorporation of new and cheaply exploited ecological surpluses from widening commodity frontiers has long had a key role in deflating wage pressures during dynamic periods of capitalist development.[32]

Following the course of wheat, England began to increasingly tap the vast new temperate livestock frontiers by the mid-nineteenth century. Heightened flows of meat were technologically enabled by the development of new canning technologies, refrigeration, more extensive rail networks, and faster steamships, and emboldened the British Empire in a few ways. First, they helped satiate the working class physically and politically, and secure their support for the Empire. Secondly, Britain became the pivot of the First International Food Regime, which emerged after 1870, drawing in large flows of wheat and meat from the new temperate frontiers, and connecting these to other parts of Europe.[33] Thirdly, in helping to contain labor costs, Britain's command of cheaper globally sourced food staples braced its competitiveness in manufacturing. As beef consumption rose it took on nationalist and imperialist dimensions, which grew out of older class aspirations and ideas about meat giving 'strength and virility' and into a mythology placing the well-nourished British beef-eater as a basis for the reign over weaker peoples and the might of the Empire. Associations of meat with strength also involved a romanticization of the rugged figures like cowboys and gauchos on the conquered, Europeanized frontiers, where much of this beef was coming from.[34] This myth was further fortified by the nutritional science of the day, which was influenced by Liebig, who was most famous for his pioneering insights into soil science and fertilization. Liebig argued that protein was the 'master nutrient' for animals in the way that nitrogen was for plants (i.e. the biggest single factor driving or inhibiting growth), a claim which was blended into a celebration of animal protein.[35] The elevation of animal protein went on to infuse both class and nationalist aspirations in the modern world.

In short, cheap food has had an important role in paving 'the road to the modern world,'[36] and cheap meat has been an important feature in this, both as an increasingly significant wage good containing the price of labor and as a powerful symbolic goal purchasing a degree of consent.

The US west: from great livestock frontier to assembly-line slaughter

For centuries, the slaughter of wild animals was an important part of European colonial frontiers as they pushed westward across North America, with the fur trade fueling the killing of untold millions of mammals, such as beavers, raccoons, pine marten, bobcats, otters, lynx, foxes, wolves, and bears. Meanwhile, echoes of Bacon and Descartes rang out in how the 'wilderness' was understood as a dark, menacing wasteland that may have been partially inhabited *but was not owned* by an uncivilized people, and how its conquest on the frontier was celebrated in the USA and Canada.[37]

The ecology of conquest on the great western grasslands was embodied most of all by the decimation of the American bison, or buffalo, in the nineteenth century. Since before the start of the Holocene, large herds of wild buffalo had ranged across the grasslands of North America, and not long before the Euro-American onslaught there were between 30 and 60 million buffalo (a range of estimates which reflects how the population was never surveyed before it was already in steep decline). These huge populations were sustained by the great productivity of the thick tall-grass, mixed-grass, and short-grass prairies stretching from Canada to Texas, that were underlain by deep and incredibly fertile soils which had built up over millennia. The indigenous nations of the grasslands, whose livelihoods and cultures centered on the buffalo and its migrations, also tended the grasses with the occasional use of fire, keeping successional forests at bay.[38] Luther Standing Bear (1868–1939) of the Oglala Sioux captured the profound disjuncture between the indigenous understanding of their world and the spirit of the Euro-American colonization which overran it:

> For the Lakota, mountains, lakes, rivers, springs, valleys, and woods were all finished beauty; winds, rain, snow, sunshine, day, night, and change of seasons brought interest; birds, insects, and animals filled the world with knowledge that defied the discernment of man. But nothing the Great Mystery placed in the land of the Indian pleased the white man, and nothing escaped his transforming hand. Wherever forests have not been mowed down; wherever the animal is recessed in their quiet protection; wherever the earth is not bereft of four-footed life – that to him is an 'unbroken wilderness'.[39]

For the USA, the pacification and enclosure of this 'wilderness' promised to unlock the most valuable agricultural frontier ever encountered. The substitution of cattle for buffalo first began with hardy Spanish longhorns in Texas, where the cattle population erupted from 100,000 in 1830 to 3.5 million in 1860. Yet by 1865 there were still many autonomous indigenous nations spread out across the US west, along with roughly 10 million buffalo. The 'Plains Indian Wars' proved difficult and costly for the US government, so it turned to a very deliberate program of ecological warfare as an easier and cheaper route to genocide that was encapsulated by famed US general Sheridan: 'let them kill, skin, and sell until the buffalo is exterminated, as it is the only way to bring lasting peace and allow civilization to advance.'[40] The phenomenal pace of the buffalo slaughter and the reconfiguration of the landscape into farmsteads and ranches were hastened by the coming of rail (financed not only by the US government and investors but also British capital, which in turn dominated much of the flows of resource wealth). In 1869, the first transcontinental railroad was finished, and by 1890 – the year the USA officially declared its frontier 'closed' – there were over 240,000 km (150,000 miles) of track, the buffalo was almost completely annihilated, and the population of cattle had risen to about 10 million. Much as sheep devoured peasants in the early British enclosures, cattle can be seen to have devoured indigenous nations during the enclosures of the US west.[41]

Fast-growing cattle populations initially fed on the native prairie grasses, and there was some ecological continuity as one large ruminant displaced another. However, native grasses began to decline as the landscape was partitioned and cattle grazed far more intensively than had the buffalo, which led to the introduction of alien grasses. Ecological change increased further with the rise of the steel plow, which enabled the extraordinary expansion of cereal crops from both the Old World (e.g. wheat, oats, rye, and barley) and the New (especially maize). From the outset, wheat was the key cash crop of the farms built on the American grasslands, while the value of maize and other coarse grains (e.g. barley, oats, and sorghum) has always derived mainly from livestock.

Pigs were a favoured animal on the US agricultural frontier because they were hardy and multiplied relatively quickly, and as maize and other coarse grain production increased, pigs were also seen as the best animal to absorb this feed and bring it to market as flesh, because they were more efficient at converting it than cows or sheep. Thus, when the first ever large-scale system of animal slaughter, disassembly, and packing was developed near this frontier in the early nineteenth century, in Cincinnati, Ohio, the focus was on killing pigs, giving the city the unflattering moniker 'Porkopolis.' The highly specialized division of labor on the early production lines in Porkopolis 'was among the most important forerunners of the mass production techniques that swept American industry in the century to come,' before this system was carried to and expanded in Chicago.[42]

In his epic book *Nature's Metropolis*, William Cronon (1991) shows how the rise of Chicago and the rapid ecological conversions of the US west were mutually constitutive dynamics, as Chicago, especially after the railways, acted like a giant funnel for much of the capital that financed the development of new resource frontiers, and for many of the commodities and surplus value that poured out of them. This included, very centrally, both grains and livestock. From its inception, the wheat from family farmers in the US west was commercialized and tied to an international 'breadbasket' role; initially as a key part of Britain's rising dependence on imports after the mid-nineteenth century, and over time to many parts of the world. Livestock production, on the other hand, was much more constrained by space at first. In temperate regions, livestock historically tended to fatten and thin with seasonal variations in the food supply, and it was more difficult to move animals to slaughter and markets in the cold of winter. This contributed to a considerable seasonality in the supply of meat, along with a high degree of localization, as animals could only be moved so far without burning off a lot of weight and flesh could only be moved so far before spoiling. However, the dramatic expansion of rail networks meant that live animals could be shipped across both farther distances and different seasons, which served to 'smooth' the seasonality of animal slaughterhouses, while the development of refrigerated railcars and steamers and advances in shipping greatly lessened the friction of distance from slaughter to market. When these biophysical constraints were first beginning to be broken down, the incipient meatpacking industry faced another sizable barrier that might be hard to appreciate today: there was a widespread expectation among people buying meat in the USA that it would be freshly killed and butchered. Cronon describes how groundbreaking industrial meatpackers like Gustavus Swift confronted these conceptions in a variety of ways: through marketing (manufacturing demand for new, modern products such as 'dressed beef'); co-opting or destroying small-scale butchers (transforming them into wholesale distributors of processed meats); and ultimately through overwhelming price advantages. The net result was to revolutionize the geography of meat, enabling a 'great tide of animal flesh' to flow through Chicago from the fast-changing landscapes to the west.[43]

The funneling of grain and livestock through Chicago also contributed to the rise of concentrated feedlots in the US Midwest. Feedlots were designed with the basic aim of quickly putting back the weight onto cattle and pigs (mostly with maize and hay) which they lost on the journeys from farm or pasture to slaughter or live market. The expansion of rail increased the radius that feedlots could be from the end-points. Feedlots began to tie together the maize and other coarse grain production with the rangelands, both of which were booming on the deep, fertile, newly opened soils. The nature of the demand, and in particular the 'peculiar shift in British appetites from lean to fatty beef in the early 19th century,' also bears attention in order to understand how grain farming and cattle ranching in the US west were increasingly linked together into the first industrial grain-livestock complex, as Britain was both the primary source of finance capital and the predominant export market for surging cattle production.[44] Much like the consumption pattern noted earlier, marbled flesh (i.e. showing fat specks) began as a strong culinary and symbolic preference of the British elite that trickled down over time as meat became more prevalent in the diets of middle and working classes, and the rising demand for fatty beef at the heart of Empire gave a new incentive to feed maize to cattle. The result was that for a region teeming with maize, surpluses could be used not only to put back *lost* weight on cattle but to put on *additional* weight as marbled flesh, and systematically add value to them.

As Chicago became the hub connecting western livestock to eastern markets, a colossal system of animal holding, slaughter, and meatpacking emerged at the Union Stock Yards, focused on cattle in addition to pigs. The Stock Yards were, in many ways, a great symbol of the US conquest of the west and the reorganization of its productive bounty. There, an oligopoly of large meatpacking companies established new techniques of mass production such as the conveyor belt and the disassembly line that spectacularly increased the scale and speed with which animals could be killed, 'disassembled' into various body parts, and packed, as well as expanding the scope of new commodities that could be produced from animal bodies. These productive innovations went on to shape extremely influential ideas about 'scientific management' in industry, including those of Henry Ford himself. Ford pointed to the disassembly lines of the Stock Yards as an inspiration for the assembly lines he developed to produce cars, and his name came to define the era-defining dominance of this system of manufacturing and regulation in the USA and beyond.[45] Again we see plunder stoking productivity gains.

The Union Stock Yards also demolished any intimacy between people and farm animals. For workers, the industrialization of slaughter and packing involved an intellectual numbing, stemming from both the extreme simplification and monotony of the labor process and the need to be hardened to a fast-paced rhythm of killing and chopping up animals. For consumers, the system enfolded meat in a heavy veil that severed the commodity from its animal being. Cronon brilliantly explains this increasing disassociation and unconsciousness, noting how, in the past, 'one was not likely to forget that pigs and cattle had died so that people might eat,' but 'in a world of ranches, packing plants, and refrigerator cars, most such connections vanished from easy view. The packing plants distanced their customers most of all from the act of killing,' and the more people became accustomed to the attractively cut, carefully wrapped, cunningly displayed packages of meat, 'the more easily they could fail to remember that their purchase had once pulsed and breathed with a life much like their own.' Thus, he places 'forgetfulness' as being 'among the least noticed and most important' consequences of the Stock Yards, furthering 'the commodification of meat' and alienating 'still more its ties to the lives and ecosystems that had ultimately created it.' This commodification and forgetting might then be seen as a 'second death':

> Severed from the form in which it had lived, severed from the act that had killed it, it vanished from human memory as one of nature's creatures. Its ties to the earth receded, and in forgetting the animal's life one also forgot the grasses and the prairie skies and the departed bison herds of a landscape that seemed more and more remote in space and time … The new corporate order, by linking and integrating the products of so many ecosystems and communities, obscured the very connections it helped create.[46]

Yet while the lives of animals may have been obscured and forgotten, meat-eating remains a powerful symbol of human supremacy over nature and other animals, even if it generally goes unsaid. Indeed, the fact that meat consumption surged with industrialization might reflect not only increased productive capacity and availability but also a generalized cultural celebration of the deepening domination over nature.[47]

Meatification in 'development' and surplus disposal

The meatification of diets is a central pillar of the 'Western diet,' what Michael Pollan calls 'the most radical change to the way humans eat since the discovery of agriculture.'[48] In addition to extremely high levels of direct meat, egg, and dairy consumption, the Western diet is also characterized by large volumes of highly processed foods in which livestock derivatives also feature centrally, along with processed maize, wheat, and soybeans and an array of synthetic chemicals and preservatives.

Britain had been the forerunner in the modern world in shifting meat from the periphery to the center of human diets, with the meatification of diets overtly woven into conceptions of power; first, as a reflection and demonstration of class rule, and later reaching the working classes and coupled to a sense of nationalist pride and imperialist strength with the 'British Beefeater.' Beyond the nineteenth century, in places where meat remained less common, levels of meat consumption have tended to keep strong associations with class and class ascension as a marker of wealth and status. However, in some countries, such as the USA, Canada, Argentina, and Australia, meatification quickly cut across class and, in its ubiquity, became an implicit, broad-based national expectation, as it had over a longer period of time in Britain. The rise of the fast food industry in the USA served to further imprint this everyday expectation on popular culture in the West, with innovators like Ray Kroc of McDonald's ingeniously tying the growth of cheap, mass-produced meat to the explosive boom in suburbia and automobility, and capitalizing on people's increasing time-stress. In a sense, the casually entitled McDonald's hamburger-eater came to replace the proud imperial British beef-eater, as fast food became so imprinted in the American psyche and in everyday rhythms.[49]

In the influential narrative about world development given by modernization theory, the USA and Britain were the apex of a universally attainable transition to modernity culminating in societies of 'high mass consumption.'[50] While this theory seems more implausible than ever today, the notion that all nations are striving to ascend some sort of shared pathway – or a developmental 'ladder' out of poverty – remains an enduring one, as does the conflation of the meaning of development with increased consumption.[51] Within this general narrative, the meatification of diets is an important if underappreciated indicator of modernization. Put another way, the climb up the 'animal protein ladder' is part and parcel of the climb up the 'development ladder,' and patterns of rising meat consumption at the national scale have been very tightly linked to patterns of rising affluence, with industrialized countries consuming meat at vastly higher levels and the world's poorest regions at the bottom of the meat consumption spectrum (this broad picture comes into clearer focus later in this chapter).

As in the nineteenth century following Liebig, national aspirations to increase meat consumption have been influenced by nutritional claims about animal protein. In essence, the argument has been that animal protein is better than plant protein, and that plant-based diets tend to be centered on carbohydrates and provide an inadequate quantity and quality of protein. In the USA, this case was vigorously promoted by the livestock and meatpacking industries in the early twentieth century, together with the US Department of Agriculture (USDA), and became ingrained in the national nutritional guidelines which foregrounded the importance of heavy meat, egg, and dairy consumption.[52] The purported superiority of animal protein has been used as a veritable trump card by the champions of industrial livestock production, pulled again and again to justify this course – even as evidence about the negative health impacts of meat-centered diets began to mount, a point that is developed more fully in Chapter 4.

This disjuncture reflects the fact that soaring livestock production and consumption were, at root, not about nutrition; rather, they were driven at a more fundamental level by the economic pressure to expand the scope for capital accumulation in agriculture and food. To appreciate this, it helps to start with the enormous grain surpluses that began emerging across large parts of the temperate world as industrialization, high-yielding seeds, and increasing input intensity brought great productivity gains. The nature and unaccounted costs of these productive changes are a major focus of the following chapter, but for the discussion here it is sufficient to focus on a central economic problem posed by chronic surpluses or gluts: they deflate prices and earnings for farmers, threatening their livelihoods and ultimately continued growth in the sector as a whole. To be clear, a chronic grain surplus does not mean that everyone is being fed. Rather, it is something that exists in relation to *effective demand*, which is essentially the desire plus the ability to purchase a commodity. It means, in very simple terms, that hungry people who can't pay don't register. In the USA, the matter of large chronic grain surpluses meant that there was easily enough being produced to meet the nation's demand, in addition to the wheat exports that had been entrenched in the breadbasket of the Midwest from the start. Well into the twentieth century, the demand for grain was mostly as food, though some was fed to overwintering livestock and some to put back or add weight before slaughter. To continue increasing productivity beyond this effective demand and rates of human population growth would be economically self-defeating. Thus, as the USA developed the most bountiful agricultural system the world had ever known, the question of *surplus absorption* became an inescapable one. This is sometimes described as a question of *surplus disposal*, but *surplus absorption* better reflects how the ultimate challenge was not to simply get rid of surpluses but to find ways of profitably absorbing them on an ongoing basis.[53]

One route to surplus absorption was for governments to buy and hold a share of the harvest to keep supply more in line with demand, and thereby stabilize prices for farmers. But this obviously establishes a considerable fiscal burden for the state, and there is still an unresolved question of what to do with swelling stocks. Destroying food is politically unpalatable, among other things (though this didn't stop it from happening in Europe). Another route to surplus disposal was for governments to purchase a share of the harvest and send it elsewhere as aid, subsidizing the consumption of those who otherwise did not have effective demand for it – some of whom may have been hungry, some of whom were not but shifted their diets in response to the cheap food before them. This was a very politically expedient course for the USA, especially as food aid could double as a geopolitical tool in the Cold War, and great volumes of wheat surpluses began streaming to the global South from the mid-twentieth century onwards. Yet while aid and subsidized trade did help to firmly establish commercial markets over time, this was still only a partial resolution to the surplus problem.

To unlock the barrier to increasing grain production there had to be a more profitable way to soak up chronic surpluses, and the key that emerged was to cycle them through fast-rising populations of concentrated livestock. The trigger for this was chicken production. In 1910, the average chicken flock on a US farm had about eighty birds, and almost 90 percent of farms kept at least a few chickens. In the 1920s, in the Delmarva Peninsula of the eastern USA (Delaware–Maryland–Virginia), an accidental experiment in rearing thousands of chickens in a small space using concentrated feed set off a wave of innovations in warehouses, hatcheries, artificial incubators, feed regimes, and debeaking machines over the next few decades, which involved the rise of some soon-to-be corporate giants like Perdue and Tyson. This take-off was famously signaled by Herbert Hoover's promise during the 1928 presidential election campaign to put 'a chicken in every pot and a car in every garage,' and 'by the start of the 21st century the average American consumed 100 times more chicken than at the start of the 1930s.'[54] As will be examined further in Chapter 3, the industrialization of poultry farming inspired a similar and now highly globalized process with other animals, most notably pigs, while large dairy barns and commercial feedlots also shifted cattle diets increasingly toward concentrated feed. For beef cattle, the pattern of 'priming' on grass and 'finishing' on grain expanded dramatically in the twentieth century.

Because of the nutrition burned in the metabolic processes of animals, a lot of feed is needed to produce a lot less meat, eggs, and dairy. However – and this is critical to their surplus absorption capacity – livestock commodities can then be sold at a higher price owing to the various cultural and perceptual values people attached to them, such as the purported superiority of animal protein. Thus, the meatification of diets was a way of dramatically increasing the effective demand for industrial grains. In this, it became the linchpin in transforming the chronic grain surplus from a price-deflating millstone into a steadily growing source of low-margin earnings for large farmers, processors, and traders. Roughly two-thirds of the incredible boom in grain production that occurred in the USA and Europe between 1950 and 1985 went into animal feed.[55]

Further, this dynamic also gave rise to the explosive growth of industrial oilseed production, and of course opened a range of increasing value-added opportunities in livestock production, processing, and retailing. For the USA, the surplus absorption function of animal feed was also extended abroad, a course that has been followed more recently by Brazil and Argentina over the past two decades. US exports of maize and soy found ready demand in Europe after the Second World War, helping fuel the growth and industrialization of livestock production there, while the US Feed Grains Council and USAID had to work more deliberately to cultivate demand for feed imports in parts of the global South. This ranged from the use of counterpart funds, other export subsidies, and low-interest loans to recipient countries, to more intangible advocacy of USAID reports and health promotion that trumpeted the nutritional value of animal protein and defined rising meat consumption as a marker of development. The support given to promote the intensification of livestock and the growth of feed imports meshed well with the desire of some developing countries to expand their supply of meat.[56] Often, this promotion started with grain-fed poultry systems geared mainly toward middle- and upper-class consumers, and over time direct US meat exports also crept upwards.

Frances Moore Lappé was the first to identify feed conversion losses and the increasing flow of industrial grains and oilseeds through concentrated livestock as a major global environment and development problem.[57] She argued that whereas livestock had once been 'protein factories' in the sense of producing protein in ways that didn't compete with crops, concentrated livestock fed on grains and oilseeds were like '*reverse* protein factories' in the sense that they effectively destroy a large share of the protein and other nutrition contained in these crops, while contributing to great volumes of unhealthy animal fat. This inherent feed conversion inefficiency is made worse by the fact that the smaller amount of nutrition which emerges is then consumed disproportionately by the wealthy in a world of persistent hunger. The nutritional losses of reverse protein factories get magnified still further by the fact that many people, especially those with meat-centered diets, consume far more protein than their bodies actually need. This means that not only are large shares of plant proteins and other nutrients lost as they are cycled through livestock, but large amounts of the ensuing animal protein serve no real nutritional function for people who already have much more than enough. Taken together, Lappé argued, these patterns of agricultural production and food consumption represent the systematization of waste.

Lappé was also clear that this waste cannot be trumped by the nutritional 'mythology' of animal protein.[58] As noted, the crux of the protein value of eggs, milk, and meat lies in the fact that they contain well-balanced bundles of essential amino acids that human bodies must take in, which makes them easily usable. On the other hand, many sources of plant protein are deficient in one or more essential amino acids, and since any single deficiency limits the effectiveness of the package as a whole they are *in themselves* less usable. Yet to use this as the basis for defining protein quality is a fundamentally false premise, since people rarely depend on just one source of plant protein (and if they do, protein deficiency is just one part of a bigger dietary problem). So instead of focusing on the bundle of essential amino acids contained in a solitary grain, oilseed, pulse, nut, or vegetable, Lappé emphasized, the real object of analysis should be the bundle of amino acids contained in typical *combinations* of foods eaten together in meals, and with varied plant-based diets it is not at all difficult to combine proteins in complementary ways that meet bodily needs for essential amino acids.

This was only the beginning of the nutritional case for plant-centered diets. Over time, increasing scientific evidence came to link the Western diet – with its high levels of saturated fat, cholesterol, calories, and unnatural chemical additives and residues – to a range of negative health outcomes, which were made worse by sedentary lifestyles and limited exercise. This correlation is broadly encapsulated in terms of 'diseases of affluence,' and includes rising levels of obesity and much higher risks of a range of cardiovascular diseases, type 2 diabetes, osteoporosis, and some cancers. This picture becomes even more worrying in light of a range of other public health problems associated with industrial livestock production that are developed in Chapter 4.[59]

The perilous dependence on cheap grain imports

The flipside of the aggressive export promotion used to manage the booming industrial surpluses was that it fundamentally altered food security in many countries of the global South, which came to increasingly depend on importing cheap grain. In 1950, Africa, South

Asia, and Southeast Asia were home to fewer than 900 million people, or about 35 percent of humanity, and were largely food self-sufficient, running net surpluses in agro-trade.[60] Only sixty years later, these same regions were home to over 3.3 billion people, almost four times more people and nearly half of humanity. The export of the high-input, high-yield productive model of the Green Revolution was a big part of this population growth in some Asian countries, nowhere more so than India, which became more food self-sufficient despite increasing from 372 million to over 1.2 billion people between 1950 and 2010 (although many remain hungry in India, it is much more a result of differential entitlements than of aggregate production).

Populations grew even faster in Africa and in some other Asian countries, but without the same gains in yield and productivity as in India. Instead, rising flows of cheap grain imports came to help sustain rapid population growth in many poor countries, as well as being entrenched partly as a result. These flows led to increasingly market-based or commoditized food security, including among many small farmers, and widespread dietary shifts toward various wheat flour products such as bread. For their part, recipient governments were often keen to accept food aid and subsidized trade as part of a deliberate emphasis on keeping food cheap, in the belief that this would assist their climb up the 'development ladder' and foster urbanization and industrialization by effectively subsidizing labor costs. The prioritization of cheap food also influenced domestic agricultural policies in a way that tended to privilege urban consumers (and urban stability) over rural producers, contributing to worsening rural poverty.[61]

The erosion of food self-sufficiency also had much older roots in the colonial period. At the center of this were European interests in extracting commodities like sugar, cotton, coffee, tea, cocoa, groundnuts, and palm oil from tropical and semi-tropical regions, and wheat from the Punjab region in South Asia. This growth was often attached to a confluence of local landholding and commercial elites, and sometimes layered onto peasant economies through exploitative tax regimes, both of which served to undermine the various practices that African and Asian societies once used to defend against climatic variability. Although these transformations culminated in a series of catastrophic famines in the late nineteenth century,[62] the combination of colonial power and local elite interests managed to maintain a durable grip over large areas of the best arable land, with production focused on a small range of export-oriented commodities – a legacy that persisted far beyond independence. Making this colonial inheritance much worse after the 1960s was the fact that tropical commodity exports suffered protracted declines in their relative earnings, with declining terms of trade a factor in the series of debt crises that unfolded across the global South from the early 1980s onwards.[63]

European colonialism initiated profound changes to shifting cultivation and pastoralism across the semi-arid tropics, with especially damaging effects across dryland regions of Africa. The resilience of these traditional practices had depended upon mobility, long fallow periods, and open access to extensive rangeland, but the progressive enclosure of the commons into sedentary farms and ranches and the barriers posed by colonial (and later national) borders increasingly disrupted relations between farmers, herders, animals and land. The movement of livestock lessened as herding routes narrowed or were cut off entirely. This led to more intensive grazing and compaction and gave land less time to recover, especially as livestock populations soared, including in highly arid regions like the Sudano-Sahelian drylands. Cattle, sheep, and goats are the primary livestock animals reared across Africa, and between 1961 and 2010 their population grew from 352 million to 894 million, a multiple of more than 2.5, slightly slower than that of the human population, which grew by a multiple of 3.5. Yet in a remarkable conceptual reversal of cause-and-effect, as soil conditions worsened Western 'experts' frequently portrayed this as a 'tragedy of the commons,' and called for still more enclosures.[64]

The onset of structural adjustment programs (SAPs) in the 1980s and 1990s was another major factor in the continuing erosion of food self-sufficiency across much of the global South. SAPs were a ubiquitous prescription designed in large measure to manage the debt crises of Southern states in ways that would ensure the repayment of loans to the financial sector in the industrialized world. As part of the broad-based assault on state expenditures, funding for things like agricultural research, subsidized credit, public seed banks, extension and training, and domestic marketing services were all targeted for big cuts, along with the dismantling of state-led redistributive land reform programs. At the same time, agro-export expansion was encouraged and markets were opened to a greater range of imports.

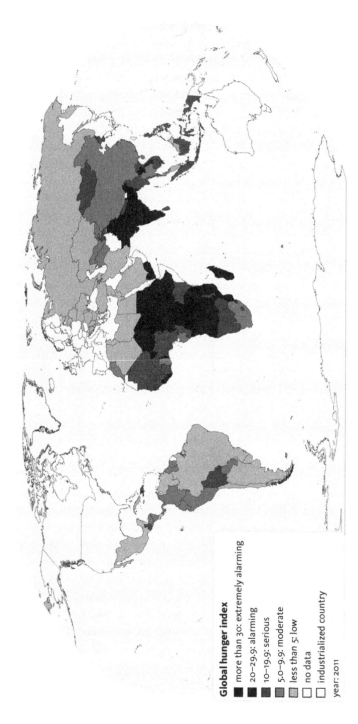

Global hunger index

- ■ more than 30: extremely alarming
- ■ 20–29.9: alarming
- ■ 10–19.9: serious
- ■ 5.0–9.9: moderate
- ▨ less than 5: low
- □ no data
- □ industrialized country

year: 2011

2.1 World hunger distribution (2009) (*source:* Global Hunger Index IFPRI 2010)

Meat consumption per capita

- less than 13 kg
- 13–23 kg
- 23–34 kg
- 34–49 kg
- 49–61 kg
- 61–74 kg
- 74–88 kg
- 88–103 kg
- 103–37 kg

2.2 World meat consumption per capita (2009) (*source:* FAOSTATS 2013)

The rose-coloured promise underpinning these policies was that by maximizing exports and foreign exchange earnings while liberalizing domestic markets, countries would optimize the efficiency of their production and in turn their net food supply. Unfortunately the purported 'free market approach to food security' has proved to be a chimera, having contributed to mounting food imports.[65]

Although there is much more than enough food produced to feed everyone on earth, the population of chronically undernourished has for decades been estimated to hover between 800 and 900 million. In 2009, this leapt to more than 1 billion people amid soaring global food prices – one clear indication of how market-based food security has become.[66] In addition to being the world's leading cause of mortality, protracted malnutrition can have especially debilitating impacts in early childhood, as diets deficient in essential micro-nutrients, fats, and minerals (as are common where the poor depend heavily on a small range of grains that are rich in carbohydrates but little else) can lead to the stunting of brain and body development, with long-term individual and societal implications.

The large majority of undernourished people live in Africa, South Asia, and Southeast Asia, which dominate what IFPRI calls the 'hot spots' of world hunger (see Figure 2.1) and contain fifty of the sixty-six Low Income Food Deficit Countries (LIFDCs) listed by the FAO in 2012, led by Africa with thirty-nine.[67] It is also important to recognize that the world's poorest countries tend to have the largest shares of their populations engaged in agriculture, as high as two-thirds of the total in the world's Least Developed Countries (LDCs), with small farmers, the rural landless, and their families by far the biggest group suffering from hunger and malnutrition. In the face of food aid, and later trade liberalization, many small farmers have simultaneously become dependent upon flows of cheap grains and impoverished by its impact in dampening domestic market conditions. Wheat has long comprised over two-thirds of total cereal imports in the world's LIFDCs, followed by maize and rice. Almost all of the world's wheat exports flow from a small number of temperate countries (e.g. the USA, Canada, Australia, Russia, Ukraine, and France), as does the world's maize (e.g. the USA, Argentina, Brazil, Ukraine, and France), with most of it controlled by a handful of large companies like ADM, Bunge, Cargill, and Dreyfus.

Champions of industrial agriculture frequently point to the scale of hunger, malnourishment, and food import dependence in Africa, South Asia, and Southeast Asia – where there are collectively 2.4 billion more people today than in 1950 – to frame both the Green Revolution and the temperate-to-tropical flows of cheap industrial grains in humanitarian terms, as though they have rescued multitudes from hunger and starvation. Accordingly, the need for temperate breadbaskets to continuing 'feeding the world' is made to appear both noble and unavoidable, especially with most of the world's future population growth projected for Africa and Asia, and almost all of it in cities. But a converse problematic can also be posed: has this really been a sustainable way of feeding so much growth, and can it continue?

This question permeates much of the following chapter, which argues that the celebration of industrial efficiency – and by extension the 'free market approach to food security' – hinges on a very incomplete picture. Not only has the global playing field in agricultural trade been tilted by *explicit* state subsidies in rich countries but the comparative advantage of industrial surpluses is also *implicitly* subsidized by an array of unaccounted environmental costs rooted in intractable biophysical contradictions. When these costs and contradictions are unpacked, the notion that food security should be organized around perpetual, long-distance flows of cheap grains appears delusional.

For now, however, these flows are a central part of the polarization of diets that is summed up well by Philip McMichael: 'as wealthy consumers dine "up" on animal protein, the working poor dine either on food aid grains or the low end of the food chain: low-protein starchy diets, or little at all.'[68] This uneven picture can be seen clearly at the world scale in Figures 2.1 and 2.2, which reflect near inverse mirror images of contemporary patterns of relative hunger and per capita meat consumption.

The continuing race up the animal protein ladder

For many decades the world production of meat and eggs has grown faster than that of other major food groups and outpaced human population growth, radically changing diets. A central argument of this chapter has been that this dietary revolution is embedded in dominant conceptions of development, and of what it means to be a society of 'high mass consumption,' in Rostowian terms. A common way this aspiration has been, and continues to be, framed is through claims about the superior nutritional value of animal protein, as though people are biologically wired to eat more and more meat, and be stronger and healthier for it. However, another key argument is that the uneven meatification of diets cannot be reduced to a biological impetus, as it has also been fired by motivations that have nothing whatsoever to do with necessity or health. These include the demonstration of class, connotations of imperial power, and, most fundamentally, the role of rising livestock production in profitably absorbing chronic grain and oilseed surpluses and hence enabling further growth and capital accumulation in agriculture. Indeed, this also increasingly means ignoring the great many health problems that the meat-centered Western diet is implicated in (to say nothing, for now, about its distributional, environmental, or ethical dimensions).

With or without a compelling nutritional rationale, it is widely assumed that the race up the animal protein ladder will continue, unevenly, in the coming decades. One reflection of this can be seen in the ongoing global expansion of fast food chains like McDonald's, Burger King, KFC, and Pizza Hut, which constitute both an antithesis of healthy diets and one of the most iconic symbols of US capitalism and consumer culture.[69] It is notable that the openings of McDonald's restaurants in the former Soviet bloc and in China in 1990 were treated as major, newsworthy events and great signals of the marketization of these economies, with China and other fast-industrializing parts of Asia having become an especially important site of fast food growth. It is also telling that *The Economist* chose the Big Mac as a ubiquitous proxy of purchasing-power parity between different currencies in its well-known 'Big Mac Index,' a measure which also doubles as a symbol of global market integration.

As emphasized at the outset of this book, while the per capita consumption of livestock products has risen almost everywhere over the past half-century, the process has been extremely uneven. To start at the widest scale, people in 'developed countries' (not counting the former Eastern Bloc) consume over three times as much meat, over four times as much dairy, and almost twice as many eggs as do people in 'developing countries.' At the scale of nation-states, there is a strong positive correlation between per capita GDP and the per capita consumption of meat.[70] Meat consumption disparities within countries are difficult to unravel, but it is generally accepted that the prevalence of cheap animal products in developed countries means

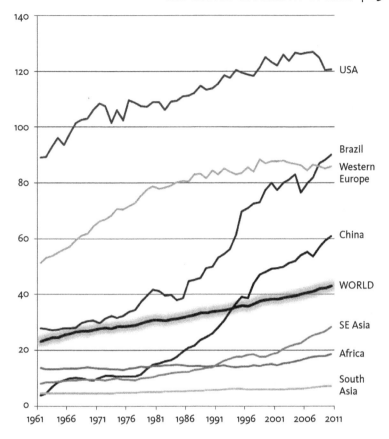

2.3 Per capita meat consumption, 1961–2010, selected examples (kg/person) (*source*: FAOSTATS 2013)

that the volume of consumption is no longer defined by class, with class instead marked in diets in a variety of other ways, like access to fresher, healthier, more diverse, and less chemical-laden foods. But because large class disparities in meat consumption remain in fast-industrializing and low income countries, the full extent of global inequality in meat consumption is considerably greater than national averages can reveal.

Still, in spite of this blurring of internal inequalities, some national and regional examples help to shed more light on the broad contours of the uneven geography of meat (see Figure 2.3). In 2010, annual per capita meat consumption was 121 kg in the USA, 113 kg in Australia and New Zealand, 104 kg in Argentina, 99 kg in Canada, and 86 kg in western Europe.[71] With just 12 percent of the world population, these countries accounted for, by volume, almost one third of world meat consumption, over one third of world meat production, and over two-thirds of meat exports. They also accounted for even larger shares of world dairy consumption, production, and exports, and had per capita egg consumption and production levels (over 14 kg) well above world averages, though not as dramatically as with meat and dairy.

At the other end of the spectrum of per capita meat and egg consumption are Southeast Asia (23 kg meat and 7 kg eggs in 2010), Africa (18 kg meat/3 kg eggs), and South Asia (7 kg meat/3 kg eggs). With almost half of humanity, these regions consumed only 16 percent of all meat and 17 percent of all eggs in 2010, keeping in mind that low national averages conceal internal disparities. Per capita consumption of dairy is also much below world averages in Southeast Asia and Africa, but in South Asia it is only slightly below the world average, reflecting in part the influence of the Hindu religion and the fact that India's large cattle population is mainly used for traction, fertilizer, fuel, and dairy, rather than beef.

However, global dietary change is occurring most quickly between these poles, in fast-industrializing countries. At the forefront of this growth are China and Brazil, as is evident in Figures 2.3 and 2.4, which highlight some of the major trends in per capita meat consumption and total meat production over roughly the past half-century. Together, with under a quarter of humanity, China and Brazil produced 7 percent of the world's meat in 1961, but 35 percent in 2010.

In China, per capita meat consumption vaulted from 4 kg to 61 kg between 1961 and 2010. Given that this was coupled with dramatic population growth, China's total meat production grew by an astounding factor of 31 in a mere half-century. China is now home to just over half the world's pigs and produces one third of all meat and two-fifths of all eggs; it alone produces more meat and almost twice as many eggs as did the *entire world* a half-century ago. Under Mao, Chinese agrarian policies centered on redistributing land, increasing per capita grain production, and maintaining food self-sufficiency. While livestock production slowly intensified, it was not until around 1980 that the huge volume increases in meat, eggs, and dairy began to take off, along with arguably the greatest industrial revolution in world history (China's take-off in meat production, and its global weight, both

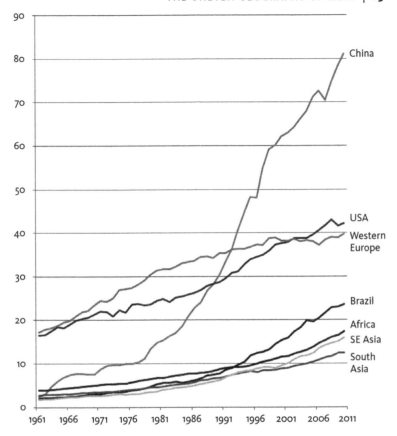

2.4 Meat production by volume, 1961–2010, selected examples (million tonnes) (*source*: FAOSTATS 2013)

appear dramatically in Figure 2.4). This rapid meatification reflects not only China's spectacular industrialization and economic growth but also how the authoritarian capitalist state made the increasing consumption of animal protein an explicit development objective.[72]

Ironically, this objective flies directly counter to the advice of the celebrated *China Study*, a long-term research project centered on traditional plant-centered Chinese dietary habits and epidemiological patterns. A central conclusion was that the healthiest diets are those based on a wide variety of plant foods and minimal or no animal foods, encapsulated in the claim that humans are essentially a vegetarian species.[73] This counsel unheeded, the rapid change in Chinese diets has been accompanied by fast-rising levels of obesity and other chronic health problems associated with the Western diet. Also somewhat ironic is the fact that the eruption of livestock production and populations in China roughly coincides with the inception of the One Child Policy (1979), a strict program of population control motivated partly by fears about biophysical limits and food self-reliance. Now, in order to feed half the world's pigs, China has become by far the world's leading importer of soybeans, and a similar fate could soon befall its self-sufficiency in basic grains owing to the rising use of crops for feed, the loss of agricultural land to industry and degradation, and the depletion of aquifers which irrigate large areas of the bountiful North China Plain.

In Brazil, total meat production increased eleven-fold between 1961 and 2010, fueling a dramatic increase in per capita meat consumption, from 28 to 91 kg in a half-century, and a recent boom in meat exports. From 2000 to 2010 alone, Brazil's meat exports quadrupled and its share of the world total rose from 6 to 16 percent. Brazil is now the second-largest meat-exporting country in the world, and the largest exporter of beef. This growth is based on both a highly competitive industrial grain-oilseed-livestock complex on its best arable land, and expansive ranching on its worst, the grounds of the razed Amazonian rainforest – each of which took off in the 1960s. Beginning in the 1960s, considerable state investment and incentives targeted at national and transnational capital alike helped incite the rapid industrialization of grain and livestock production and processing as well as a move into industrial soybeans.

The 1960s were also when the Brazilian frontier started expanding into Amazonia, beginning one of the greatest ecological transformations in world history, with momentous GHG emissions and lost sequestration capacity. A confluence of multilateral and bilateral loans and grants, strong support from the military state, and national and transnational investment unleashed a frenzy of development, including massive highway and dam-building, extractive industry projects, small-farmer resettlement (rather than land reform on good arable land), and land conversion from forest to pasture. Of this, cattle pasture has been by far the biggest land use, and from the 1960s into the 1990s, Amazonian beef was mainly consumed in the industrializing south of Brazil. Although thin soils support only very low stocking densities, large estate holders benefited handsomely from subsidies and tax and credit incentives, as well as being motivated by exceptionally cheap land and speculative hopes that it might contain resource wealth.[74]

In the early 1990s, Amazonian ranching began to take on a new export dimension, driving the growth of the cattle population from 27 to 64 million in little more than a decade (1990–2003). This dynamic has strong parallels to the process of tropical deforestation in Central America between the 1960s and the 1980s, when the cattle population there nearly doubled as much of the region's tropical forest was cleared for pasture, fueled by cheap beef exports to the USA as well as financing from the World Bank and the Inter-American Development Bank. Cattle ranching remains a leading force in Amazonian deforestation, but since the mid-1990s Brazil's race to expand soybean production and exports has also pushed it into the frontier areas of Pará, Mato Grosso, Acre, and Rondônia. There soybean production has often taken over already cleared land, enabled by heavy fertilization, but it can also be seen as a factor in deforestation for its role in spurring more road development and crowding out smaller-scale farmers.

The story of soybeans connects the courses of China and Brazil. In the 1990s, soybean production began quickly expanding in southern Brazil, as well as in adjoining Argentina, Paraguay, and Bolivia, morphing into a huge expanse that has been dubbed 'the Soybean Republic.'[75] This growth is linked to both the increase in industrial livestock in the region, especially Brazil, and to an export boom in soy-meal feed, especially to China, where the industrialization of livestock has necessitated rising feed imports.[76] From 1990 to 2010, Brazil's soybean exports rose from 4 to 26 million tonnes, while China's soybean imports shot up from 2 to 57 million tonnes, more than half the world total.

Soybeans clearly reflect how the trajectory of meatification is entwined with heavy flows of grains and oilseeds, the overwhelming basis of animal feed.[77] The great majority of the world's coarse grains, soybeans, and canola/rapeseed are fed to animals, and in 2010 446 million ha were devoted to these crops – about one-third of the world's harvested land. The land devoted to coarse grains and oilseeds increased by roughly 30 percent over the past half-century, and the ratio of agricultural land devoted to these crops is much higher in the heartlands of the industrial grain-oilseed-livestock complex. On a world scale, the expansion of feed crops over the past half-century has overwhelmingly centered on maize and soybeans. From 1961 to 2010, the total area planted in maize grew by more than half and the total area planted in soybeans more than quadrupled, accompanied by tremendous yield gains (and, as will be emphasized in the following chapter, tremendous input usage), with the result that global maize production more than quadrupled and world soybean production grew more than eightfold.[78] Maize and soy are also the principal feed crops in international trade, which for decades was dominated by the USA, mainly to Europe, but is now also marked by rising competition from southern South America, with growing markets in China and Asia. Since 1961, world maize exports grew sevenfold and world soybean exports grew eightfold, and more than one third of world soybean production is now traded.

In recent years, the fast-rising production of industrial agrofuels has emerged as a new and powerful dynamic augmenting the role of animal feed in profitably absorbing grain and oilseed surpluses. The agrofuel boom has generated vociferous criticism, centered on the role of agrofuel production in the volatility of world grain and oilseed markets, and by extension the problems of food insecurity in LIFDCs, as well as the dubious environmental claims.[79] Rather than a source of 'green energy', critics have emphasized how industrial agrofuels have a low energy return on energy investment (i.e. almost as much or more fossil energy goes into its production than comes out as liquid energy outputs) which implies that the land area given to industrial agrofuels would better serve the goal of climate change mitigation if it were re-naturalized to sequester more carbon. Yet as important as these dynamics are, the volume of grains and oilseeds flowing into the cars of relatively wealthier people are still much less than the global volume that is flowing into animals, which are also disproportionately consumed by relatively wealthier people.

Further, the production and flow of industrial grains and oilseeds are bound to intensify with continuing meatification, since industrial livestock production is expected to account for virtually all future global growth in the volume of meat, eggs, and dairy.[80] Another important dynamic is how industrialization is driving a major shift in the relative composition of world livestock production. In 1961, ruminant animals accounted for about half of all meat produced, primarily cattle (39 percent) and secondarily sheep and goats (8 percent). Since

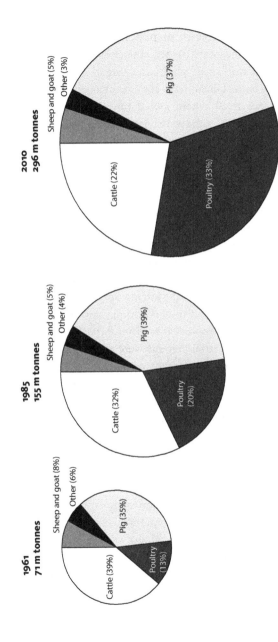

1961
71 m tonnes

Sheep and goat (8%)
Other (6%)
Cattle (39%)
Pig (35%)
Poultry (13%)

1985
155 m tonnes

Sheep and goat (5%)
Other (4%)
Cattle (32%)
Pig (39%)
Poultry (20%)

2010
296 m tonnes

Sheep and goat (5%)
Other (3%)
Cattle (22%)
Pig (37%)
Poultry (33%)

2.5 Relative world meat production by animal group: three snapshots this time, ruminant production has largely kept pace with human population growth while falling to just over a quarter of all meat, a relative decline that appears clearly in Figure 2.5.

Significant global increases in pasture-fed ruminants are highly unlikely, owing to the scale of desertification and land degradation unfolding on the world's drylands, the threats posed to the quality of pasture and animal health by climate change, and the fact that there are few areas left where global rangeland could conceivably be expanded – at least without driving further forest clearance, the prevention of which is an unqualified imperative for climate change mitigation. And while the intensification of ruminant stocking densities may be possible on some high-quality pasture and mixed farms, it would come at the steep cost of increasing methane emissions.

In contrast to the slower growth of ruminants, over the past half-century annual pig meat production more than quadrupled and annual poultry meat production (predominantly chicken) rose more than tenfold, such that pig production rose slightly from 35 to 37 percent of world meat production and poultry leapt from 13 to 33 percent (see Figures 2.5 and 2.6). Industrial systems are the main force behind this growth, as their share of total world pig and poultry production has risen quickly in recent decades. In *Livestock's Long Shadow*, it was estimated that industrial systems were responsible for more than half of all pig meat and 70 percent of all poultry meat, along with the growth of semi-intensive forms of production at intermediate scales.[81] These levels have surely since increased, as world pig meat production increased by 10 percent and world poultry production shot up by 21 percent from 2005 to 2010.

Poultry is also the leading source of growth in meat exporting, increasing almost sixfold by volume between 1990 and 2010, to over 15 million tonnes, which represents almost two-fifths of world meat exports. In 1961, meat exports accounted for only 5 percent of total world production and by 2010 exports had risen to 13 percent of world production. The exceptional growth in poultry production relates to the fact that poultry birds amass weight from feed less inefficiently than do ruminants. And because birds are the smallest and most industrialized farm animal with the fastest 'turnover time,' this translates into a staggering number of individual beings trapped in conditions akin to living hell. These far-reaching changes to animal populations and living conditions are another aspect of the changing

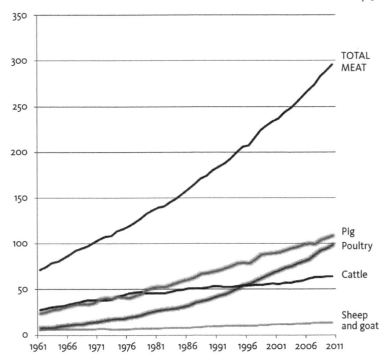

2.6 World meat production by animal group, 1961–2010 (million tonnes)

geography of meat, but to make sense of them it helps to first examine the industrial-grain-oilseed-livestock complex as a system in motion, where attention turns in the following chapter. This systemic framework should also help to make it clear why meatification not only reflects global inequalities, as has been emphasized in this chapter, but seriously extends them.

The framework starts from understanding how biophysical problems are created or exacerbated, and then overridden, in the course of industrialization. From this, a complex system of flows of inputs and technologies can be seen, which opens up an ability to assess resource budgets and pollution loads. An important argument running throughout this analysis is the need to problematize the narrow way that efficiency gets defined, which relates to the triumphant competitiveness of industrial systems. When we appreciate this system of flows and unaccounted costs, the tremendous productivity in industrial monocultures appears less a stunning achievement of technological genius (which of course it still is at some level) and much more an extremely precarious foundation for human civilization. The cycling of industrial grains and oilseeds through concentrated livestock then greatly magnifies these contradictions, a crucial dynamic the ecological hoofprint seeks to highlight.

3 | THE INDUSTRIAL-GRAIN-OILSEED-LIVESTOCK COMPLEX

Scale imperatives: mechanization, standardization, and simplification

A degree of ecological simplification is inherent in all agriculture, as it entails stopping natural succession from unfolding and increasing the abundance of some species while reducing or eliminating others. However, as emphasized in the preceding two chapters, the incessant pressure to compete, grow, and accumulate under capitalism has pushed the expansion and simplification of farming landscapes to radical new extremes. In this chapter, attention turns to the industrialization of agricultural production and the biophysical instabilities that are established or exacerbated, and the ways that these get overridden. This focus on instabilities and overrides is necessary to first understand the resource demands and pollution loads of industrial monocultures, and then the ways these get magnified through industrial livestock.[1]

To start with, it is necessary to consider how competitive pressures are entwined with the pursuit of economies of scale. Because the productivity of labor and its relative cost in production are fundamental to competitiveness in capitalism, one of the most elemental system-wide tendencies is for capital to search for technological innovations that increase output per worker, from assembly lines and industrial robotics in manufacturing, to tractors, combines, pesticides, and higher-yielding seeds in agriculture. This implies that the nature of productive technologies tends to reinforce existing social relations. In a general sense, to achieve economies of scale and displace labor with capital, the process of production must be standardized in terms of both physical space and the nature of work. In agriculture, this means that rather than tailoring agricultural practices to bioregions, bioregions have to be transfigured to fit a set of practices and technologies.

The industrialization of grain harvesting began in the 1830s with Cyrus McCormick's invention of a mechanical grain harvester and John Deere's invention of the steel plow. As David Montgomery puts it, these new technologies 'helped revolutionize farming and reconfigure the relation between American land, labor, and capital,' vastly increasing the amount of land that a family farmer could work.[2] Both diffused rapidly with the expansion of railways as the USA raced across its westward frontier, and had an invaluable role in helping prairie farmers cope with shortages (and the ensuing high costs) of labor at harvest time. At first, animals were still needed for traction, but the rise of combustion-powered farm machinery soon displaced animals from this key historic function, and further expanded the scale of plowing, planting, and harvesting that was possible.

Large machines obviously do not work well on small fields with a mix of crops and small, varied livestock populations grazing or scavenging here and there. Instead, they need big volumes of the same thing that can be sown, grown, and harvested across expansive areas at the same time. Thus, the physical separation of animals from fields and their concentration into factories and feedlots is necessary for mechanization and economies of scale in cultivation, part of an organizing logic that wiped out attention to biological cycles, species complementarity and intercropping, and animal multifunctionality. Mechanization and standardization also struck at historic soil conservation practices like land terracing and hedgerows.

In the decades following the Second World War, continued innovation in farm machinery was coupled with momentous genetic advances in high-yielding crop varieties, which contributed to the rapid narrowing of both crop diversity and control on a world scale. A good reflection of this is that a single indigenous village in Mesoamerica 'may maintain more kinds of maize than the [US] Corn Belt ever heard of.'[3] These new enhanced varieties drove a further surge in global agricultural productivity, along with the ongoing conversions of land for agriculture and the explosion of agro-inputs, which will be discussed soon. This is very much in line with Jason Moore's insistence that 'intensive capitalization and extensive appropriation form a dialectical unity.'[4] The net result was a doubling of total world food production in the second half of the twentieth century.

As emphasized in Chapter 2, the booming productivity of industrial monocultures and the ascension of factory farms and feedlots were mutually reinforcing, with the rapid growth of livestock populations having a pivotal role in fortifying chronic grain and oilseed surpluses. First, it enabled continuing growth when this would otherwise have deflated prices (even with aid, trade, and dumping in foreign markets), albeit still at low margins that continued to erode the viability of many small farms. Secondly, these surpluses enabled livestock populations to increase far beyond former densities on integrated farms. Together these helped to unlock prospects for further accumulation in agriculture, which was boosted further still by the treadmill of inputs that has been necessitated by these industrial transformations.

Consequently, the dualistic productive environments of the industrial grain-oilseed-livestock complex – vast monoculture fields of maize, wheat, soybeans, barley, sorghum, oats, and rapeseed/canola dotted by spaces of concentrated pigs, poultry, and cattle – must be seen to be organized by a unitary logic. So while there is a much longer record of confined livestock rearing in different regions,[5] the industrialization of livestock under distinctly capitalist imperatives began only recently. From its origins in the USA, with cattle and pigs first pushed onto concentrated feedlots in the Midwest and chickens next pushed into large sheds on the Delmarva Peninsula, systems of industrial livestock production began a rapid spread across large areas of the temperate world following the Second World War. Since the 1980s, these systems have also increasingly expanded into tropical areas, and parts of countries like Brazil, China, Thailand, and India.

Although the higher value of livestock products relative to grains and oilseeds makes it profitable to burn large volumes of usable nutrition in the metabolism of animals, there remains an inexorable pressure to increase levels of labor productivity and enhance the rates at which feed is converted to flesh, eggs, and milk. These have propelled the rising density of animal populations within highly automated spaces, which reduce both infrastructure and labor costs per animal. Corporate-led livestock science has also vigorously pursued selective breeding to: make animals grow, reach sexual maturity, reproduce, and lactate faster; become more uniform; and augment the relative size of more valuable body parts, such as poultry breasts. Just as with crops, this process of genetic enhancement has driven a radical narrowing of animal breeds. On a world scale the FAO's Global Databank for Farm Animal Genetic Resources lists more than 7,600 livestock breeds, and reports that 190 have recently become extinct and that 1,500 are at risk of extinction,[6] though this only hints at the profound narrowing of 'enhanced' breeds used within industrial systems. The increasing uniformity of animal bodies supports multiple objectives, abetting the standardization of animal enclosures, the speeding pace of slaughter lines, and the growing scale and consistency of meatpacking operations.

More than any other species, chickens have been at the vanguard of the technological innovations in industrial livestock production. A fundamental part of this was their genetic specialization into meat 'broilers' and egg 'layers,' reared in distinct systems. For broilers and later turkeys, it was found that thousands of birds could be reared together on a single crowded floor. For layers, automation gave rise to the most extreme form of animal confinement, the battery cage, which began to be commercially manufactured in the 1930s in order to collect non-damaged eggs from growing hen populations. By the 1950s, growers began cramming three birds into tiny spaces initially intended for one, and as early as 1962 an industry trade magazine described 'the modern layer' as being 'only a very efficient converting machine' between feed and egg.[7] The battery cage disseminated widely from the USA, and though it has since been contested in a number of settings, most notably the EU, legislative victories won by animal welfare organizations have generally brought only modest gains in the minimal area afforded to each hen (caging has never worked for birds destined for meat because it causes too much damage to the flesh).

Another important part of the mechanization and standardization of livestock production is the subdivision of different life phases, wherein animals lose all agency over reproductive activity and all ability to maintain maternal and familial bonds. Animals are effectively placed on fast-moving but spatially disaggregated production lines, which are integrated by large companies intent on outsourcing the lowest-margin, highest-risk phase: the growing. At the start of these lines are specialized sites for breeding and hatching which treat the breeding stock as veritable reproductive machines, locking females into near-constant states of pregnancy or lactation, with the nursing of young either cut short or cut off entirely.

In industrial hatcheries, specialized breeder flocks never see their young, as eggs are artificially incubated, hatched, and chicks sold off to growers in large bundles (with the exception of male layer chicks, which are promptly destroyed, as discussed below). In industrial pig breeding sites, sows are inseminated and confined for the duration of their sixteen-week pregnancy, at best in small group pens and at worst in gestation crates, individualized enclosures so tight they cannot turn around. As with battery cages, animal welfare organizations have targeted gestation crates as a particularly extreme apparatus, and have won a series of bans and phase-outs around the world. Sows are next moved to farrowing enclosures to give birth and nurse their litter for one to three weeks, as compared with three to four months under natural conditions, before they are returned for another cycle of insemination. Meanwhile, abruptly weaned piglets are sent off to growers and finishers, sometimes to different buildings within a single setting ('farrow-to-finish' operations) and sometimes to different operations entirely. Though cattle remain the least industrialized of the 'big three' livestock animals, the growing scale and mechanization of dairy production have led to rising densities in many regions, as has the practice of 'finishing' beef cattle on feedlots before slaughter, most dramatically in western North America.

Another key dimension of the industrial grain-oilseed-livestock complex which must be considered is its role in the spatial and conceptual distancing of most people from the systems which provide their food. On one hand, prevailing social, ecological, and inter-species relations of production get buried in extremely complex and opaque market dynamics. On the other hand, cheap and copious food comes to appear as clear evidence of the superior efficiency of the system as a whole, with meat having an especially potent ideological effect given the mythologies that surround animal protein and which connect to the role of food as a crucial wage good. The result is an assurance that the course is not only inevitable but advantageous, which in turn helps to maintain and extend consent – and with it, inertia.

A central aim of this chapter is, therefore, to deconstruct this illusion of efficiency.

The promise of industrial efficiency

The conception of efficiency in industrial capitalist agriculture is drawn along two basic, interrelated lines: labor productivity and yield, which have been widely portrayed as normative goals for agricultural development, along with promises that they will be optimized by competition. As large machines displace working people, the process establishes a positive feedback in which mechanized farmers become much more competitive than smaller-scale farmers in terms of labor productivity, driving many out of agriculture. As this capital investment grows (often accompanied by deep indebtedness) amid low unit values, the pressure to keep expanding persists. Skewed subsidies toward large farmers have also been an important part of this story in a number of major industrial countries, with the USA the most extreme case.[8] For champions of industrial agriculture, high-yielding monocultures are celebrated for having liberated hundreds of millions of people from the poverty and drudgery of peasant agriculture, and as having saved billions of people from starvation. Related to this, labor productivity in agriculture is given as a key foundation for development itself. Output per farmer did indeed increase to an astonishing and highly uneven degree across the twentieth century, and the disparity in labor productivity between high- and low-input agricultural systems is now of the order of 2,000 to 1.[9] Today, farmers make up only about 4 percent of the total workforce across the industrialized countries in the Organization for Economic Cooperation and Development (OECD), whereas farmers continue to comprise by far the largest segment of the workforce in most of the world's poorest and most food-insecure nations. In addition to the obvious disparities in mechanization, leading industrialized countries tend to have the greatest crop yields.

It is instructive to briefly consider the US agricultural system owing to its overall weight in world agriculture, its extraordinary advances in labor productivity, and the fact that it is home to many of the key corporations driving leading-edge technological development. In the late twentieth century, an average US farmer cultivated roughly fifteen times more land than a century before,[10] and benefited from much greater relative increases in capital investment. Today farmers represent less than 2 percent of the US workforce, a small number that is still somewhat deceiving, as fewer than 300,000 farms account for the great majority of all production, led by the more than 80,000 farms that are larger than 800 ha (~2,000 acres). The tendency of fewer and larger farms to dominate production is also reflected in the fact that one fifth of US landholders control more than four-fifths of all irrigated land.[11]

US grain yields per hectare are roughly twice the world average, 2.5 times those of South Asia, and almost five times those of Africa, differentials that are even greater when the focus shifts to coarse grains alone. With fewer than one in every 500 farmers worldwide, the USA produced roughly one sixth of the world's cereals between 2000 and 2010 (including almost one third of all coarse grains, led by maize) and over one third of the world's soybeans.[12] Great volumes of these coarse grains and soybeans are then fed to animals, as are their exports. This growth partly reflects the fact that the combination of carbohydrate-rich maize and protein-dense soybean meal works well to promote animal growth. It also reflects how the remarkable productivity gains of coarse grains and oilseeds have been enabled – in an economic sense – by the surplus absorption capacity of livestock, as emphasized in Chapter 2. This role of feed in absorbing surpluses does not, however, mean that conversion losses are taken as a given; on the contrary, as will be stressed later on, one of the most fundamental forces driving innovation in industrial livestock production is the pressure to increase the rates at which animals yield flesh, eggs, and milk.

Just like grains and oilseeds, US-based corporations have been at the vanguard of industrial innovation and productivity gains in livestock. In the USA, the livestock sector is dominated by an even smaller number of operators than with industrial monocultures, yet they account for more than one seventh of the world's meat production. In 2007, fewer than 8,000 mega-farms were responsible for 87 percent of all pigs sold, turning over an average of almost 23,000 animals per year, following a tenfold decline in the number of US farmers raising pigs that took place over just a half-century. The growth of industrial poultry has been even more stunning, as more chickens are now killed in a *day* than were killed in an entire *year* less than a century ago. In 2007, just over 11,300 mega-farms were responsible for 89 percent of all broiler chickens sold, turning over an average of almost 700,000 birds per year. Individual broiler sheds regularly house between 30,000 and 50,000 birds, with large operations having many sheds on a property. Cattle remain much less densely populated, though this too is changing. It was not long ago that viable dairy herds in the USA could number fewer than 50 head, but industrial dairy operations now typically range between 1,000 and 5,000 and can even top 10,000 head, while more than half of the nation's beef production gets fattened on a few hundred massive western feedlots.[13]

As with grains and oilseeds, extraordinary increases in labor productivity in the USA have been accompanied by yield gains in individual animals that have risen above world averages. Between 1961 and 2010, the slaughter weight of the average chicken in the US was 68 percent heavier than a half-century earlier, a cow was 59 percent heavier, and a pig was 46 percent heavier, while the average dairy cow produced almost three times more milk per year and the average layer hen produced one quarter more eggs per year. In 2010, chickens in the USA were 24 percent larger at slaughter than the world average, pigs were 16 percent larger, cows were 62 percent larger, while a layer hen annually yielded 53 percent more eggs and a dairy cow yielded more than eight times more milk. Conversely, the average chickens, pigs, and cows in Africa and South Asia are between one quarter and one half smaller than world averages. Countries with highly industrialized livestock sectors have generally achieved the greatest yield gains, and it is notable that in recent years Brazil has surpassed the USA in terms of both pig and chicken yields.[14]

Industrial yield gains are amplified by the dramatic acceleration in how fast animals are being turned over, which essentially means speeding reproductive rates and shortening lifespans. Whereas wild cattle, boars, and jungle fowl can live twenty years or more, and cattle, pigs, and chickens often live for many years on mixed farms, beef cattle started on grasses and finished on feedlots can now be brought to commercial slaughter weight in eighteen months, industrialized pigs in as little as six months, and broiler chickens in a mere *weeks*. For industrialized broiler chickens, the speeding time to slaughter means that in addition to growing two-thirds bigger than a half-century ago, they are putting on roughly four times more weight per day. For industrialized layer hens, the speeding of reproductive activity means that they now lay almost an egg a day, over vastly shortened lives, in contrast to traditional farm hens, which typically lay thirty to 100 eggs a year and wild jungle fowl which lay around thirty eggs a year.[15]

In the end, if labor productivity and the yield of individual plants and animals are accepted as the pillars of agricultural efficiency, then the gains of the industrial grain-oilseed-livestock complex are clear. However, beyond these narrow metrics lies a much more complex and problematic picture, at the heart of which is the failure to account for a vast ecological burden. To unpack this burden, it helps to approach it at two basic levels: first, by focusing on industrial grain and oilseed monocultures, and next turning to sites of industrial livestock production, which are bound together by heavy flows of feed. The key to this approach in both cases is to consider the biophysical instabilities that are generated in the course of mechanization, standardization, and simplification, the ways that these get overridden, and the resource budgets this entails. When viewed in this way, the soaring volumes of cheap meat flowing from the industrial grain-oilseed-livestock complex can be seen to greatly magnify the land, water, energy, and other resources needed for agriculture, and the ecological burden that ensues.

Problematizing efficiency: instabilities and overrides in industrial monocultures

Celebratory accounts of economies of scale typically leave out or downplay big parts of the story, including the undervalued costs of energy (both *in situ* and in moving things over space) and ensuing emissions and pollution loads. This is especially true in agriculture, where mechanization and standardization are far more difficult than in other industrial settings, as the far-reaching simplification of environments intensifies the biological and physical challenges inherent in farming and establishes new problems.

Central to this are the soil problems that were at the basis of how Marx conceived of the metabolic rift. Some peasant agriculture has been remarkably durable, effective not only in maintaining but also in enhancing soil fertility, though the exhaustion of soils from unsustainable practices also has an old history that has been a factor in the decline of many civilizations. Yet whether previous practices were sustainable over the long term or not, industrial agriculture serves to greatly accelerate the loss of soil organisms and nutrients, depleting soils at least ten times faster than it is formed in the temperate world, and much faster still in the tropics.[16]

Part of this is rooted in the diminished ground cover in monocultures relative to more diversified small farms, which can employ a range of more labor-intensive soil conservation practices. The decline in ground cover simultaneously increases the erosive impacts of rain and wind while reducing soil moisture retention, made worse by annual cycles of tillage and the compaction caused by large machines in the course of fertilizing, spraying, and harvesting (although annual tillage is increasingly being replaced by 'precision' or no-till seeding, where seeds are inserted directly into the ground, which helps to maintain a degree of ground cover). The loss of organic material is further exacerbated by the decline of rotations, fallow cycles, and livestock manure, and as a by-product of proliferating chemical pesticides. But at the same time, the ability to respond to the loss of soil is inhibited by shortened time horizons associated with intense competition, small margins, large capital investments, and the frequency of high debt loads.

Another basic biophysical problem posed by monoculture production is that it expands the range of undesirable organisms which may have once had benign or beneficial roles in more diverse agroecosystems. In short, the definition of pests widens, at the same time as the loss of diversity weakens previous interrelations that once controlled their population. These vulnerabilities grow further with the genetic homogenization bound up in the diffusion of new varieties of high-yielding crops, which have also served to displace one of agriculture's most basic regenerative cycles: seed saving and selection. As the International Commission on the Future of Food put it in its *Manifesto on the Future of Seed*, 'until very recently, seed has resisted basic principles of capitalist market laws, the most important barrier being the nature of the seed, which reproduces itself and multiplies,' making it 'both a means of production as well as the product itself' – which is not to say that seed was never purchased before this time.[17] While conventional seed enhancement occurred by naturally crossing different varieties within the same species, creating seeds that could reproduce and be saved and replanted, in practice farmers were increasingly propelled into markets for seeds owing to the diminishing returns from seed progeny as well as the cost efficiencies and time savings from large-scale plant breeding (though because of the nature of innovation and the fact that farmers maintained control over the progeny, there was a prospect of democratic control and decentralized innovation).

In itself, the desire for higher-yielding plants and animals is obvious and indisputable; obviously every farmer would be happy if each plant and animal on the farm grew bigger. Indeed, improving yields has been a central objective of peasant farmers over the ages. However, as Jan Douwe van der Ploeg emphasizes, enhancing yield in peasant farming has always involved not only plant breeding but highly localized ecological knowledge and, crucially, the *intensification of labor* geared toward improving the soil. In industrial monocultures, this is effectively reversed: yield gains are part of a process of reducing the local specificity of agriculture and the intensity of labor in farming, as well as being implicated in impoverishing the soil.[18]

Another important dimension of high-yielding monocultures is that varieties were designed under optimal conditions and require more water to augment growth, in contrast to the more variable conditions under which traditional varieties were developed. High-yielding seeds are, in effect, thirstier. Water demands grow further owing to the loss of ground cover and the declining organic content and moisture retention in monoculture soils, and are anticipated to grow further still with the higher temperatures and aridity associated with climate change.

Finally, the process of mechanization, standardization, and simplification utterly transforms the demand for energy in agriculture. For most of agrarian history, the friction of distance was pronounced, limited by both perishability and the restraints that relying on biological energy set on movement. This means that work and movement were mainly fueled by solar energy conducted through relatively localized biomass (i.e. from both farms and nearby ecosystems) and 'strictly constrained by the physiological ability of animal metabolisms to convert food into work,' placing 'well-defined biological limits' on both 'the total quantity of work that people or animals could perform in a day' and the general 'speed of movement.'[19] As landscapes become more industrialized and specialized, food must necessarily move farther and farther over space.

To transcend these limits of work and movement with combustion-powered machines requires dense packets of combustible energy, with far more calories than could be sustainably harvested from living biomass. This establishes a reinforcing and expanding sequence. External sources of energy are needed to enable mechanization and economies of scale, powering the specialization of vast monoculture landscapes and even entire regions, seen at its most striking in places like the Corn and Wheat Belts of the USA and the 'Soybean Republic' in southern South America. This scale and specialization then amplify the demand for external sources of energy to power the movement of goods, as inputs and outputs must be transported across longer distances to and from farms, especially as these flows are organized by increasingly large and centralized corporate intermediaries.

In sum, industrial grain and oilseed monocultures operate in dramatic contrast to both natural cycles in self-organizing ecosystems, and to the relatively closed-loop cycles that are managed within diverse, low-input agro-ecosystems. This results in a range of bio-physical barriers to continued productivity. The general systematic response is to override these problems with the repeated application of external inputs, which amount to a series of perpetual short-term fixes that must frequently be moved over considerable distances. Yet these *biophysical overrides* not only fail to resolve the basic contradictions necessitating their use, which makes them like a treadmill, but over time they can serve to make problems much worse, more like a quickening treadmill. This is powerfully reflected in the fact that the tremendous rates of yield growth discussed earlier have been far surpassed by the growth in industrial agro-input usage, as discussed below. Thus, in place of organic cycles, new flows of non-renewable materials are established, along with new flows of inorganic wastes and GHG emissions.

Overriding soil mining The modern understanding of soil chemistry and fertilization is indelibly associated with the advances made by Justis von Liebig in the nineteenth century. One of Liebig's most crucial discoveries was the 'Law of the Minimum,' which deciphered how plants need a certain mix of nutrients and how their growth is constrained by whatever nutrient is least abundant in relation to its requirements, with nitrogen, phosphorus, and potassium the most culpable controls on plant growth, and in farming landscapes more broadly. Nitrogen was a particular concern since most crops deplete nitrogen in soils. This is because plants are incapable of extracting nitrogen from the atmosphere, and instead must rely on certain bacteria – which exist only on certain plants – to fix and convert nitrogen into usable forms that can then cycle in soil organic material.

Through history, farming cultures tended to appreciate the importance of intercropping and using rotations with leguminous plants that have nitrogen-fixing bacteria in order to enrich soil fertility. But as these practices were broken and monocultures with nitrogen-depleting crops proliferated, the danger soon became clear. Having established how particular nutrient deficiencies constrain productivity, Liebig then showed how injections of these nutrients could, where they were scarce, drive great yield gains, a discovery that effectively 'opened the door to seeing the soil as a chemical warehouse through which to supply crop growth.'[20] Although declining soil fertility stems from the loss of biological complexity, organic content, and a range of nutrients, the expansion of industrial fertilizers was overwhelmingly focused on the 'big three' nutrients that are the greatest constraints to plant growth.

Around the period of Liebig's great breakthrough, a new, unlikely resource emerged on the world stage: guano, bird droppings aged into a nitrogen- and phosphorus-rich fertilizer. The large-scale export of guano began from Peru and later Chile to Europe, followed by the USA setting out to annex small islands around the world containing this relatively rare resource, in a scramble that has been dubbed 'guano and nitrate imperialism.'[21] While most guano reserves were used up very quickly, they gave clear evidence of how concentrated doses of key nutrients could keep organically depleted soils productive, ultimately helping to set the course for industrial fertilizer development – and with it, the decline of historic soil conservation practices, leguminous rotations, and integrated livestock populations.

The game-changing advance in overriding declining soil fertility occurred in the early twentieth century, when Fritz Haber invented a process for manufacturing synthetic nitrogen fertilizer and Carl Bosch commercialized it. In the Haber-Bosch process, nitrogen and hydrogen from the air are combined under high temperatures and pressure, which involves a tremendous demand for energy. Commercial manufacturing took off in the immediate wake of the Second World War, partly owing to the easy conversion of plants that had been geared to making nitrogen bombs, and this boom crucially underpinned the great yield gains of the twentieth century, placing it among the most influential technologies ever established.[22] The Haber-Bosch process continues to account for the greatest volume of industrial fertilizer on a world scale, predominantly using natural gas.

After nitrogen, the depletion of phosphorus and potassium from soils is the next largest constraint on crop growth, and their application in concentrated forms has therefore served to greatly enhance crop growth. This entails another large fossil energy budget: first, in the mining and material extraction of phosphate ore and potash; and secondly, because the uneven geographic distribution of these resources means that these fertilizers are regularly shipped over long distances. Potassium is much more abundant than phosphorus in the earth's crust, and considerably easier to process into fertilizer, in particular since the manufacture of phosphorous fertilizer involves large volumes of sulphuric acid. High-grade phosphate ore reserves are very unevenly distributed on a world scale, as only a few countries contain most of what remains, and this might well pose another considerable resource challenge for industrial agriculture in the coming decades.[23]

Fossil energy can be seen to be systematically linked to both the degradation of soils and the manufacture of a few key nutrients which are injected back into them. On a world scale, the total volume of chemical fertilizers consumed increased more than fivefold from 1961 to 2010, from 31 to 178 million tonnes, led by synthetic nitrogen fertilizer, which grew by a factor of nine. Since the early 1990s, nitrogen fertilizer has accounted for roughly three-fifths of the total volume of fertilizer consumed. The USA has the highest levels of industrial fertilizer consumption per farmer, as 0.25 percent of the world's farmers account for more than one tenth of the world's annual fertilizer consumption. China's surge is also very notable. In 2010, China consumed almost one third of the world's industrial fertilizers, compared with only 2 percent a half-century earlier. Beyond the fertilizer treadmill, the primary industrial innovation to reduce soil erosion in monocultures is no-till seeding, which alleviates the need for annual tillage and leaves more ground cover. However, though this might slow erosion it does not alter the essential biophysical contradictions of industrial monocultures, and has not stopped the steady growth in the total annual consumption of chemical fertilizers on a world scale, which grew by roughly one third between 2000 and 2010.[24]

Overriding pest problems The heightened vulnerability to a wider definition of pests within high-yielding monocultures is overridden by massive volumes of synthetic chemical pesticides, comprising herbicides (for weeds), insecticides, fungicides, bactericides, and disinfectants. As with fertilizers, the use of synthetic chemicals drastically increased after the Second World War, owing in part to their immense capacity for displacing labor while opening a new realm of profit-making in the conversion of chemical weapons plants (though the strong connection between agro-chemicals and chemical warfare persisted long after[25]). Pesticide consumption also grew at a rate that dwarfed yield gains, rising by roughly a factor of ten over the second half of the twentieth century, with fossil energy central to this exploding scale in both manufacturing and transportation.

Again, however, fundamental problems are never resolved, and another treadmill is established. Once it is set in motion, problems tend to deepen for a number of reasons that include: the damage inflicted by broad-spectrum chemicals on previous natural controls and on the biology of soils; the development of resistance over time in the face of repeated applications; and the loss of knowledge about non-chemical approaches. New pesticides are then needed to adjust to fast-evolving new threats, such as chemical resistance in insects and weeds. Jason Moore calls this the 'superweed effect' to encapsulate the escalating unpredictability associated with the fact that 'superweeds are advancing faster than agro-capitalism can run,' with shorter and often more toxic chemical fixes required.[26] Here, the image of a treadmill fails in some ways, as responses are hardly straightforward.

Overriding limits to crop yield (or limits to accumulation in agriculture?) High-yielding seeds can be seen as a twofold override, as crop breeding surpasses the yield limits of traditional varieties while annual purchases override the rupture of historic seed saving and selection cycles. However, the yield gains from conventional enhancement started slowing in the 1980s, and in response some of the world's leading agro-input TNCs began to develop sophisticated techniques for combining particular genetic traits in ways that could not occur in nature, even crossing DNA sequences between plant and animal species. The rise of genetically modified (GM) crops came with big promises that it would ignite a new wave of yield gains and help solve world hunger, at the same time as the ability to patent 'the products, processes, and even the genes themselves ... rendered such technical development extremely lucrative.'[27] That is, the proprietary nature of the research, the seeds, and the patent protections together deny any potential to save, breed, or replant seeds, and hence bind farmers to the repeated purchase of seeds and chemicals more forcefully than with conventionally enhanced crops. Thus, critics have long held that the genetic modification of crops is motivated, in considerable measure, by a desire to override the limits to capital accumulation posed by the regenerative nature of the seed.[28]

After two decades of GM crop development, some major currents are clear. First, GM crop sales have been dominated by a small number of TNCs such as Monsanto and DuPont, augmenting their control over the world's commercial seed markets. Secondly, development has been heavily concentrated on three major feed crops – maize, soybeans, and canola – which in turn permeate industrial livestock production and processed foods. Feed has provided a way around consumer fears about GMOs, in turn helping to diffuse their place in the food system. As Hattie Ellis suggests, feed has been an essential 'money-spinner for the GM industry: if people won't eat it, give it to animals.'[29] Thirdly, GM crops have diffused widely across some of the heartlands of the industrial grain-oilseed-livestock complex, especially North America, the southern cone of South America, and parts of China. Fourthly, GM crops have failed to ignite another yield revolution, with the two predominant traits in commercial GM crops being tolerance for a particular agro-chemical (e.g. Monsanto's *Roundup Ready*® varieties that are designed for use with its broad-spectrum herbicide) and in-built pesticides (e.g. Bt varieties that are designed to express a particular bacterial toxin that poisons insect pests).[30] This has led to a shift in GM advocacy, away from claims about yield and toward assurances about pest and climate overrides, in that they reduce chemical inputs and could support climate change adaptation by engineering traits for drought tolerance and heat stress (i.e. 'climate proofing' seeds).

However one might view these modified promises for GM crops, what is clear is that the absence of new yield gains has impeded further advances in agricultural labor productivity – one major factor now threatening the continuing supply of cheap food which has been so central to accumulation on a world scale.[31]

Overriding water constraints The heightened irrigation demands associated with thirstier seeds and drier soils have been met by a range of engineering fixes. As noted in Chapter 1, even in ancient times some irrigation water moved across considerable distances, but it was not until the second half of the twentieth century that engineering advances overwhelmed virtually all limits to the scale of rivers and freshwater ecosystems that could be tamed and harnessed for agriculture and energy. The pumping of underground aquifers provides a vital override in some highly productive regions, though in many instances rates of withdrawals are so much faster than rates of recharge that this is akin to a non-renewable resource.[32] Another underappreciated aspect of the water override is the energy budget associated with moving it against gravity, from large-scale aquifer mining to micro-scale diesel and electric pumps that tap many small reservoirs around the world and direct surface water in ways in which it could not otherwise flow.

Overriding the friction of distance The inability of local, renewable stores of biomass to power mechanization and long-distance flows of inputs and outputs is primarily overridden by substituting them with ancient, irreplaceable stores of fossilized biomass. The notion of 'food miles' is an increasingly popular way of marking the oil that is embedded in the long-distance movement of food, which necessarily grows with industrialization and the specialization of landscapes. Here, it is important to recognize that rail and coal did not displace horses and grass because they were more efficient in the sense of energy return on energy invested, but rather because 'they could consume vastly greater quantities of fuel much more quickly, and thus had much higher limits for work, speed, and endurance.'[33] Oil has been the chief source of energy enabling both combustion-powered machinery like tractors and combines on ever bigger farms, and combustion-powered transport moving inputs and outputs across ever greater distances, now sometimes from one side of the earth to the other. The rising distance that food moves is also entwined with the need to encase it in more durable parcels, with more energy and materials needed for processing and packaging.

The through-flow of industrial monocultures The practice of farming in relatively localized, closed-loop biophysical cycles has defined any durable agricultural system and civilization. As these organizing imperatives are broken, age-old problems are exacerbated and new ones established, and industrial productivity comes to hinge upon an array of biophysical overrides that are frequently sourced across long distances. Figure 3.1 depicts this transformation into an increasingly linear or through-flow process. The pivotal role of fossil energy is reflected in the fact that at least 2 calories of fossil energy are embedded in a single calorie of food energy contained in industrial maize, wheat, or soy, which is sometimes described in terms of the fact that we are effectively 'eating fossil fuels.'[34] Thus, while food miles can provide a valuable tool for drawing attention to the despatialization of industrial food, they should not obscure the energy and material flows that go into producing it. Rather, to assess the carbon budget of industrial grains and oilseed means considering not only how far the end product has moved but also asking questions such as how were its fertilizers and pesticides produced and how far have these external inputs moved.

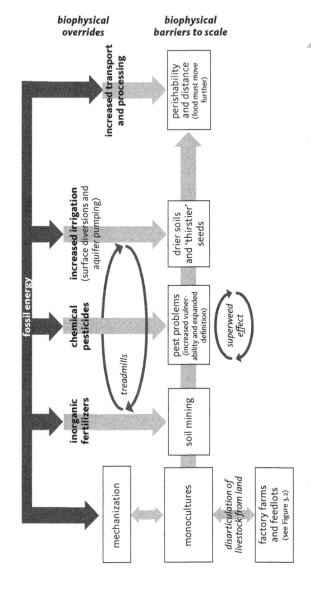

3.1 The through-flow of industrial monocultures

Approaching industrial grain and oilseed production this way helps to make sense of the many external resources and un- and under-accounted costs that are subsidizing high yields and high output per farmer. In the first instance, this strikes at the narrow conceptions of efficiency discussed at the outset of this chapter. It also establishes a basis for understanding why it is such a big problem to be cycling massive and growing volumes of these crops through livestock.

The magnifying effect of industrial livestock, part I: burning usable nutrition

A central argument in this book is that the scale, pace of change, and unevenness of meatification constitute a powerful vector of global inequality, environmental degradation, and violence, with industrial livestock production increasingly driving the rapid growth of meat production and consumption on a world scale. The focus on industrial monocultures so far in this chapter is an important building block in this case. Feed crops already command a large share of the world's arable land, and this pull on feed would have to rise further for the trajectory of meatification to continue growing as projected. The 'reverse protein factory' effect that Lappé first signaled remains one of the most fundamental imbalances in the distribution of the world's food supply, as cycling humanly edible grains and oilseeds through animals to produce flesh, eggs, and milk destroys much more protein and other usable plant nutrition than it contributes to human societies. And as she also stressed, this inherent nutritional wastage effectively magnifies the land area that must be devoted to industrial monocultures, together with all of their attendant instabilities and overrides – an insight that has been fortified again and again.[35]

Yet this should not suggest that relative levels of nutritional wastage are fixed, as much attention has been given to reducing feed conversion losses on a world scale. Losses have been reduced in two primary ways. The first is through a species-level shift toward poultry birds and pigs, monogastric animals that convert feed to flesh better than cattle and other ruminants. Indeed, the superior feed conversion of chickens is a central part of why they are the cheapest, most industrialized, and fastest-rising segment of world meat production. The second way is through innovations in livestock science geared at speeding the turnover time of animals. Ruth Harrison captured the essence of this pressure a half-century ago in her suggestion that 'a few days knocked off the tiny life span of the broiler chicken is greeted with enthusiasm by the industry.'[36] Since then, about a month more has been 'knocked off.' This pressure is reflected in a series of attempts to override the bodily limits and biorhythms of animals.

Overriding limits to animal yield Efforts to increase bodily yield start from the control that is exerted over the sexual activity and reproductive lives of animals. While husbandry has always involved a degree of intervention in animal reproduction, this has been transformed into a relation of utter domination, with extremely invasive procedures routinized and performed again and again upon the small minority of the population that is cast into near-constant cycles of breeding. Intensive control over reproduction involves two essential goals: to accelerate the development of bigger, faster-growing, and more uniform animals, and to churn out more material for the hurtling conveyor belts. The transformation of bodies is so radical that copulation is physically impossible for genetically enhanced turkeys, nearly impossible for broiler chickens, and increasingly difficult for pigs. Specialized breeding populations are also necessitated by the fact that most of their offspring are killed before reaching sexual maturity.

Another extreme outcome of the genetic transformations can be seen in layer hatcheries, where male offspring are deemed a waste product upon their birth. That is, because layer chickens are biologically programmed to pump out eggs rather than to quickly add flesh, it is not economically worth the feed and other inputs needed to grow males. This population, which numbers in the hundreds of millions of birds each year, is promptly electrocuted, chopped up alive, gassed, or simply trashed in plastic bins and left to die through suffocation or starvation. The genetic specialization of dairy cattle is a similar deterrent against rearing male offspring to adult weight, though their flesh is given value as veal by coupling extreme confinement with nutritionally deficient diets (the use of veal crates to produce anemic flesh pre-dates the rise of industrial dairy operations, but this practice has grown with them).

Both the speed of conveyor belts and the physical barriers to reproduction impel artificial insemination technologies, which were again pioneered with poultry birds and later advanced into industrial pig production, taking off with pigs in the 1990s, and quickly becoming dominant. Industrial pig breeding now involves purchasing boar semen from an external site or collecting it from a small number of boars, then injecting this into breeding sows with a specialized inseminating catheter. Hormone shots have also been developed to speed the transition of sows from lactation to reinsemination and the next round of pregnancy. Ultimately, just as with seeds, high-tech propagation and the commodification of new genetic varieties lead toward a narrowing of control over the breeding stock which populates industrial systems. As with crops, the pursuit of advances beyond conventional genetic enhancement has spun into the qualitatively different process of crossing genetics across species.

The goal of increasing bodily yields has also been instrumental in the design of industrial environments. Intensive confinement within seasonally heated spaces means that animals burn less feed than if they were moving around or struggling to regulate their body temperatures during colder times of the year, in turn ensuring that more is directed to weight gain, gestation, laying, and lactating. The seasonal heating of enclosures is especially needed in temperate regions for animals like chickens and pigs which originally evolved in the tropics, while heat lamps and pads are essential to warm infants in hatcheries and nurseries in the absence of their mothers.

Bodily yields have also been extended by manipulating animals' sense of day and night. This began with the layer industry, which played on the natural biorhythms of hens (i.e. rates of egg-laying rise with longer days and shifts in hormonal balances) and found that it could establish continual laying cycles by creating an illusion of extended daylight and twilight, boosted by adding vitamins A and D to feed. Another extreme practice devised by the layer industry is known as forced molting, in order to override the productivity decline in physically exhausted hens ('layer fatigue'), which cannot maintain the warp-speed pace of laying for much more than a year. Chickens naturally shed their feathers every year, and it can take four months before they are regrown and laying resumes. It was found that sudden reductions in light and feed can shock hens' bodies into defeathering more quickly, thereby quickening the onset of a second but shorter intensive laying cycle. Once laying rates slow down, between one and two years, industrialized layers are deemed to be physically 'spent' and are slaughtered for low-grade flesh, mostly destined for a range of processed foods. Forced molting has been successfully challenged by animal welfare organizations, again most conspicuously in the EU.

In some other cases, it has been abandoned out of pure economics: it can be more cost-effective to simply kill and replace a flock after their productivity first wanes than to endure the fallow time between laying cycles for the prospect of a less productive second round.

The development of hormone injections is yet another means to promote unnatural levels of bodily growth and milk production. In the USA, for example, repeated hormone injections have been key to the doubling of the annual milk that is produced by the average cow, to an extent that total national milk production has continued increasing while the total population of dairy cattle has fallen over the past half-century. However, human health concerns have stopped the diffusion of the hormone regime devised in the USA (most notably recombinant bovine growth hormone, or rBGH) from diffusing as widely as other practices. As with poultry birds, the dramatic acceleration in productivity takes a huge toll on the bodies of dairy cattle, and after their yield wanes they are similarly converted from bodily machines to low-grade flesh.

Finally, the pressure to enhance feed conversion means that animals' basic need to eat is denied for a period prior to slaughter, so as to reduce the wastage of undigested feed that would not add any value to the end commodity. This has also led to some mind-boggling experiments with non-nutritional additives such as cardboard, sawdust, and newspaper, in the hope that cheaper fillers can help to put on weight.

Unyielding metabolism A host of factors influence the rates at which individual animals convert feed to flesh, eggs, and milk, including differences in animal genetics, breeds, feed regimes, conditions of confinement, and the cocktails of pharmaceuticals discussed below. Calculations of feed conversion rates also depend upon whether measurements account for the populations of breeding animals, the animals that die in production and transport, and those that are condemned post-mortem owing to damage or disease. A range of metrics might also be used, from crude weights (i.e. 10 kg of feed goes into 1 kg of flesh) to differential conversions of usable protein, carbohydrates, fibre, and micro-nutrients – recalling the exaggerated focus on protein.[37]

For the purposes of this discussion, it is sufficient to say that while ratios of feed conversion have improved and may well advance further, this ultimately butts up against inescapable biophysical limits.

As with chemical fertilizers, pesticides, irrigation, and enhanced seeds, there comes a time when yield gains are maxed out, because no matter how intensely animals are immobilized and transfigured, a significant share of feed will be burned off as energy, excreted, and go into non-edible body parts. Even with industrial broiler production, where feed-to-flesh conversion ratios are the lowest (2–3:1 by weight), somewhere between half and two-thirds of all feed is lost to metabolic processes. Ratios of feed conversion losses are at least twice as high for pigs and many times higher for beef cattle, with the grain-fed steer long recognized as the pinnacle of inefficiency. Of course, defenders drape these losses in the claim that what emerges in flesh, eggs, and milk is nutritionally superior to the feed going in, which is problematic for reasons discussed in Chapter 2, and for more reasons that are developed below.

It is also very important to recognize that any gains in feed conversion must be set against the great increases in the scale of production. Put more simply, while individual animals in industrial systems generally convert feed faster than they did a few decades ago, there are many billions more of them. This means that nutrition is getting burned more efficiently, but at much greater volumes. This general dynamic reflects the Jevons Paradox that typifies industrial capitalist production, in that overall volume increases in resource use tend to accompany efficiency gains.[38]

Finally, the gains in feed conversion ratios have also come at the expense of a range of other inputs and ecological costs which are developed below, to say nothing yet of the profound ethical concerns.

The magnifying effect of industrial livestock, part II: more instabilities and overrides

The impacts and regressivity of industrial livestock production grow further in light of how, just as with monocultures, another set of interlocking instabilities are generated and then met by another set of overrides. To appreciate this, it helps to consider the key problems that emerge in the course of mechanizing, standardizing, and biologically simplifying livestock production.[39] These challenges run even deeper with animals than with crops, as they are complicated not only by physiology but also by animals' behavioral, intellectual, and emotional capacities, and with this their ability to suffer. Here, these dynamics are mainly considered in light of the challenges posed to the treadmill of production; Chapter 4 picks up their significance with respect to inter-species relations and responsibilities.

The acceleration of selective breeding for traits like size (in general, and of more valuable body parts), appetite, and rapid growth has altered the genetic make-up of animals used in industrial systems in ways that effectively lock in chronic circulatory and musculoskeletal problems. Unnaturally large and fast-growing bodies with excessive fat put increasing strain on hearts, lungs, bones, joints, and tendons, which is augmented by animals' lack of mobility. One extreme manifestation of weakened cardiovascular systems is the proneness to sudden heart attacks and ascites syndrome (referred to as 'leaking liver' or 'water belly') in broiler chickens, the latter occurring when cardiovascular systems fail to pump enough oxygenated blood for fast-growing bodies, and oxygen-depleted blood returning from veins becomes stuck and then seeps backwards into organs like the stomach or liver, having a suffocating effect. The strain of abnormally heavy bodies on weakened bones and joints is augmented by the rigid surfaces of concrete, slatted steel, and wire mesh, the design of which is determined above all by waste removal demands (as compostable bedding has to be regularly removed from stalls, which is increasingly difficult, laborious, and costly as animal populations grow). Many animals in industrial systems suffer from osteoporosis, and some can barely stand, much less walk. Fragile leg and hip bones are vulnerable to fractures, especially when they are forcefully grabbed and jerked in moving the animals to another stage in the extended conveyor belt.

The nature of industrial production also heightens vulnerability to infection. On mixed farms with relatively small populations, animals build up their immune systems through lengthy periods of nursing, access to diverse and physiologically suited food sources, routine exercise, and exposure to fresh air, sunlight, and daily and seasonal variations. Seasonality in cold climates also necessitates the development of thicker fur and denser feathers to help regulate body temperatures (though obviously some degree of protection from the elements, especially the cold, has long been provided). In contrast, animal immune systems are compromised by a number of features of industrial production, including the truncated weaning of infants, the lack of exercise, poor air quality, and the denaturalization and narrowing of diets. In general, dietary change is hardest on grain-fed cattle, as ruminant digestive systems have evolved to ferment grasses, stalks, and other roughage like hay, and the substitution of grain alters the microorganisms and acidity levels and leads to a range of digestive problems, including rampant diarrhea. Thinner coats and feathering also make skin more prone to chafing within tight enclosures and increase the loss of body heat. Thus, while the increased demand for heating stems in part from the drive to reduce metabolic losses, it becomes self-reinforcing as the external defences of animals weaken.

The greatest source of air pollution is the large concentrations of excrement, which emit levels of ammonia that damage respiratory systems and produce rampant skin lesions and abscesses on chickens. The alkalinity of ammonia regularly burns chicken's eyes (known as 'ammonia burn,' which can end in blindness), legs ('hock burn'), and breasts. Excrement and animal respiration contribute to humid ambient environments, and the contaminated air can become especially stifling during hot spells. Filthy and densely populated environments create favorable conditions for the growth of infectious microbes, the presence of flies, mites, lice, and other pests, and the rapid spread of air- and fluid-borne disease vectors, while large concentrations of feed are enticing to rodents. As a result, systems of industrial livestock production must be on constant guard against a long list of infectious diseases such as swine and avian influenza, listeriosis, salmonella, Escherichia coli (E. coli), campylobacteriosis, coccidiosis, cryptosporidiosis, streptococci, giardia, Marek's disease, and mastitis.

Environmental and physiological problems are further compounded by what livestock science typically defines as animal 'stress' – a guarded way of describing deep psychological problems. Rather than simply stress, Mason and Singer insist, it is more accurate and telling to acknowledge that animals are suffering from boredom, frustration, and fear from being packed into noisy and reeking spaces, and from being deprived of elemental desires to move around, explore, have social interactions with other animals, and maintain familial bonds.[40] Dismal psychological states of being not only reduce the general health of animals but routinely lead to neurotic behaviors. Some neuroses are not necessarily anti-productive, such as continuous preening or chewing on cages, but others are, as when chickens peck at and pigs bite crowded neighbors. Chickens are social but territorial birds that establish group hierarchies (the 'pecking order'), and hens have very strong desires to find private nesting spaces before laying eggs, while pigs are highly intelligent and social animals that want to root around, explore, and by and large interact with other pigs. In both cases, group infighting is limited where there is adequate space, but aggressive and even cannibalistic behaviors can emerge when animals are put into constant proximity to one another.

The enclosure and soaring density of animal populations transform manure from its functional role as fertilizer into a major waste management problem. An average pig, for example, excretes much more (and more potent) waste each day than does an average person, to an extent that a large industrial pig farm can rival the volume of human sewage from small cities. Such levels of biowaste simply cannot be composted naturally or healthily absorbed on nearby farmlands, nor clearly can animals contribute to spreading it themselves. Further, it is not only a matter of quantity, as the quality of potential fertilizer is compromised by excessive concentrations of nutrients and the presence of infectious pathogens and pharmaceutical and chemical residues. In short, there are quantitatively much larger flows of wastes and qualitatively more complex treatment challenges, while treated wastes have to move farther for fertilizer applications.

The disarticulation of animals from land is also entwined with the need to move feed and water across greater distances. In simple terms, instead of animals having to move to get all or most of their food and water, these must be brought to them (for water, this also relates to the loss of roughage in diets with the shift toward dry feed concentrates). The energy associated with the movement of feed is compounded by the specialization of both monoculture and livestock production over large areas. Within the USA, for example, there are a number of major factory farm and feedlot belts – some of which roughly overlap with major feed-producing regions, some of which do not. A large share of the US pig industry is heavily concentrated in 'Corn Belt' states like Iowa, and secondarily in North Carolina; the broiler chicken industry is heavily concentrated in the US Southeast, south of an arc stretching from Arkansas to the Delmarva Peninsula; beef cattle feedlots are heavily concentrated in the southern Great Plains; and central and southern California is a major site of both factory farms and feedlots. This geography appears vividly in a valuable website (www.factoryfarmmap.org) run by Food and Water Watch. Where the spatial separation of livestock operations from major feed-producing regions occurs it is influenced by a mix of factors, including weak environmental and labor laws, the ability to pay workers at lower wages, and warm weather to reduce heating costs.

As emphasized in Chapter 2, there is also increasing movement of feed on a world scale, at the head of which are the large exports of maize and soy from countries like the USA and Brazil to China and parts of Europe. Finally, the expanding geography of animal conveyor belts, between specialized sites of breeding and growing and large centralized industrial slaughter and packing plants, means that increasing numbers of animals must be transported during their shortened lives, when in the past they would largely only move over relatively short distances, and under their own power. The centralization of processing facilities along with the consolidation of corporate power also tend to increase the distance that meat, eggs, and dairy products end up moving between sites of production and consumption, especially with the rising international trade in livestock products.

As with monocultures, the general systematic response to the problems posed by the nature of industrial livestock production is to technologically overpower them. Together, this amounts to an array of biophysical, physiological, and psychosocial overrides, establishing more input treadmills with more short-term risks and long-term costs.

Overriding chronic health problems and disease risks There is a basic tolerance for frail, unhealthy, and highly stressed animals in industrial livestock production, provided yields are high. The clearest reflection of this is the high rates of disease and mortality that pervade industrial poultry and pig barns. In a given growing cycle, pre-slaughter death rates regularly run on the order of 5 percent or more in an average large-scale poultry shed, which translates into many thousands of birds over a year. The fact that on-site incinerators for dead birds have become common exemplifies the ubiquity of this loss-of-life-turned-disposal problem. But the tolerance for a given level of losses should not downplay the challenge of managing chronic health problems and disease risks and containing losses within acceptable levels, for which antibiotics, vaccines, vitamins, and other additives comprise the central override, delivered through feed, water, manual shots, and mechanized injection and spraying systems.

Pharmacological innovation has been inseparable from industrial livestock production ever since antibiotics, vaccines, and vitamin additives enabled the initial expansion of poultry sheds. The principal function is to override the damaged immune systems and heightened susceptibility to respiratory diseases within individual animals, along with the risks of infectious disease spreading among dense and genetically alike animal populations in bacteria-laden environments. Drugs also override a range of other frequent problems, such as the diarrhea common to piglets after their premature weaning and to cattle as their digestive systems are unsettled by so much grain, while feed additives are used to fortify diminished colors (e.g. flesh, egg yolks) and weakened egg shells.

As antibiotics proliferated they were found to have the productive side effect of suppressing intestinal bacteria and enhancing digestion, and from this they quickly came to be seen as another means to override limits to yield, promoting weight gain and extending milking and laying cycles. In the USA, where these dynamics took root, the volume of antibiotics used in livestock production now dwarfs the amount directly consumed by humans, with the majority given at a 'sub-therapeutic' level; that is, a regular low-level dosage in the absence of a particular illness. However, owing to the clear risks associated with the pharmaceutical treadmill (discussed below), there has been rising opposition to the explicit use of drugs for growth promotion, and here again the most extreme industry practices have been tempered somewhat in Europe, where legislation has been designed to ensure that drugs are used only in response to a specific disease.

Chemical pesticides and disinfectants are another significant override for the magnified disease risks in production, aimed at containing the bacteria, insects, and rodents that thrive amid dense concentrations of animals, excrement, and feed. Insecticides are applied through ear tags, hand-held sprayers, and aerial 'misting' systems from the rafters of buildings (and on feedlots, occasionally from low-flying aircraft), while targeted rodenticides help to protect feed from mice and other rodents. The decontamination of filthy enclosures involves a combination of harsh antiseptics and high-pressure hot water. As with many overrides, responding to one problem adversely affects something else, and the presence of airborne pesticides and cleansing agents further worsens the ambient environment.

Finally, the recent emergence of 'bio-securitization' as a concern for industrial livestock operations speaks to the severity of infectious disease risks and pathogen mutation. That is, the great threat of pandemic disease jumping from pig and poultry populations to humans has heightened the physical security of sites against risks of bio-terrorism and the need for information and communication technologies to rapidly assess and communicate risks. Large-scale livestock operations are also increasingly installing decontamination procedures for workers to pass through to inhibit contagion.

Overriding psychosocial stress From an economic standpoint, the stress animals endure is worrying only to the extent that it contributes to chronic health problems or damaging neurotic behaviors. A basic goal, then, is to make anxious or fearful animals more languid, which is partly accomplished as a by-product of proliferating pharmaceuticals. The deprivation of light is also used for this effect in some cases, swinging the other way from how extended periods of light are used to stimulate bodily activity as with laying. However, drugs or extended periods of dimness and darkness cannot fully negate aggressive behaviors such as repeated pecking or tail-biting, which have been met with systemic physical mutilations – or what might be seen as the disfigurement override.

This includes practices such as debeaking (or 'beak-tipping'), toe-cutting, needle-teeth-clipping, ear-notching, tail-docking, dehorning, and castration, which are overwhelmingly performed without anesthetic. Again, the poultry industry illustrates this basic logic pushed to an especially extreme form, as early techniques for blunting beaks with blow torches and hot blades were quickly turned into rapid-fire debeaking machines. Workers operating these machines today regularly dismember one beak every four seconds.

Overriding unusable concentrations of biowaste In designing factory farms, a central imperative is to manage vast flows of feces and urine with minimal labor inputs. This starts from either grated or hard surfaces of concrete and steel, so that biowastes can either seep through or get rinsed away into channels. It also entails great volumes of freshwater for spraying these enclosures, which mixes with feces, urine, food scraps, and other wastes to form a slurry material that ends up in large storage facilities, where bacteria break it down into less-polluting elements. Yet slurries still regularly contain unhealthy concentrations of nutrients and risks from pathogens and pharmaceutical and agro-chemical residues, and their lower quality as fertilizer (compared with either traditionally composted manure or synthetic fertilizers) and bulky character (with associated transportation and energy costs) tend to restrict its movement. At the same time, neighboring agricultural landscapes can only absorb so much, and so often, while the slurry is generated steadily throughout the year. Together, the limits to local applications and transportation over significant distances mean that much of the slurry generated in factory farms accrues in great adjoining pits, euphemistically termed 'lagoons,' which can exceed 100,000 m^3.

One way of mitigating the excessive concentrations of phosphorus in slurry is by reducing its presence in feed mixtures. However, this risks weakening skeletal strength, which can become an economic problem (quite apart from any concern for animal well-being) if too many broken limbs lead to premature deaths or slow down fast-moving slaughter lines. In other words, there is a fine balance between moderating the pollution load of excrement and compromising the production itself. A more dramatic override has also been developed: the so-called Enviro-pig^{TM}, genetically engineered to produce manure with less phosphorus. In blaming the nature of pigs rather than the nature of production and animal populations, and ostensibly 'fixing' this through genetics, this innovation, Jonathan Clark argues, is a striking new way of representing ecological problems and exerting power over animals.[41] Among the many contradictions is the prospect that if individual pigs are made to produce less waste it could help enable still higher populations, another case of the Jevons Paradox. Meanwhile, a literal end-of-pipe override is the design of backpacks for cattle in order to capture methane from their flatulence.

Powerful ventilation is another essential override for indoor enclosures, in order to flush out the unhealthy concentrations of ammonia, other gases, and germs, and draw in fresh air. In locations with cold winters, the need for ventilation is complicated by the desire to conserve the energy used in heating buildings, forcing operators to weigh the build-up of contaminated air against the significant heat losses associated with regular ventilation. Although ventilation systems have a crucial role in making the ambient environment livable for most animals, they hardly resolve all respiratory problems and infectious disease risks, and it speaks to the severity of the chronic air pollution that the loss of power or malfunction of these systems can quickly have a lethal effect.

Finally, there is an energy budget built into all of this, in order to run slurry pumping systems, processing equipment, off-site transport, and spraying, as well as automated ventilation systems. Yet another partial override can be seen in attempts to capture methane from lagoons in order to produce electricity.

Overriding the friction of distance As with monocultures, fossil-energy-powered transport is indispensable to the movement of an expanded array of inputs to sites of production, namely feed, pharmaceuticals, and chemicals. As noted, sites of industrial livestock production also call on a large volume of water beyond their immediate vicinity, since animals cannot seek out water themselves, obtain less moisture in dry feed concentrates than they would from plants in more natural and diversified diets, and most of all since enclosures must be frequently washed down. Thus, water infrastructure is another dimension of how the historically heavy friction of distance in agriculture must be overridden.

Fossil-energy-powered transport also enables increasing distance between sites of breeding, growing, and slaughter, and increasing food miles between sites of production and consumption. Owing to the rising scale and corporate consolidation of slaughterhouses, the final journey to slaughter alone is now often many hundreds of kilometers long and occurs in tremendously crowded and sometimes extremely hot or cold conditions, since maximizing animals per load and eschewing temperature controls save on fuel costs. As with all welfare regulations, poultry birds have the weakest protections in their transport conditions, and more than five thousand broiler chickens can be crammed onto a typical transport truck in one load to the slaughterhouse. In addition to being exposed to the elements, animals are deprived of food and water, as this would take up space and fail to add anything to the weight and value of the body parts about to be processed. The hardship is especially great over long hauls in hot summers or cold winters, yet though transport conditions inevitably lead to some injuries, 'downers' (animals too weak or injured to make it to the slaughter line under their own power), and deaths, these losses are accepted, within certain bounds, as a matter of course. Put another way, as in production a degree of wastage is simply absorbed in the cost savings from economies of scale.

Though temperature controls in transport can be ignored while animals are living, they cannot be ignored after animals are killed or after eggs and milk are obtained, as livestock products demand more refrigeration than raw or processed cereals, oilseeds, and many other sources of plant-based nutrition. Thus, the fuel budgets contained in the food miles for meat, eggs, and dairy products are amplified by the energy associated with running mobile refrigeration units.

Overriding post-slaughter wastes The structural wastage associated with so many unhealthy animals extends from the significant pre-slaughter mortality rates to the flesh that is damaged in transport and on slaughter lines and to that which is condemned post-slaughter owing to disease. Some of the flesh that is unfit for human consumption is redirected out of waste streams, along with non-edible body parts such as internal organs, bones, and feathers, and the instantly superfluous male layer chicks. These diverted wastes are rendered and added to a variety of lower-grade products, including pet food, fertilizers, and protein supplements that are fed back to livestock, the latter yet another aspect of the broader systemic pressure to enhance rates of feed-to-flesh conversion. But there is still great pressure to salvage for human consumption as much flesh from unhealthy animals as possible, which has led to a variety of processing and handling techniques. Injections of coloring and flavoring additives, such as sodium nitrates (which also act as a preservative), are one basic post-slaughter method for overriding substandard appearance and taste, along with the development of an immense range of highly processed meats, from hot dogs to chicken nuggets to hamburgers, which regularly contain pieces of many animals along with assorted fillers and coagulants.

Like factory farms, slaughterhouses are extremely thirsty spaces, with large volumes of water and disinfectants needed to rinse away the splattered blood, guts, and excrement from various surfaces and machines, and to rinse off carcasses. After rinsing, different methods of cooling are then used to stop the growth and spread of dangerous bacteria among freshly slaughtered carcasses. For poultry, there is a divide between the use of air chill systems, as are the rule in Europe, and chlorinated water chill systems, as are dominant in the USA, with the latter having the economic advantage of being cheaper and soaking up water to inflate the weight of the flesh. The most high-tech override for food-borne disease risks is irradiation, which entails sending short pulses of high energy (X-rays, gamma rays, and electron beams) through carcasses. Yet even in the USA, where irradiation was first approved for commercial use on meat in the 1990s, it remains rarely used owing to high costs and consumer fears.

The 'disappearance' of animals from sight and mind Finally, it is important to recognize that this transformation in production is not only linked to radical changes in diets but also to a profound loss of consciousness about the animal lives it involves. For most of the history of agriculture, human populations were overwhelmingly rural and lived close to the animals being consumed; indeed, this often meant a familiarity with the individual animal the flesh, eggs, or milk came from. Most people would regularly see or interact with livestock in their daily rhythms, while consuming from them far more sporadically than today. Thus, without sentimentalizing or homogenizing attitudes toward the consumption of livestock, the nature of animal lives and deaths would have been known, and harder to set aside when eating their products. The industrialization of livestock production and the expanding physical distance between animals, people, slaughter, and markets have radically changed this, and established, as William Cronon puts it, a 'deeper and subtler separation – the word "alienation" is not too strong – from the act of killing and from nature itself.'[42]

The through-flow of industrial livestock production Taken together, the disarticulation of animals from land and the practices which make up systems of industrial livestock production establish a series of intractable problems. These include: weakened circulatory, musculoskeletal, respiratory, and immune systems in animals; omnipresent risks of contagion; reproductive difficulties; stress-induced behavioral pathologies; and massive amounts of unusable biowaste. As with monocultures, contradictions are never resolved but are instead overridden at every turn. Overrides involve varying combinations of antibiotics, vaccines, hormones, insecticides, disinfectants, artificial inseminators, physical mutilations, heating, lighting, ventilation systems, large volumes of water, slurry pumps, sprayers, and lagoons, along with the energy needed to transport things over greater distances. In sum, industrial livestock production emerges as another through-flow process, depicted in Figure 3.2, with contradictions and overrides driving perpetual flows of external resource inputs and polluting outputs, and fossil energy again coursing through the system as a whole.

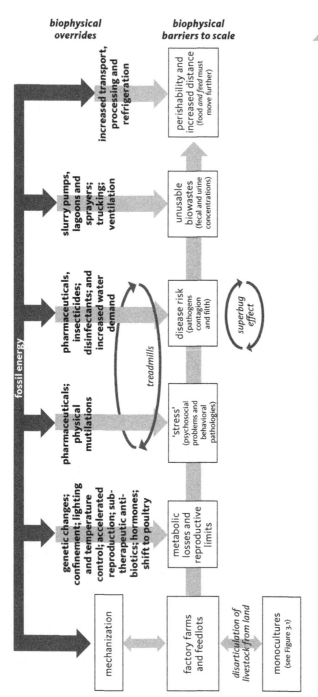

3.2 The through-flow of industrial livestock production

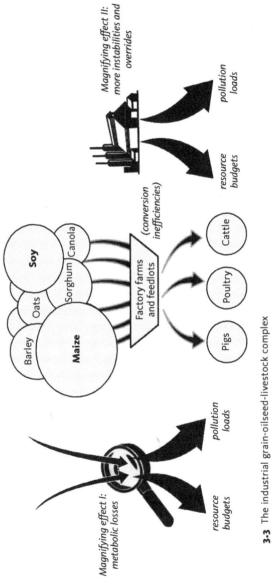

3.3 The industrial grain-oilseed-livestock complex

Approaching industrial monocultures and industrial livestock production in parallel (compare Figures 3.1 and 3.2) helps to underscore their linearity and the narrow ways in which problems are framed and overridden, and to make sense of their resource budgets and pollution loads. Ultimately, however, these through-flow processes converge as part of a unitary complex of production, depicted in Figure 3.3, and it is here that Chapter 4 picks up, adding up the great burden that is the ecological hoofprint.

4 | CONFRONTING THE HOOFPRINT: TOWARDS A SUSTAINABLE, JUST, AND HUMANE WORLD

The ecological hoofprint

The introduction to this book noted how attention to the burden of industrial livestock production is increasing, but generally still pales in relation to its magnitude. For most, this system of production remains hidden in plain sight, entrenched in simplified and standardized landscapes, in food, and in everyday life. One basic reflection of this can be seen in the assumption that industrial livestock production and the meatification of diets are destined to continue increasing, which is part of the influential claim that the world's food supply must double by 2050 to meet future demand.

But this trajectory is not only about silence and inertia. The bounty of cheap meat has also been widely celebrated as a, if not *the*, definitive marker of agricultural modernization. In this rosy depiction, humans are omnivores (and the more animal protein the better) and science and technology have simply enabled the ramping up of an age-old interrelation between humans and domesticated animals. Such benign imagery is neatly encapsulated in the boast that animal 'protein has never been more affordable,' as a factory farm operator put it to Jonathan Safran Foer; though, as Foer counters, this cheapness is made possible only by the systematic failure to count the multidimensional costs, 'which make the [real] price historically high.'[1]

Part of the goal of the ecological hoofprint is, like the ecological footprint before it, to draw attention to the resource budgets and pollution loads that are embedded and under-accounted for in production and consumption. This chapter starts by adding up the burden of industrial livestock production in terms of land, water, atmosphere, and public health, building upon the conceptual framework developed in Chapter 3 in which industrial monocultures and factory farms and feedlots were understood as dual through-flow processes that are characterized by their own sets of biophysical instabilities and overrides, and then bound together by the metabolic losses that are inherent in cycling rising volumes of feed through rising populations

LAND

magnified monoculture area

- ⅓ of arable land and metabolic losses to feed
- role in the decline and fragmentation of ecosystems
- more soil degradation and fertilizers
- more pesticides, toxicity, and risks from 'superweed' effect
- contributes to the spread of GMOs

'islands' of concentrated contaminants

- fecal lagoons and slurries
- feedlot wastelands

WATER

magnified consumption and diversions

- feed crop irrigation and metabolic losses
- sites of concentrated livestock
- large-scale slaughterhouses

magnified pollution

- more nutrient loads from fertilizers and animal biowastes
- more pesticides and toxicity
- pharmaceutical residues
- magnifies cultural eutrophication and persistent toxins in aquatic ecosystems

ATMOSPHERE

magnified GHG emissions

- expanded feed crop production (especially fertilizers)
- powering machinery and factory farms
- moving animals and feed within spatially disaggregated conveyor belts
- more ruminant flatulence and animal respiration
- moving outputs further in specialized landscapes
- more energy in refrigeration and cooking

reduced carbon sequestration capacity

- in biologically impoverished landscapes

localized airborne pollutants and wretched 'smell-scapes'

PUBLIC HEALTH

magnified diet-related chronic disease

- 'diseases of affluence'

magnified long-term eco-health risks

- bioaccumulation of persistent toxins
- declining micro-nutrient content in soils and foods
- drug-resistant 'super-bugs'
- GMO uncertainties

magnified infectious disease risks

- viral pandemics jumping species
- foodborne bacteria

INTER-SPECIES RELATIONS

scale and acceleration

- exploding populations
- rapid turnover time
- genetic reconfiguration

domination of animal lives

- extreme sensory deprivation and monotony
- chronic pain and suffering
- routinized bodily mutilations
- invasive manipulation of reproduction

silent violence

- distancing and invisibility of animal lives and deaths in consumption

THE DEGRADATION OF WORK

manufacture of instruments of violence

psychological trauma

- immersion in suffering-filled environments
- routinized mutilations
- fast-paced killing and packing floors
- spillover into households and communities

health risks

- high rates of injury, repetitive stress, and job turnover
- immersion in polluted environments

4.1 The ecological hoofprint of industrial livestock production

of concentrated animals. As was emphasized, the burning of usable nutrition has had a vital role enabling continued growth and capital accumulation in agriculture by profitably absorbing grain and oilseed surpluses and increasing markets for animal feed and value-added meat, eggs, and dairy products. The net result is that the burden of industrial livestock production must be seen through both its role in magnifying the spatial expanse, resource budgets, and pollution loads of industrial monocultures, and in the resource- and pollution-intensive sites of concentrated animals that dot the landscapes of the industrial grain-oilseed-livestock complex.

One fundamental implication of this is that consumption disparities are tied to lopsided environmental impacts, again much like the ecological footprint. However, the burden of industrial livestock production must also be understood in a different, relational way; first in terms of the commodification of animals and next in terms of how this reverberates in profoundly dehumanizing work. Figure 4.1 depicts the main contours of the ecological hoofprint together, though they are more entangled than this. Ultimately, I hope, this might help cut through the blind spots and illusions that surround cheap meat, and dispel the pretense that industrial livestock production is anything like a mere technological amplification of age-old interrelations.

Land While rates of feed conversion have generally improved, a given amount of usable nutrition can always be obtained from much less cultivated land if crops are directly consumed than if they are cycled through livestock to produce food, owing to metabolic losses. Thus, any use of 'highly productive croplands to produce animal feed, no matter how efficiently, represents a net drain on the world's potential food supply,' and this drain now sits under roughly one third of the world's arable lands.[2] The extension is that the meatification of diets necessarily expands the land area needed for cultivation, a dynamic that for decades has centered on maize and soybeans. With this, it is also ultimately a factor in the decline and fragmentation of forests, wetlands, and native grasslands, and in impoverishing habitat for other species.

More land in grain and oilseed monocultures means more artificial fertilization, which both masks and accelerates the long-term degradation of soils. This also expands the ecological burden of industrial fertilizers. Phosphate fertilizer production generates highly toxic wastewater ponds, as chemical solutions are needed to extract the mined product and large quantities of unusable waste are generated for every unit of fertilizer. Above-ground potash mining leaves behind open-pit wastelands, and below-ground potash mining creates extensive underground mines which pose risks for water table contamination and land subsidence. After it is applied to fields, not all of the nutrients get taken up in crop growth, which effectively turns them into pollutants as they course across landscapes and into waterways.

Expanded monoculture production also means more pesticides and persistent toxins circulating in the environment, which reduces the organic matter, microorganisms, and invertebrates in soils and heightens risks of resistance emerging over time (the 'superweed effect'). Added to this are the pharmaceutical and chemical residues and array of microbial pathogens contained in animal biowastes, as treatment fails to remove all risks entailed in using slurry as fertilizer. As Jason Moore puts it, 'every leap forward in labour productivity (more chickens per working hour) also represents a leap forward in toxification (more poisons per dollar) and the creative responses of extra-human nature to the disciplines of capital (more weeds per ha).'[3] As discussed, industrial livestock production is also heavily tied to the expansion and associated risks of GMOs, as the large flow of GM crops through factory farms and feedlots has been one way of skirting consumer fears (along with staunch opposition to clear labeling wherever they have spread).

As discussed in Chapter 1, the amount of arable land on a world scale is expected to decline in absolute terms owing to land degradation and climate change, which will be intensified on a per capita level by continuing population growth. Thus, it is impossible to overstate the urgency of maintaining and in many instances rebuilding soil health in the world's cultivated landscapes, a challenge that is entwined with the need to stop all further conversions of land for agriculture. This is most urgent in the tropics, and nowhere more so than on the frontier of the Amazonian rainforest, where high-input soybean monocultures are a growing part of the land-use matrix, along with continuing clearance for low-density cattle ranching. Beyond the need to sustain cultivated soils and prevent the further loss of self-organizing ecosystems lays the more ambitious goal of consciously shrinking the land area in agriculture, the prospect of which is developed below.

Finally, the land burden should also be seen to encompass the industrial wastelands of livestock sheds, fecal lagoons, and feedlots. The massive surpluses of excrement contained at these sites – the primary physical output of all the squandered nutrition in feed crops – pose risks to surrounding soils and water. The durability of lagoon lining varies, with earthen structures especially susceptible to slow leakage or sudden rupture, while feedlot runoff is almost impossible to contain.

Water As discussed in Chapter 2, agriculture is by far the greatest consumer of freshwater on a world scale and thus the leading force altering aquatic ecosystems and drawing down underground reservoirs. Industrial livestock production plays a major part in this, starting with feed crops, which account for roughly half of agriculture's total freshwater consumption in industrialized countries; again, with much effectively wasted through feed conversion losses. Added to the water used in feed crops is the increased supply needed for drinking, flushing away wastes from industrial enclosures, and cleaning the kill-floor, disassembly lines, and carcasses at slaughterhouses. Thus, although precise volumes vary considerably between species, industrial meat, eggs, and dairy contain much more embedded water per unit of nutrition than if it were derived directly from grains or oilseeds.[4]

Industrial livestock production is also a leading source of freshwater pollution wherever it has a prominent place in landscapes. The nutrient loads and persistent toxins associated with feed crop production are augmented by the leaching of porous or ruptured lagoons and the dense concentrations of manure on feedlots. Over time, contaminants build up in groundwater, streams, rivers, lakes, estuaries, and coastal marine environments, as well as in fish, amphibians, and other organisms. One widespread problem is cultural eutrophication, which occurs when too many phosphates, nitrates, and other nutrients are added to water bodies, fostering the growth of algal blooms that deplete oxygen concentrations in water, shade out sunlight, produce damaging toxins, and can ultimately have devastating effects upon trophic webs.[5] Large-scale slaughterhouses, processing plants, and tanneries generate additional volumes of hazardous wastewater that is high in organic content from residues of animal flesh, blood, skin, feathers, undigested food, and excrement. This discharge tends to be more strictly regulated and managed than animal biowastes on factory farms and feedlots, where the task (and costs) of sanitation is cast downstream to water treatment facilities or externalized onto ecosystems. Finally, given the extent to which the industrial grain-oilseed-livestock complex hinges on fossil energy, it can be seen to contribute to the rising water pollution as extraction becomes more hazardous through shale oil and gas fracking, tar sands extraction, and deep ocean drilling.

An obvious extension of the water hoofprint is that continuing meatification is bound to increase the demand for freshwater withdrawals and the ensuing pollution loads, at the same time as this trajectory is becoming less and less tenable in the context of irrigation-affected land degradation and with the looming threats to supply posed by climate change.

Atmosphere More than two decades ago, Jeremy Rifkin first drew attention to the impact of what he called the 'modern cattle complex' on the atmosphere.[6] It is now widely recognized that livestock production is responsible for the lion's share of agriculture-related GHG emissions and ranks among the largest causes of climate change of any economic sector.[7] In the most commonly cited estimate, global livestock production – considering both extensive pasture and industrial livestock production – is implicated in almost one fifth of all anthropogenic GHG emissions, including especially large contributions of methane and nitrous oxide (see Figure 4.2). The atmospheric impact of pasture centers on its role in the conversion of forests and other ecosystems, the loss of organic matter in soils, and the enteric fermentation of ruminant animals, which makes their flatulence a major source of global methane emissions.[8]

Industrial livestock production increases agriculture's atmospheric impact in a range of ways. As with the expansion of pasture, the additional land devoted to industrial grain and oilseed monocultures entails

GHG emissions	Total (in CO_2 equivalent)	Carbon dioxide	Methane	Nitrous oxide
Percentage of world total	18% (including role in deforestation and pasture degradation)	9% (not considering respiration)	37%	65% (including feed crops)

4.2 Estimated total livestock-related GHG emissions (*source*: Steinfeld et al. 2006)

GHG emissions in the process of biologically simplifying landscapes, as well as a long-term decline in the carbon sequestration capacity of landscapes owing to the reduced biomass in plants and the degradation of soils. Feed conversion inefficiencies mean that more fuel is needed to power farm machinery and irrigation pumps, manufacture and transport more fertilizers and chemicals, and run processing facilities, which collectively magnify the CO_2 emissions embedded in monoculture production. This also magnifies the considerable nitrous oxide emissions that stem from the use of nitrogen fertilizer.

Fuel consumption and emissions rise further as a result of the specialization of landscapes, the separation of sites of breeding and growing, and the centralization of processing facilities, which means that animals, feed, and various inputs must move much greater distances than in the past across the spatially disaggregated conveyor belts. Although poultry and pigs are smaller emitters than ruminant animals in relative terms, their explosive growth in numbers involves rising CO_2 and methane emissions from respiration and from vast manure and urine loads, which grow further with the energy consumed in transporting and spraying slurries. The large energy budgets needed to build (e.g. concrete, steel, and machinery) and operate hatcheries, nurseries, factory farms, slaughterhouses, and processing plants (e.g. in heating, cooling, lighting, ventilating, spraying, incinerating, treating wastes, monitoring conditions, running machinery on the kill-floor and disassembly lines, air- and water-chilling systems, and pasteurization and refrigeration units) are also tied to an atmospheric impact; though this is contingent on how power is generated either on-site or within a given electricity grid. The heightened need to refrigerate meat, eggs, and dairy in comparison with plant-based nutrition extends energy budgets in yet another way, from processing and transportation to retail markets and household storage, as well as being tied to more of the powerful emissions associated with refrigerant gases. Added to this is the generally higher demand for energy in cooking flesh.

While the net energy budget varies from species to species, the fundamental point is that industrial meat, eggs, and dairy products tend to require much more fossil energy per unit of edible nutrition as compared with plant-based sources. In the USA, for instance, Pimentel and Pimentel calculate that 2.2 kilocalories (kcal) of fossil energy are embedded in the production of 1 kcal of plant protein from industrial monocultures, and a staggering 25 kcal of fossil energy embedded in 1 kcal of animal protein from industrial production. There is considerable variation in this, with industrial broiler chicken production the least inefficient converter of fossil energy inputs to animal protein output (4:1 kcal), followed by turkey (10:1), pig (14:1), milk (14:1), and beef (40:1), assuming with milk and beef a diet of combined feed and forage.[9]

Beyond fossil energy and climate change, industrial livestock production also generates air pollutants that have more localized impacts. Lagoons, feedlots, and slurry applications release airborne viruses, bacteria, fungal spores, and gas concentrations (especially ammonia and a range of sulfur compounds) that can be noxious to humans and animals downwind and are frequently marked by nauseating 'smell-scapes'.

Public health problems As discussed in Chapter 2, nutritional claims are a central but problematic part of the way that the meatification of diets is celebrated as a goal and measure of development. Although nutritional science is a highly complex field, with many variables to consider over uncertain timescales, strong scientific evidence connects the heavy consumption of animal products to heightened risks of obesity, cardiovascular disease, and other so-called diseases of affluence, while indicating clearly that diversified plant-centered diets dramatically reduce these problems. Nowhere are diseases of affluence more rampant than in the USA, where a greater share of the population is overweight and chronically medicated on prescription drugs than anywhere in the world. Thus, rather than moving toward American-style, meat-intensive diets, Barry Popkin argues that health research points in the exact opposite direction: to the 'need for a major reduction in total meat intake, an even larger reduction in processed meat and other highly processed and salted animal source food products, and a reduction in total saturated fat,' which not only reduces risks to begin with but can help reverse entrenched health problems.[10]

At the same time, it is important to recognize that some of the risks to public health posed by industrial livestock production extend far beyond the point of consumption, from heavy meat eaters to vegans alike. The consumption of pesticides is enlarged through the scale of feed production and through their use in factory farms and on feedlots. As noted in Chapter 3, this increasing consumption heightens the risk of resistance emerging, and with it a need for not only more chemicals but also the continuing development of new ones to encounter unpredictable mutations.

Some pesticide residues end up in the human food supply via the feed crops cycled through livestock, and some circulate in eco-systems after running off from monoculture fields and feedlots. Once released into the environment, these persistent toxins bioaccumulate as they move up trophic webs, a dynamic Rachel Carson famously first identified and likened to a low-intensity chemical war on the natural world.[11] Humans are surely not immune from this war, though the number and diffusion of pesticides make their bearing on the proliferation of cancers difficult to definitively connect.[12] The complex impact of pesticides on public health also relates to their role in the declining micro-nutrient content of industrial foods. This stems from the loss of organic matter and nutrients in soils, the elimination of micro-nutrient-rich plants that are targeted as weeds, and the focus on certain macro-nutrients in the design of high-yielding seed vari-eties. For instance, maize historically provided considerable nutritional value, not only in the traditional milpa system but in the plant itself, and continues to do so where it remains a primary food staple and where a diversity of traditional varieties persists – but the nutritional value of maize has been greatly diminished as enhanced seeds have been designed for high carbohydrate content.[13]

There has been much written about how the spread of GMOs contains many potential but as yet unknowable risks for both human health and for ecosystems as new organisms disperse and cross with non-GM crops and wild relatives, and how containment is very difficult after the proverbial horse has been let out of the gate. The depth of these uncertainties is why much of the world maintains strong precautionary positions against the release of GMOs, which entails a heavy burden of proof on those seeking to introduce things like new biotechnologies to show that they are benign in the long term prior to their release. Permissive regulatory regimes, in contrast, are characterized by shorter time frames, limited independently monitored trials, and conditions where it is easier to get something released than have it pulled back. Such regimes have enabled crops to spread widely throughout agricultural landscapes and food systems in some of the heartlands of the industrial grain-oilseed-livestock complex, including the USA, Canada, Argentina, and parts of Brazil and China.[14]

Just as with industrial monocultures, the biophysical overrides used in factory farms and feedlots cannot contain all of the problems they create, and over time new and greater risks are established. Residues of antibiotics, hormones, and some infectious bacteria end up in the water supply through regular practices like the use of contaminated slurry as fertilizer, and through accidental failures to contain biowastes, as in the case of leaking lagoons. Some residues also end up in industrial meat, eggs, and dairy. Over time, the chronic use of low levels of broad-spectrum antibiotics in livestock (e.g. varieties of penicillin and tetracycline) threatens to erode their effectiveness in human populations while establishing ideal conditions for stronger pathogens to emerge. Thus, critics have depicted factory farms as incubators of 'super-bugs,' with new drugs needed to combat antibiotic resistance. Especially dangerous health risks are posed by viral diseases capable of hopping from farm animals to humans, which has generated a number of recent scares about the potential for global swine and avian influenza pandemics – something Mike Davis has likened to 'the monster at our door.'[15]

The massive scale of slaughter and processing facilities increases the risks of pathogens spreading from the kill-floor to the packing process with so much blood, flesh, and fecal matter circulating along fast-moving lines, and various post-slaughter treatments cannot override all food-borne bacteria. Disease transmission risks also stem from the pressures to render the flesh of 'downers' and other condemned animals along with the non-edible parts of slaughtered carcasses, such as bonemeal, into saleable materials such as protein feed supplements and fertilizers. Mad cow disease (officially called bovine spongiform encephalopathy in cattle, and Creutzfeldt-Jakob disease when transmitted to humans) is the most dramatic illustration of the dangers of rendering practices, as it arose in the course of feeding ground-up cattle parts back to cattle.[16] Health hazards expand further where public oversight has been eroded by deregulation and funding cutbacks to government inspection agencies, as has occurred to a dramatic extent in the USA since the 1980s. The frequent presence of bacteria like salmonella and E. coli in animal foods is responsible for pervasive food poisoning and gastrointestinal illnesses. While much low-level incidence goes unrecognized and unreported, systemic food safety risks leap out from time to time whenever there are large-scale recalls of highly contaminated animal products from particular packing plants.[17]

The polluted ambient environments of factory farms are not only a major managerial challenge, as described in Chapter 3, but heighten risks of respiratory and other related illnesses for farmers and farmworkers. Airborne health hazards can also reach into downwind communities, and the accompanying smell-scapes constitute an unquantifiable psychosocial stressor for nearby residents. Beyond the chronic discomfort and health concerns lies the economic risk of decimated property values. Negative public health impacts are a major reason why many communities are beginning to oppose the siting of new industrial livestock operations in their vicinity. The differential capacity of communities to resist, in both political and economic terms, can perpetuate a common environmental injustice in which hazardous facilities are disproportionately located near poorer communities and regions – which not coincidentally also provide a bigger pool of cheap labor. This is widely recognized as one contributing factor to the increasing regional specialization of industrial livestock production in the USA, and its gravitation toward poorer regions in pockets of the South and Midwest.[18]

Ultimately, the health burden of industrial livestock production is overwhelmingly externalized: passed downstream, downwind, and through the belly, with the costs of dealing with chronic disease, antibiotic resistance, and food-borne illnesses transferred onto consumers and governments. Some of these costs spin into increasing demand and profits for the pharmaceutical industry and private healthcare providers, while other costs fall on public water treatment facilities and healthcare systems. Simply put, 'even if you don't eat this stuff yourself, you pay the taxes for the hospitals that will cope with the fall-out.'[19] Added to these are the costs of having areas of land and water so polluted they have lost all recreational value. In sum, a range of private and public health-related expenditures help to subsidize the cheapness of industrial meat, eggs, and dairy products.

Yet, with boundless irony, the driving forces behind industrial livestock production have insisted that risks of infectious disease are actually best contained on factory farms and have tried to positively identify them as having greater capacity for 'bio-security.'

The commodification of animals From 1961, around the time neo-Malthusian ideas were emerging as a powerful narrative in environmentalism, to 2010, the human population grew by a factor of roughly

2.3. Over this same period, the world's livestock population grew by a factor of 3.5 and the annual number of animals slaughtered per year leapt almost eightfold (the fact that more animals are killed every year than are present on earth at any one time results from the accelerating 'turnover time' from birth to slaughter weight). Although industrial livestock production is responsible for less than half of world meat production by volume, factory farms house a majority of all farm animals on earth at any one time and are responsible for an even larger share of the more than 64 billion farm animals killed every year. This is because, as noted in Chapter 2, over 70 percent of all meat now comes from pigs and poultry, and a rising share of both comes from industrial production. Poultry birds, predominantly chickens, are the most industrialized and fastest-growing livestock sector by volume and involve by far the greatest number of individual animal lives and deaths given their smaller size and rapid turnover time. More than any other species, broiler and layer chickens embody the violence of industrial livestock production, and occupy a fast-expanding place in the global food economy. Between 1990 and 2010 alone, the annual volume of world chicken meat production increased almost 2.5 times, and the annual number of chickens killed leapt from 25 to 56 billion.[20] With industrial livestock production projected to account for virtually all of the continuing growth in meat consumption in the coming decades, and chickens in the vanguard, this would push the annual number of animals slaughtered upwards of 120 billion or more. In light of the enduring fixation with the 'population bomb' in mainstream environmentalism, the lack of attention to the livestock population bomb is especially unconscionable.

Part of this blind spot relates to the widespread neglect of consumption inequalities within segments of environmentalism. Another part no doubt relates to the derogatory views of livestock animals as languid and stupid and less worthy of moral concern than wild animals or pets, species in which people tend to be far more willing to acknowledge brainpower, intentionality, and consciousness. However, such views have no basis in comparative ethology and, to the contrary, all evidence indicates that livestock animals have similar cognitive abilities and 'the same capacity for emotional complexity and intensity as did their evolutionary ancestors,' including clear expressions of affection, happiness, sadness, and fear, and strong desires to interact socially and with the natural environment.[21] There is, very simply, no cognitive or moral basis for affording differential rights to different species, the essence of what Peter Singer famously called 'speciesism.'[22] Rather, the conditions animals face are determined only by the amoral logic of capital, with the aim of packing industrial spaces as densely as possible and churning out flesh, eggs, and milk as fast as possible.

Environments of concrete and steel lead to extreme sensory deprivation and monotony. Animals are cut off from daily and seasonal rhythms and the ability to breathe fresh air, play, explore, or find food, sun, or shade, and are faced with frustrated co-inhabitants instead of families, social groups, and playmates. Painful musculoskeletal, cardiovascular, and respiratory disorders add to the misery in these crowded, noisy, reeking, and artificially lit spaces. The collective 'stress' and ill-health are acknowledged only to the extent that they impair production, and are then overridden in a variety of ways, including through routine, unanesthetized bodily mutilations. Mason and Singer depict this as a sort of schizophrenia; on one hand, dismissing the notion that animals suffer from stress, and on the other hand, devoting considerable scientific resources to figure out technological responses to behavioral pathologies.[23] To be sure, some practices such as selective castrations, branding, and dehorning have older histories, but the scale and scope of mutilations have increased dramatically, with new forms developed in response to specific problems posed by industrialization, such as assembly line debeakers capable of processing one chick every four seconds. Beyond these hellish spaces are the harsh conditions of transport, in hunger and thirst and sometimes in extreme heat or cold, before the terrifying encounters with prodders, shacklers, and stunners on the kill-floor. Though most animals are rendered unconscious before slaughter, the speed of the lines contributes to some reaching late stages on the line, including those of scalding and skinning, while still conscious.[24]

Successful legal battles have tempered some of the most extreme industry practices in certain jurisdictions, achieving reforms such as so-called 'enhanced' battery cages and more humane slaughter practices. Here, the more 'enlightened' regulatory regimes of the EU are often set against more 'backward' US regimes (though US regulations vary from state to state). But welfare reforms have not challenged the fundamental imperatives organizing production or the differential bases of most animal protection laws, with livestock everywhere subjected to conditions and practices that would be deemed cruel and illegal if inflicted upon most other animals. In fact, efforts to reduce the extent of psychosocial distress through industrial design might reflect an *economic* as much as an *intrinsic* concern for animal welfare, in the hope of reducing losses, reducing the expense of other overrides, and allaying potential consumer anxieties.

To critics, the celebrated contribution of Temple Grandin is a case in point. Grandin, who is autistic, is famed for having become a successful industry consultant and animal science professor, roles through which she helped to design or modify a large number of US slaughterhouses as well as other practices and environments, in ways that have made these industrial spaces less stressful for cattle and pigs. These innovations have undoubtedly enhanced the welfare of animals at some level, to the extent that Grandin has been lauded by the well-known animal advocacy organization People for the Ethical Treatment of Animals. But for others, these reforms can hardly be seen to advance the interests of animals in the long run, because they essentially enhance the operative logic of capital by reducing certain losses and helping improve public opinion while doing nothing to change (and perhaps even serving to increase) the overall number of animals now confined to only slightly less miserable lives.[25]

In the end, legal and technological reforms have barely dinted the systemic violence inflicted on animals in industrial livestock production. Instead, animals can be seen to have been transfigured into an interchangeable mass, something approximating crop-like material (insentient flesh) or bio-productive machines (yielding eggs and milk, then ultimately low-grade flesh). Bob Torres calls them 'super-exploited living commodities,' in that they have been reduced to 'nothing more than the means to the end of profit in contemporary capitalist production. Their particularity, their interests in not suffering, their desires to be free and to live as beings in the world are all subjugated – *en masse* – to the productive ends of capital.'[26] In this, there are striking parallels to their depiction as morally insignificant automata infamously given by René Descartes, as noted in Chapter 2.

This discussion should not imply that industrial livestock production is the only realm where animals are treated as insentient commodities. Animals are commercialized on a large scale in vivisection, where they are brutalized in the extreme, in secrecy with little legal protection, and with bodies that have been engineered into mutant forms conducive to disease and even patented (e.g. OncoMouse,

Knockout Rat). However, industrial livestock production dwarfs all other forms of animal commodification in terms of populations, and in terms of the scale with which people encounter animals on a daily basis. In reflecting on the practical achievements of animal protection in the USA, Peter Singer noted that any 'modest gains' for animals in some realms 'are dwarfed' by the explosive population growth in factory farms, which 'is by far the greatest source of human-inflicted suffering on animals.'[27]

The nature and scale of production, I suggest, amount to a revolution in inter-species relations. That is, however one interprets the 'ambiguous contract' of livestock domestication discussed in Chapter 2, its cultural variations, and all of the ethical complexities wrapped into the co-evolved interdependence between humans and domesticated livestock animals, there is a unitary set of organizing imperatives that is fast wiping out old practices and principles of animal husbandry. Torres again summarizes this well: 'While it is certainly the case that animal exploitation could exist without capitalism, the structure and nature of contemporary capital has deepened, extended, and worsened our domination over animals and the natural world.'[28] Further, as suggested near the end of Chapter 3, this revolution is not only about the fact that historically unprecedented numbers of animals are being raised and killed for human consumption in historically unprecedented ways, but also relates to how these relations – and the moral responsibilities that attach to them – are pushed into the collective unconscious of modern societies.

Today the primary way that billions of people are connected to animal lives is through torrents of cheap meat, eggs, and dairy products, at the same time as they know or think little about the conditions under which these distant animals have lived and been killed. This immeasurable but invisible pain and suffering might be seen as yet another externalized cost that subsidizes cheap meat, eggs, and milk.

The dehumanization of work The commodification of animals in production translates into wretched working environments and labor processes.[29] As Chapter 3 emphasized, the pressure to substitute capital for labor and pursue economies of scale shapes how industrial enclosures and slaughterhouses are organized. Some of the violence of production is therefore contained in the design and manufacture of a range of technological innovations such as large-scale incubation units, debeaking machines, macerators for male layer chicks, battery cages, gestation crates, veal stalls, mechanical feeders, poultry shed incinerators, artificial inseminators, vacuum-like milking pumps, hanging shackles, automated throat slitters, defeathering machines, and scalding tanks.

As the animal conveyor belt is disaggregated and farmers are forced to organize productive environments in very specific ways with given sets of technologies, they are effectively reduced to contract 'growers' while the corporation integrating the process outsources a considerable share of the risk. Yet however mechanized reproduction, growing, killing, and packaging have become, there will always be limits to technology in handling animals at various stages. Part of this stems from the fact that animals tend to squirm, kick, or otherwise resist domination when they are fearful or in pain, and human dexterity, adaptability, and reflexivity are needed to respond to this unpredictability, especially since there is a need to prevent damage to the end product. Human labor is needed for a wide range of grim tasks such as artificial insemination, castration, debeaking chicks, tail-docking pigs, dehorning cattle, sexing layer chicks and discarding males, separating infant piglets and calves from mothers, removing dead birds from cages and flocks, catching chickens on broiler floors, loading animals in and out of transport systems, shackling animals to slaughter lines, firing stun-guns, and slicing throats. There are also limits to how much packing lines can be mechanized, with workers needed for such tasks as deskinning, deboning, eviscerating, and sectioning carcasses.

The handling of animals in factory farms presents injury risks for workers, especially when performing invasive and painful procedures. Added to this are the health risks associated with the chronic exposure to polluted air moist with bacteria, fecal emissions, insecticide sprays, and other chemicals. The unhealthy nature of these environments is marked not only by the omnipresent stench but by decontamination showers for exiting workers. However, the greatest injury risks are experienced on fast-moving kill-floors, where workers encounter large numbers of writhing animals, and on fast-moving packing lines, where workers must make quick and repeated cuts. This produces some of the highest rates of workplace accidents, repetitive stress disorders, stress and injury leave, and job turnover among forms of industrial labor – as well as being among the lowest paying (in the USA, this labor force is heavily drawn from recent migrant labor).

Beyond the physical health risks and insecurity lies an untold psychological burden from inflicting painful and deadly acts as a routine part of the labor process, and from the immersion in environments filled with so much suffering. People involved in designing and manufacturing these spaces and instruments have a degree of physical separation from the nature of their intellectual and physical labor, but workers in factory farms, slaughterhouses, and packing plants are constantly faced with the anguished cries of animals, the visible expressions of confusion and distress, and the immediacy of bloodshed. To cope, most workers try to detach themselves emotionally while a few lash out with rage, as reflected in a litany of sadistic acts that have been documented in US slaughterhouses, from gouging eyes to stomping, beating, and sodomizing wounded animals. Investigative journalist Gail Eisnitz documents the violence of slaughterhouses with great detail and chilling force, including the psychotic extremes.[30] A recent US-based study also found a strong relation between the proximity to industrial slaughterhouses and an increasing prevalence of sexual violence and other crimes. From this, the authors suggest that the psychosocial impacts of these work environments and labor processes could well be spilling out into households and nearby communities. They call this the 'Sinclair effect' to mark how Upton Sinclair vividly portrayed the spillover violence of Chicago's colossal slaughterhouse complex at the turn of the twentieth century in his epic novel *The Jungle*.[31]

On one level, there is nothing unique about workers having their labor defined as repetitive, mind-numbing tasks that are tiny fragments of the overall production process, and losing something of their being as the scope of work gets smaller and smaller. In industrial livestock production, however, workers lose more than this. As Jonathan Safran Foer puts it: 'human beings cannot be human (much less humane) under the conditions of a factory farm or slaughterhouse. It's the most perfect workplace alienation in the world right now.'[32]

A dangerous and regressive course and the need to rethink efficiency

An important aspect of Chapter 3 was the analysis of the narrow way that efficiency and in turn competitiveness are defined in industrial capitalist agriculture. In essence, the combination of fossil-fuel-powered machines, industrial fertilizers, synthetic pesticides, pharmaceuticals, systems of intensive confinement, and high-yielding seeds and animals has greatly enhanced labor productivity, and this translates into relatively cheap food in comparison with more labor-intensive systems. With respect to livestock specifically, it strains the imagination to consider the lengths to which further efficiency gains will be pursued through industrial design, genetic modification, pharmacological development, feed additives, and biowaste recycling – especially if the annual number of slaughtered animals continues growing toward 120 billion in the coming decades. The arc of this future innovation (and its associated greenwash) is suggested in such things as Enviro-pig™, flatulence-catching backpacks for cattle, and systems to capture methane emitted from fecal lagoons and burn it as a source of energy.

A basic assumption that underpins this framework is a view that science and technology cannot resolve the biophysical contradictions of a system where incessant growth and accumulation are the fundamental motive force, and biological standardization and simplification are a basic organizing principle. Nor can science and technology prevent large volumes of usable nutrition from being burned in the metabolism of animals. At most, future innovations might reduce inputs such as feed, chemicals, pharmaceuticals, and energy, and wastes such as manure and emissions per unit of output, though even this is uncertain in the long run given some of the unpredictable biological responses to biophysical overrides, such as 'super-weeds' and 'super-bugs.' Further, any per unit resource and pollution reductions could easily be canceled out by increases in the total volume of production (recall the Jevons Paradox), especially in light of the magnitude of projected growth. It is clear that the enormity of the ecological hoofprint cannot be engineered away.

As was emphasized at the outset of this book, the trajectory of industrial livestock production and the meatification of diets reflect global inequalities and extend them, particularly as these bear on climate change and food security. The need for urgent and ambitious mitigation efforts overarches all prospects for world agriculture, and the longer this is delayed the greater the risks that changes such as increasing heat, aridity, and rainfall variability will imperil agricultural livelihoods and production across large areas. These risks are already at hand in many of the world's poorest regions that are home to a large share of the world's chronically hungry and undernourished population, and climate change is clearly poised to exacerbate the problem of food import dependence laid out at the end of Chapter 2. This vulnerability is further compounded by other demand- and supply-side pressures. On the demand side, world market prices for basic food staples face pressure from the rising volumes of grains and oilseeds used for livestock feed and, more recently, for agrofuels. On the supply side, production costs face pressure from the approaching resource limits that will make key biophysical overrides more expensive, as with increasingly difficult and expensive oil and gas extraction and declines in high-grade phosphorus reserves.

The biophysical dimensions of the ecological hoofprint alone point to the need to redefine agricultural efficiency, away from the pathological economic logic underpinning the industrial grain-oilseed-livestock complex and toward a new ecological rationality that simultaneously considers both on- and off-farm dynamics. On farms, an ecologically rational conception of agricultural efficiency would mean minimizing the outflow of GHG emissions, persistent toxins, harmful nutrient loads, and other pollutants, while enhancing the long-term fertility of the soil, reducing erosion, and fostering soil formation, nutrient cycles, and moisture retention. In a nutshell, productivity would be delinked from resource-intensive machinery and overrides. Effective farming with few external inputs is much more biologically diverse, and entails cultivating multiple crops in mutually beneficial ways, managing natural controls on pests, and striving to enhance soil biota. It is also much more labor- and knowledge-intensive, and involves a range of things, such as: managing more but smaller planting and harvest cycles; selecting and saving seeds; using pasture-fed animals for traction; digging in agricultural wastes; terracing slopes; and conducting and sharing localized ecological research. This might be broadly called *bio-intensive* farming, whether low-input or organic.[33]

But agricultural systems must also be understood outside of the land they physically occupy, and take into account whether they serve to expand or contract the total area and water resources needed for food production, as this impinges on the potential space left for self-organizing ecosystems. From this angle, ecological efficiency centers on the goal of maximizing nutritional output per hectare of arable land, which should be defined as well-balanced combinations of essential macro- and micro-nutrients in contrast to fixating on the mythologized protein hierarchy. Again, small, bio-intensive farms come out superior to high-yielding monocultures. Bio-intensive farms are able to produce more total nutrition per land area than monocultures owing to their capacity to grow a bigger range and overall number of plants through intercrops, even if individual plants are lower yielding, and there is compelling evidence of their benefits from a wide range of settings.[34] This output is also bound to have lower chemical residues and greater micro-nutrient content than monocultures that have been genetically enhanced around a few macro-nutrients. Finally, the fact that the rural poor make up almost two-fifths of humanity is another reason that industrial monocultures could never serve to minimize agricultural land, even if they were more efficient in terms of nutritional output, as there is no indication that this population could find productive work in other sectors and purchase all of their food needs.

The goal of maximizing nutritional output per land area also points squarely at a major focus of this book: that the product of roughly one third of the earth's arable land is being funneled down a net nutritional drain, and that this wastage is wired into the logic of the system, as the capacity of industrial livestock production to profitably absorb grain and oilseed surpluses has enabled their continuing expansion. Clearly, then, if this nutritional drain could be closed with bio-intensive farms progressively displacing the industrial-grain-oilseed-livestock complex, the overall land area needed for agriculture would greatly shrink (provided that, in the absence of more fundamental changes, this funnel is not merely shifted to the nutritional black hole of industrial agrofuels). In addition, given the large water budget of monocultures and industrial livestock operations, such a transition would also greatly reduce agriculture's overall pull on freshwater ecosystems and enhance the efficiency of the water that continues to be drawn upon for irrigation, as more ground cover means more moisture retention, less evaporation, and fewer risks of salinization.

While this book has not focused on extensive herding, it is important to recognize that the pursuit of ecological efficiency, climate change mitigation, and biodiversity conservation also calls into question some of the roughly one quarter of the earth's land area in pasture. As discussed in Chapters 1 and 2, the expansion of pasture has been heavily linked to both tropical deforestation and desertification, and there is a desperate need to halt and then reverse these processes, starting wherever pasture sits on razed rainforest soils.

Outside of the moist and arid tropics, pasture is usually treated as either an inexorable or benign use of land where it occupies regions with soils and climates that are ill suited for long-term cultivation but where native or introduced grasses can thrive. The ecological case for pasture grows where effective management can build soils and enhance carbon sequestration to an extent that resembles these processes in natural grasslands. However, this is partly offset by the fact that the global ruminant population is a major source of methane emissions, and where pasture occupies quality arable land ecological efficiency would generally favor cultivation.

The idea of reducing the area in crops and pasture is an un-abashedly radical one, particularly since crops and pasture can appear as immutable features of a landscape, as can be seen in the common terminology of 'permanent crops' and 'permanent pasture' to define these land uses. But any hopes of confronting climate change and biodiversity loss impel thinking in radical ways and on big scales. To shrink the land given to agriculture and pasture could open some space for the renaturalization of forests, native grasslands, wetlands, riparian zones, streams, and rivers, which has the potential to make an enormous contribution to both biodiversity conservation and climate change mitigation. The ecological case for bio-intensive farming is now increasingly being taken up by the global peasant movement Vía Campesina as part of its broader advocacy for small-farm livelihoods. This is positioned in the context of mitigating agriculture's role in climate change with the slogan that small farming can 'cool the earth.'

An ecologically rational conception of efficiency thus turns a basic tenet of modernization on its head: rather than technology displacing labor in large monocultures, there is a need for labor and knowledge to displace mechanization. This is not to romanticize the difficult balances that peasant households are typically faced with, especially when trapped in exploitative social relations, nor does it imply that deindustrialization is an objective in itself that would necessarily unfold into more equitable social relations. In the course of rethinking efficiency, ways must be found to ensure equitable outcomes that valorize the labor, skill, and ecological services of bio-intensive farms – a big subject beyond the scope of discussion here.[35] What this analysis makes clear, though, is that dismantling the industrial-grain-oilseed-livestock complex is at the very center of any hopes of making world agriculture more sustainable, socially just, and humane.

Entwined with this is the clear need to drastically reduce the world's livestock population. On a hopeful note, this presents a relatively easy target, at least in practice, and particularly in comparison to human demographic change. Whereas human population change unfolds slowly over generations (witness the confidence demographers have in projecting that the world population will top 9 billion by 2050), the 'livestock population bomb' could be almost instantly imploded. Since most farm animals on earth today live very short lives, enormous planned reductions to this population could unfold over the course of a single year merely by ceasing to violate animal bodies with artificial inseminators.

The de-meatification imperative – to what ends?

The meatification of diets has long been a marker of class ascension and a dietary aspiration of development, from British lords to US suburbia to China's burgeoning urban elites and middle class. This dietary transition has become ever more entwined with industrial livestock production, which for decades has been the driving force in the volume increases and which will account for virtually all future growth should it materialize. The lens of the ecological hoofprint helps make it clear why this amounts to a major vector of inequality, degradation, and violence that must be confronted. So, rather than assuming that the meatification of world diets will continue and seeking to double world food production, there is a need for a fundamentally different starting point: the 'de-meatification' of diets.

But to what ends? Should people in rich countries aim to reduce their per capita annual consumption of meat (~80–120 kg) to the world average (~42 kg in 2010)? Is the current average across most of the global South (well under 30 kg) a better, and fairer, target? Or are these levels already too high? In general, critical writing on industrial livestock production tends to culminate either in an appeal to eat less and only 'humane' or 'sustainable' meat that has come from well-treated animals on mixed farms, or to be vegetarian (no flesh) or vegan (no animal products). This has begun creeping into mainstream environmental thinking, with some organizations now making broad appeals for people to eat less meat or giving more concrete suggestions to cut out meat one day a week, as in 'meatless Mondays.'[36] Of course, such appeals hardly do justice to the scale of de-meatification that is needed, so the tactical question is essentially whether they risk giving a false sense of satisfactory change or are an effective starting point to get people thinking critically about their diet.

Complicating matters further is the fact that growing consumer consciousness is also translating into new high-value niche markets for livestock products branded in terms of sustainability, to an extent that that some of the world's largest TNCs have begun trying to capitalize. Perhaps the clearest indication of this is the Global Roundtable for Sustainable Beef (www.sustainablelivestock.org), which draws support from some giants in the in areas of fast food (McDonald's), retailing (Wal-Mart), agro-chemicals (Dow), animal pharmaceuticals (Meerk), and grain-oilseed-livestock production (Cargill), alongside large-scale beef producers' alliances (e.g. the National Cattlemen's Beef Association, Canadian Cattlemen's Association), and some influential mainstream environmental NGOs (e.g. the Rainforest Alliance; the National Wildlife Federation; and the World Wildlife Fund).

The argument for some but less meat, eggs, and dairy production and consumption rests on claims about the functionality of livestock on low-input mixed farms and on quality pasture that is ill suited for cultivation, coupled with enduring claims about the nutritional superiority of animal protein. On the production side, as discussed in Chapter 2, functionality involves such things as the role of livestock in making productive use of fallowed land in rotations, post-harvest crop stubble, and household wastes, returning concentrated nutrients to the soil, providing traction, and helping balance the seasonality of crop harvests. This is the dominant position held by farmers, in agro-ecology, and by many in local food movements, who view eating meat, eggs, and dairy from mixed farms as an essential part of eating within their 'foodsheds' and by season, especially in higher latitudes as growing seasons shorten. Simon Fairlie, a noted authority in the field of permaculture, presents a clear case for the necessary biophysical function of livestock on mixed small farms, which he argues makes some meat 'a benign indulgence.'[37] From this position, the fundamental ethical concern is to ensure that animals live reasonably good lives up to the point of slaughter, including making every effort to ensure a quick death that is as free of pain and fear as possible.

Michael Pollan is a prominent voice framing this in terms of consumption, having famously described humans as omnivores who are now greatly over-consuming meat. For Pollan, while some level of meat consumption is defensible on agricultural and nutritional grounds, this is very far from justifying the levels of meat consumption in the industrialized world. In fact, with respect to nutrition, he notes that if there is one 'point of universal consensus' in nutritional science it is about 'the benefits of a plant-based diet,' imploring people to eat 'mostly plants' as one of his essential food rules.[38] At the same time, he also champions the small, mixed livestock farmers who are holding out against the onslaught of industrial production, and appeals to conscious consumers to actively support those who could provide the foundations for rebuilding sustainable mixed farming systems. The fact that so many of these farmers are economically beleaguered is one reason why vegetarians and vegans are sometimes viewed with varying degrees of animosity – as actual threats to more sustainable and humane production – by people who are intensely critical of the industrial grain-oilseed-livestock complex.

This animosity is returned by some vegetarians and vegans. For instance, Howard Lyman likens a meat-eating environmentalist to 'a philanthropist who doesn't happen to give to charity,' and Jim Motavalli argues that 'future generations will find the idea of eating meat both morally absurd and logistically impossible,' insisting that environmental limits will drive an 'inevitable vegetarian revolution.'[39] Advocates of vegetarianism stress the fact that it is not only possible to live very healthfully without meat, by balancing the intake of plant-based nutrients, but that the weight of nutritional evidence shows it to be much healthier than meat-centered diets.

As the necessity of meat consumption fades, the moral inconsistency of speciesism – killing some animals while loving and revering others – becomes inescapable for ethical vegetarians. Here, it is important to stress that this objection to killing does not deny the possibility that livestock animals can be treated with consideration and respect on mixed farms, as vegetarianism by its very nature accepts the multifunctional role of livestock in agriculture in the willingness to consume eggs, milk, and wool. From this position, the moral imperative is to treat farm animals as well as possible in taking non-flesh products and in demanding some labor. In its most idealized terms, the hope is that the ambiguous contract described in Chapter 2 can be softened so that livestock animals can live out their natural lifespans in a mutually beneficial relation, something akin to what humans share with companion animals. Along these lines, Foer argues against consuming animals while writing in heroic terms about the concern given by some small-scale livestock farmers (as well as by micro-slaughterhouses concerned with humane killing practices).[40] To ethical vegans, even if such relations are possible in theory, which some will grant and some will not, it should not obscure their rarity in practice. Instead, vegans stress the fact that a rising share of eggs and dairy come from industrial systems which contain the same biophysical contradictions as industrial meat, which makes this similarly unsustainable, as well as tying it to some of the cruelest features of factory farming. As a result, there is a militancy within some vegan politics that targets vegetarianism as much as meat eating, with the essential argument being that if people choose to not eat meat for environmental or moral reasons this same logic should compel them to go vegan.[41] Finally, veganism does not grant that livestock animals have a necessary function in agriculture today, as the historic precedent of livestock in mixed farming systems is seen to provide little guidance for the future. That is to say, for most of the Holocene the human population was only a few hundred million people and, to vegans, directly consuming the product of photosynthetic activity is a fundamental part of the radical new ecological efficiencies that will be needed to contain the magnitude of change in the Anthropocene and sustainably feed an increasingly urbanized world of 7 going on 9+ billion people.

Ultimately, the conceptual framework of the ecological hoofprint can't settle intense debates about whether people should eat some but less meat, none, or no animal products at all. Part of this stems from the difficulty of looking forward on fast-shifting ground, as agricultural societies have never lived through the anticipated scale and pace of climatic change. In this context, hopeful bio-intensive innovations will be diverse and unpredictable, combining agro-ecological science, traditional knowledges, organic experimentation, and open-sourced information sharing.[42] Another part of this restraint stems from the fact that the moral basis of the 'ambiguous contract' itself was not the subject of analysis. Instead, one of the things that the ecological hoofprint makes loud and clear is that the ethical dilemmas and responsibilities bound up in millennia of co-evolution are being obliterated by the imperatives of industrial capitalism and the violence of commodification – which points to the fact that confronting this must be the absolute strategic imperative whether one believes sustainable and humane livestock is possible and desirable or not.

Finally, there are good reasons not to prescribe universal 'food rules,' as Julie Guthman makes clear.[43] To stop here can risk exaggerating the impact of individual consumer choices ('voting with your fork') as an end in itself, which can absorb too much attention, drop off into self-satisfaction, or wash away the need for ongoing critical reflection and political commitment. This is not to downplay the importance of food choices in the least; rather, it should be clear that one goal of the ecological hoofprint is to challenge people to think about them.[44] However, I also hope that if it succeeds in helping people think through all that is embedded in the meatification of diets and the system of production driving it, the implications will be seen to extend much farther than this. As Frances Moore Lappé put it so well: 'To ask the biggest questions, we can start with the most personal – what do we eat? What we eat … ties us to the economic, political, and ecological order of our whole planet.'[45]

The spirit of capitalism made flesh[46]

Commodities contain bundles of socio-ecological relations that are obscured when people encounter them in markets. In other words, it is difficult to understand how any given commodity gets produced or priced, leaving people to fixate on commodities at a surface level – a tendency Marx called 'commodity fetishism.' This incomprehensibility is an important part of the durability of capitalism, at the same time as the relentless drive to subject the whole of the world to the commodity form leads to many uneven and violent outcomes.

There is clearly a powerful fetishism that surrounds meat, which is widely perceived as a desirable object while little or no thought is given to the nature of its production. Yet food, and especially the flesh of other animals, might still be seen to have special potential to stir consciousness about the systemic injustices that are a silent part of everyday life, much as Lappé suggests. And in this sense, the ecological hoofprint might not only provide a means to understand the burden of industrial livestock production but also a lens through which to see the violence of capitalism as world-ecology, a totalizing way of organizing nature.[47]

There are many reasons why confronting industrial livestock production should be a pillar of environmental and social justice struggles, and in the nascent climate justice movement. Appreciating the scope of the ecological hoofprint might also have a key role in widening and connecting anti-systemic movements in line with what John Sanbonmatsu calls meta-humanism: a challenge to progressive political traditions that insists on the need to expand the sphere of moral concern beyond historically anthropocentric bounds, with 'ethical practice grounded in attentiveness to suffering' in all animal life. For Sanbonmatsu, empathy has been mistakenly dismissed when it should in fact provide the essential 'mode of perception' and basis for 'moral judgement' in radical theories of praxis. Extending this to animals, he argues, has the potential to 'awaken within ourselves a healthy form of self-love – a love for the kind of being we *could* become. Only by attending to the monsters we make of ourselves in inflicting ceaseless and unspeakable brutality and violence against the minds and bodies of other sensitive beings-in-the-world, might we begin to construct a new narrative about who and what we are.'[48]

It might be hard to imagine a new narrative of biospheric humility gaining wide traction in a world where selfish and avaricious behavior is so deeply entrenched in the way that societies are organized. But it is similarly hard to see any hope of rebuilding a more sustainable, just, and humane world without it.

NOTES

Introduction

1 The production and trade statistics used in this book are summarized from the excellent resource provided by FAO Statistics Division, *Production and Resource STAT Calculators*, which starts in 1961. FAOSTATS (2013).

2 FAO (2011a, 2006a). Dutch researchers make a case for why the common projections of growth in meat consumption in the coming decades could well be too low. Keyzer et al. (2005).

3 National statistics for meat consumption were derived by adding production and imports together and subtracting exports.

4 Schneider (2011); FAO (2009a); Nierenberg (2005).

5 FAO (2011b).

6 Delgado et al. (1999).

7 Rostow (1990 [1960]).

8 Tilman et al. (2011); Neumann et al. (2010).

9 Weis (2013, 2010a, 2007).

10 Singer (2002 [1975]); Lappé (1991 [1971]); Harrison (1964).

11 Some of the most influential examples are: Rifkin (1992); Mason and Singer (1990 [1980]); and Robbins (1987).

12 Steinfeld et al. (2006). See also: FAO (2011a, b, 2009a); Nellemann et al. (2009); Delgado et al. (1999).

13 Black (2008).

14 FAO (2011b: 78); Steinfeld et al. (2006).

15 McMichael (2012); Winders (2009); Weis (2007); Friedmann (1990, 1993, 2005).

16 Weis (2010b).

17 Sassen (2013); Houtart (2010); Giampietro and Mayumi (2009); Holt-Giménez and Patel (2009).

1 Contextualizing the hoofprint

1 Montgomery (2007: 47).

2 NPP is a measure of the biochemical energy that is captured and stored by plants through photosynthesis, less the energy used in respiration, over a given area and length of time. It controls the amount of usable energy that is available to other trophic levels within ecosystems, and is assessed as the net amount of carbon assimilated by vegetation over a given land area in the course of a year. Haberl et al. (2007).

3 Flannery (2001).

4 Shiva (2008).

5 Duncan (1996). There are rare exceptions where irrigation increases plant growth beyond what would be present under natural conditions.

6 Montgomery (2007: 3, 15).

7 Pretty (2008); Altieri (1995, 1999); Gleissman (1997); Jackson (1985 [1980]).

8 Montgomery (2007); Wright (2004).

9 Crosby (1972, 1986).

10 Williams (2006).

11 Shiva (2008).

12 Montgomery (2007); Williams (2006).

13 MEA (2005: 2).

14 In their landmark study, Vitousek et al. estimated the HANPP to be 25 percent over the entire earth surface, and 40 percent over the earth's land surface. The world's ocean surface is much greater than the land surface, and it is obviously much harder to systematically

organize and appropriate the biological activity across the oceans, though on the continental shelves the HANPP might approach terrestrial levels. These are clearly complex calculations, which have spawned subsequent methodological refinements and other estimates. Haberl et al. (2007); Vitousek et al. (1986).

15 Wilson (2002: 58).

16 Nepstad (2007); Williams (2006); MEA (2005).

17 Flannery (2009); IPCC (2007).

18 Compaction results in soils with less air, less capacity to absorb and retain moisture, and increased vulnerability to erosion. Salinization is rooted in the fact that some dissolved salt gets left behind as water evaporates from the land or transpires from plants, and this can build up over time. It becomes a problem when accumulating salt concentrations begin to impede moisture uptake and yield in plants, and tends to be more acute in arid and semiarid regions where evaporation rates are high and where groundwater contains high levels of dissolved salt.

19 Geist and Lambin (2004); Dregne (2002).

20 Gleick (2012); MEA (2005); McCully (2001). Large dams are defined as 15 m or higher from the foundation, or with a reservoir volume greater than 3 million m3.

21 Mansfield (2011); Sale (2011); MEA (2005).

22 There is evidence that some species have begun migrating pole-ward and upwards in elevation at considerably faster than anticipated rates, though the scale of these migrations does not dispel the expectation that many will be unsuccessful in this process. Chen et al. (2011); MEA (2005).

23 IUCN (2012); MEA (2005).

24 Wilson (2002: 43). The range of estimates reflects the lack of data for some species. There is also a large gap between the number of invertebrates, plants, and fungi that are known and the varying estimates of the number of total species on earth. This is a big part of the uncertainty about precisely how fast species diversity is being lost and how much this has accelerated from the natural or 'background' rate of extinctions across geological history; though it is generally accepted to be by a factor of hundreds and maybe even thousands. The notion of a 'final struggle' reflects the impossibility of reconstructing lost biodiversity: 'to revive or synthesize the thousands of species needed – probably millions when the still largely unknown microorganisms have been catalogued – and put them together in functioning ecosystems is beyond even the theoretical imagination of existing science' (Wilson 2002: 130).

25 IUCN (2012); Mackey (2009).

26 Wilson (2002); Leakey and Lewin (1995); Soulé (1985).

27 Davis (2007).

28 Costanza and Farber (2002); Costanza et al. (1997).

29 Cox-Foster and Van Engelsdorp (2009).

30 NOAA/ESRL (2013).

31 IEA (2010); Heinberg (2005).

32 Of all greenhouse gases, CO_2 emissions have had the greatest impact on warming. Methane and nitrous oxide are much smaller by volume (their density is recorded in the parts per billion), but they have much greater per unit heat-trapping properties than CO_2. For commensurability, GHG emissions are generally converted to CO_2 equivalence.

33 The brief summary of climate science that follows draws from a range of sources, including: Rogelj et al. (2011); Joshi et al. (2011); Hansen (2009); Flannery (2006, 2009); Rosenzweig et al. (2008); and IPCC (2007).

34 Flannery (2009: 15); Oreskes and Conway (2010); Monbiot (2006).

35 Sale (2011); Hoegh-Guldberg et al. (2007); MEA (2005).

36 Figueres (2010).

37 Lovelock (2007: 180); Wilson (2002: 50); Kanter (2007).

38 Angus and Butler (2011).

39 Foster (2002: 137); Angus and Butler (2011).

40 Ehrlich (1971 [1968]: xii); Hardin (1968); Boulding (1964).

41 Livingston (1994: viii).

42 Meadows et al. (1972: 23, 129, 145, 178, 188). The authors were clear that their notion of 'standard run' 'assumes no major change in physical, economic, or social relationships that have historically governed the development of the world system.' In the vernacular of climate forecasting, this has become a 'business-as-usual' scenario. Probably the greatest misrepresentation of the *Limits to Growth* has been the tendency of its critics to exaggerate the rigidness of the forecasts, and to disregard the humility with which they were presented. Though it was a project on a grand scale with unabashedly ambitious aims, the authors were very explicit about the imprecision of their data, growth projections, and system dynamics. In their words, the model was 'imperfect, oversimplified, and unfinished' and unconcerned with making predictions, as the 'exact timing is not meaningful.' Nevertheless, critics liked to hold up specific milestone estimates (namely for collapse) produced in different scenarios as targets of ridicule, to discredit both the approach and findings. Meanwhile, mounting evidence has largely vindicated key aspects of the report's 'standard run' trajectory, in which collapse occurs midway through the twenty-first century. Ibid.: 21, 124, 126; Turner (2008).

43 Heinberg (2005, 2007).

44 Broomfield (2012); Colborn et al. (2011).

45 IEA (2010, 2012); Heinberg (2009).

46 Pepper (1984: 13).

47 There is an extensive literature critiquing the nature of 'mainstream' environmentalism. Some valuable sources here include: Foster (2002, 2009); Sachs (1999); Tokar (1997); Athanasiou (1996); Bookchin (1994).

48 Wilson (2002: 77).

49 Simon (1981).

50 Oreskes and Conway (2010); Foster et al. (2010); Beder (1998).

51 WCED (1987). Wolfgang Sachs (1999) thoroughly examines the political neutering and rebranding of the concept of sustainability.

52 Sachs (1999: 34).

53 Hardin (1974).

54 Wilson (2002: 23).

55 Misanthropy has also been associated with some radical strands of environmental thinking, a notable contemporary example being Derrick Jensen. Jensen is a prominent US environmental thinker who expressly seeks to destroy hope that human civilization can be transformed, and argues that committed activists should focus on smashing it so that there might be something of the natural world left from which to rebuild primeval livelihoods. Jensen (2006).

56 Bookchin (1994: 6, 17).

57 *Nature Unbound* provides an excellent survey of the complexities and tensions associated with different forms of conservation. Brockington et al. (2008).

58 Foster (2002: 102). See also: Foster et al. (2010); Foster (2009).

59 Moore (2010a: 396, 2011).

60 Moore (2010b: 233).

61 Moore (2010a: 392).

62 Moore (forthcoming).

63 Wackernagel and Rees (1996: 78).

64 Catton (1980).

65 Wackernagel and Rees (1996: 41).

66 Wackernagel et al. (2002).

67 Wackernagel and Rees (1996: 37, 57). However, instead of capitalism fundamental dynamics are described in terms of such things as: the 'philosophy of competitive expansionism'; 'selfish individualism'; the 'culture of consumerism'; 'big city life' breaking natural material cycles; an 'industrial metabolism'; and 'the human enterprise.' Ibid.: x, xi, 4, 11, 51.

68 To be fair, while some of Ehrlich's more extreme argumentation and rhetoric and his political positions on things like immigration and population control drew deserved criticism, he was never entirely oblivious to inequality. For instance, *The Population Bomb* did point to such problems as uneven resource consumption in 'over-developed' countries, nefarious US geopolitical interventions, and the repression of land reforms. Further, Ehrlich did later grant the importance of inequality more explicitly in an essay entitled 'Too many rich folks.' Angus and Butler also point out how Donella Meadows, the lead author of *Limits to Growth*, became increasingly wary over time about the overemphasis which tended to be given to population. Similarly, though E. O. Wilson sees the fate of the global environment centrally tied to the population growth of the global South and the need for population control, he does partly condition this with an acknowledgment of the scale and significance of unequal ecological footprints, even pointing to a central aspect of this book: that the rising demand for feed grains greatly expands the terrestrial demands of agriculture. He notes that at the turn of the twenty-first century, global grain production was 'enough to feed 10 billion East Indians, who eat primarily grains,' but could 'support only 2.5 billion Americans, who convert a large part of their grains into livestock and poultry.' Wilson (2002: 33); Ehrlich

(1971 [1968]); Ehrlich and Ehrlich (1989); Angus and Butler (2011).

69 UNEP (1999: 2); UNDP (1999: 79).

70 Jorgenson and Clark (2011); York et al. (2003); McLaren (2003).

71 Tony Allan describes how he acceded to the increasing use of 'virtual' because it has given the concept much more popular traction even though, in his words, it is a more 'ambiguous and nebulous' term than its 'more accurate and informative' predecessor, embedded. Galloway et al. separate the terms, using 'virtual' to represent the full burden of resources that went into a product, and embedded to reflect only the volume of inputs (e.g. water, nitrogen) that remains in the final product. My preference is to use the older terminology of embedded water and inputs more generally, as I think it conveys a stronger sense of the materiality of what went into the process of production. Allan (2011: 9); Galloway et al. (2007).

72 UN Water (2007: 10); FAO (2006b).

73 Tokar (2010); Hertwich and Peters (2009); Ackerman (2009); UNDP (2007).

74 IPCC (2007); UNFCCC (2007); UNDP (2007).

75 FAO (2011c: 3). See also: FAO (2011d); Hertel et al. (2010); Nellemann et al. (2009); Cline (2007); Schmidhuber and Tubiello (2007).

76 Tokar (2010); Brown (2008); UNDP (2007); Myers (2002).

77 Ackerman (2009: 4); UNDP (2007).

78 Ackerman (2009).

79 Monbiot (2006).

80 UNDP (2007: 13,167); Tokar (2010).

81 Ackerman (2009).

82 MEA (2005: 777); Montgomery (2007); Williams (2006).

83 MEA (2005: 2).

84 Monfreda et al. (2008); Foley et al. (2007); Steinfeld et al. (2006).

85 Steinfeld et al. (2006: xxi).

86 Nellemann et al. (2009).

87 Hall (2011); Nepstad et al. (2008); Nepstad (2007); Greenpeace (2006).

88 Steinfeld et al. (2006); Geist and Lambin (2004); Dregne (2002).

89 Vidal (2010).

90 Gleick (2012); Allan (2011); WWAP (2009); McCully (2001).

91 Postel (1999). The International Rivers Network (www.international rivers.org) is an organization that draws attention to the underappreciated costs to freshwater ecosystems that have subsidized industrial productivity on a world scale.

92 Flannery (2001: 332); Reisner (1993).

93 Montgomery (2003: 230).

94 Gleick (2012); WWAP (2009); UN Water (2007); FAO (2006b); Opie (2000 [1993]); Postel (1999).

95 As organic matter in soils dries up, the oxidization generates CO_2 emissions and the capacity to absorb carbon declines. This should also highlight the fact that the Pedosphere is a very important carbon sink.

96 Foster et al. (2010: 81).

97 De Schutter (2010a).

98 Rifkin (1992: 159, 161).

99 Sanbonmatsu (2004: 193).

2 The uneven geography of meat

1 Sauer (1972 [1952]: viii).

2 In debates over the origins of the Neolithic Revolution, a core division is whether agricultural innovation arose first from a position of relative scarcity and declining resources, or from relative abundance, with largely sedentary societies experimenting from positions of considerable surpluses of food and time. Carl Sauer made the latter case, arguing that 'the initiators of domestication required a comfortable and dependable margin above mere survival, permanent homes, and a living in communities in which they could share observations and have the leisure to begin the long range experimentation that led to domestication.' Sauer (1972: 118).

3 The human body contains different forms of protein that have varying combinations of amino acids, some of which it can synthesize, but eight of which it cannot and must therefore repeatedly consume. Healthy protein intake provides sufficient levels of all eight of these essential amino acids, as a deficiency of one or more will compromise the process of protein synthesis. Usability implies that some foods provide much more complete bundles of essential amino acids by themselves than do others. If the protein content of a food item is understood in terms of its individual bundle of essential amino acids, then eggs and dairy rank among the most complete sources of protein, ahead of meat. Lappé (1991 [1971]).

4 Sauer (1972 [1952]: 86).

5 Lappé (1991 [1971]).

6 Fairlie (2010) provides a good summary of the scope of the biophysical role that small livestock populations have in mixed farming systems.

7 Merrifield (2008: 190); Shiva (2008); Montgomery (2007); Rifkin (1992).

8 Sauer (1972: 64).

9 Ellis and Wang (1997: 191).

10 Foer (2009: 99).

11 Adams (2000 [1990]); Rifkin (1992); Spiegel (1996 [1988]); Fiddes (1992).

12 Rifkin (1992: 28); Mason and Singer (1990 [1980]).

13 Davis (2007: 148).

14 Shiva (2008); Rifkin (1992).

15 Johnson (1991).

16 Masson (2003).

17 Montgomery (2007); Wright (2004).

18 Braudel (1981: 105, 190); Sauer (1972 [1952]).

19 Rifkin (1992: 53).

20 Braudel (1981).
21 Moore (2003).
22 Moore (2010a, b).
23 Duncan (1996).
24 Rifkin (1992).
25 Noble (1999: 14, 48–9); Moore (2011).
26 Singer (2002 [1975]); Pepper (1984).
27 Rod Preece argues that interpretations of Descartes' mind–body dualism frequently exaggerate the rigidity of his thinking, which was muddied by some contradictory views about animal sensations – though Descartes did see animals as morally insignificant automata and treated them as such in invasive experimentation. Preece also argues that this view of animals as automata did not have much popular or scientific purchase beyond those practicing vivisection, which is part of his broader case that Western 'sensibilities' about the treatment of animals through history have been much more varied and nuanced than they are often portrayed. From this, he warns against overgeneralizing then vilifying 'Western culture' as the basis of animal exploitation. For instance, he notes that while 'eating animals was almost universally practised' in early modern Europe, it 'still occasioned a concern over whether one actually had a moral right to do so.' Preece (2002: 82).
28 Flannery (2001); Rifkin (1992); Crosby (1972, 1986).
29 Melville (1994); Rifkin (1992); Crosby (1972, 1986).
30 Nally (2011).
31 Braudel (1981).
32 Moore (2010a, b).
33 Friedmann and McMichael (1989).
34 Rifkin (1992).
35 Pollan (2008).
36 Moore (2010a: 395).
37 Flannery (2001); Nash (2001 [1967]).

38 Flannery (2001); Cronon (1991).
39 Standing Bear (2006 [1933]: 196).
40 Quoted in Brown (1970: 265).
41 Flannery (2001); Rifkin (1992); Cronon (1991).
42 Cronon (1991: 229).
43 Ibid.: 247.
44 Rifkin (1992: 59).
45 Cronon (1991).
46 Ibid.: 256–7.
47 Fiddes (1992).
48 Pollan (2008: 10).
49 Schlosser (2001).
50 Rostow (1990 [1960]).
51 McMichael (2012).
52 Nestle (2002); Mason and Singer (1990 [1980]); Robbins (1987).
53 McMichael (2012); Winders (2009); Cochrane (2003); Friedmann (1993); Friedmann and McMichael (1989).
54 Ellis (2007: 26); Foer (2009); Davis (2009 [1996]); Mason and Singer (1990 [1980]).
55 Winders (2009); Winders and Nibert (2004); Rifkin (1992); Berlan (1991).
56 McMichael (2012); Friedmann (1993).
57 Lappé (1991 [1971]).
58 At around the same time, claims about the superiority of animal foods were contained in both *The Population Bomb* and *Limits to Growth*, which might be part of their blind spot to the livestock population explosion.
59 Popkin (2009); Campbell and Campbell (2006); Leitzmann (2003); Sabate (2003); Barnard (1993); Chen et al. (1990).
60 The population statistics in this section are drawn from the United Nations Population Division, and the agricultural populations and the farm animal populations are summarized from FAOSTATS (2013).
61 McMichael (2012); Friedmann (1990, 1993).
62 Davis (2001).
63 Weis (2007); Robbins (2003).

64 Davis (2007).

65 Bello (2009); Holt-Giménez and Patel (2009); Weis (2007).

66 FAO (2009b).

67 The FAO's list of LIFDCs identifies poor countries that devote large shares of their foreign exchange earnings to food imports. It is based on a low gross national income (below US$1,905 in the 2012 report) and an assessment of the average volume of net food traded and an estimation of their caloric content over the preceding three years. Countries can choose to de-list themselves (www.fao.org/countryprofiles/lifdc.asp).

68 McMichael (2012: 73).

69 Ritzer (2010 [1993]); Schlosser (2001).

70 FAO (2009a); McMichael et al. (2007); Steinfeld et al. (2006); York and Gossard (2004); Popkin (2003).

71 The statistics in this section are summarized from FAOSTAT (2013). National statistics for per capita meat consumption were derived by adding production and imports together and subtracting exports, then averaging these against the total population. The statistics for western Europe aggregate the FAO groupings of northern, southern, and western Europe.

72 Schneider (2011); Nierenberg (2005).

73 Campbell and Campbell (2006); Chen et al. (1990).

74 Austin (2010); Barreto et al. (2006); Hecht (2005); Kaimowitz et al. (2004); Hecht and Cockburn (1989).

75 Turzi (2011).

76 Schneider (2011); Brown (2011); Bello (2009).

77 Roots and tubers are the only other group of crops used for feed on any scale, more so in the global South. Soybeans are the main oilseed used for animal feed, getting processed into a dense meal that is the primary source of feed protein on a world scale. Canola/rapeseed has a higher oil content and more value as an oil than soybeans, but its meal is also valued as a protein-rich feed for animals.

78 The land area devoted to canola/rapeseed has also grown dramatically, increasing roughly fivefold over the past half-century, but from a much smaller starting point than soybeans. There is more than three times as much land in soybeans as in canola.

79 Houtart (2010); Giampietro and Mayumi (2009).

80 FAO (2011b); D'Silva and Webster (2010); Steinfeld et al. (2006); Nierenberg (2005).

81 Steinfeld et al. (2006).

3 Industrial agriculture

1 This chapter examines the systemic logic, tendencies, and contradictions of both industrial monocultures and factory farms and feedlots, while keeping the technical detail to a minimum of what is necessary. The compression of complexity is an inevitable pitfall, but I can only hope that the effect is for the whole to be greater than the sum of its parts, and that what emerges is an accessible framework which helps to make sense of how different dynamics and problems fit together. To spare the reader copious endnotes in Chapters 3 and 4, points that are well established in the literature are not cited at every turn and instead a 'blanket' note is given to identify a number of key sources for particular sections. Especially valuable sources for the analysis of industrial monocultures that follows include: Sage (2012); McIntyre et al. (2009); Pretty (2008); Shiva (2008); Pimentel and Pimentel (2008 [1979]); Montgomery (2007); Pimentel (2006); Pollan (2006); Kloppenburg (2004); Kimbrell (2002).

2 Montgomery (2007: 146); Cronon (1991).

3 Sauer (1972 [1952]: 65).

4 Moore (2010a: 394).

5 Johnson (1991).

6 FAO (2007).

7 Harrison (1964: 50).

8 Winders (2009); Weis (2007).

9 McMichael (2012).

10 Montgomery (2007).

11 The statistics in this paragraph are derived from USDA NASS (2008).

12 The statistics in this paragraph are derived from FAOSTATS (2013).

13 The statistics in this paragraph are derived from USDA NASS (2008).

14 The statistics in this paragraph are derived from FAOSTATS (2013).

15 Davis (2009 [1996]); Ellis (2007).

16 McIntyre et al. (2009); Montgomery (2007); Pimentel (2006).

17 Shiva (2007: 84–5).

18 Ploeg (2013).

19 Cronon (1991: 79–80).

20 Montgomery (2007: 183).

21 Foster et al. (2010).

22 Smil (2001).

23 After it is mined, phosphate rock is nearly insoluble, and hence could not be taken up by plants for many years if it were just mechanically ground up. A chemical fix is therefore needed to fashion water-soluble phosphates. Cordell et al. (2009); Cordell and White (2011).

24 The statistics in this paragraph are derived from FAOSTATS (2013).

25 Most notoriously reflected in the relationship between DDT, dioxin, and Agent Orange. Foster (2002).

26 Moore (2010b: 247).

27 Noble (1999: 183).

28 Shiva (2007); Kloppenburg (2004).

29 Ellis (2007: 113).

30 *The World According to Monsanto* is an outstanding documentary film that provides much insight into the nature and scope of Monsanto's activity. Robin (2010); films.nfb.ca/monsanto/.

31 Moore (2010a, b).

32 Gleick (2012); WWAP (2009); Postel (1999).

33 Cronon (1991: 80).

34 Shiva (2008); Pollan (2006); Pfeiffer (2006); Manning (2004).

35 Following Lappé's seminal contribution, some other helpful sources that consider the resource inefficiencies bound up in the nutritional wastage of cycling feed through livestock include: Godfray et al. (2010); Pew Commission (2008); Halweil and Nierenberg (2008); Steinfeld et al. (2006); Nierenberg (2005); Pimentel (2004); Pimentel and Pimentel (2003); Gilland (2002); Gerben-Leenes and Nonhebel (2002); White (2000); Goodland (1997).

36 Harrison (1964: 15).

37 For cattle primed on pasture and finished on feedlots, the role of grasses in weight gain must be extracted in order to assess the conversion of feed to flesh, and there are debates about how precisely to calculate this.

38 Foster et al. (2010).

39 There is a large literature that examines the processes, contradictions, and overrides in industrial livestock production. Some key sources for the discussion that follows include: WSPA–Canada (2012); Imhoff (2011); Emel and Neo (2011); D'Silva and Webster (2010); Davis (2009 [1996]); CIWF (2009); Pew Commission (2008); Ellis (2007); Steinfeld et al. (2006); Midkiff (2004); Ervin et al. (2003); Boyd (2001); Marks (2001); Tansey and D'Silva (1999); Boyd and Watts (1997); Mason and Singer (1990 [1980]).

40 Mason and Singer (1990 [1980]).

41 Clark (2012).

42 This was written in the context of how Chicago's Union Stock Yards connected the rise of assembly-line slaughter to the fast-changing US west, but it speaks powerfully to much wider transformations. Cronon (1991: 212–13).

4 Confronting the hoofprint

1 Foer (2009: 96, 108).

2 Foley et al. (2011: 338); Pimentel and Pimentel (2003); Gerben-Leenes and Nonhebel (2002).

3 Moore (2010a: 408).

4 Some valuable sources for the discussion on the water consumption and pollution associated with industrial livestock production include: Hoekstra (2012); Mekonnen and Hoekstra (2012); Imhoff (2011); Pew Commission (2008); Heederik et al. (2007); Galloway et al. (2007); Steinfeld et al. (2006); FAO (2005); Pimentel and Pimentel (2003); Mallin and Cahoon (2003); Ervin et al. (2003); Kolpin et al. (2002); Marks (2001); Hooda et al. (2000).

5 Cultural eutrophication is the common terminology used to denote human causation. Because a low level of available phosphorus is often the key constraint on primary production in freshwater ecosystems, the injection of phosphates can have a particularly potent effect on algal growth. Livestock excrement tends to be very high in both phosphorus and nitrogen concentrations, as animals expel large shares of these nutrients from what they consume, though the precise ratios of intake to output vary with species, diet, age, and a range of other factors. Schindler and Vallentyne (2008); MEA (2005).

6 Rifkin (1992).

7 D'Silva and Webster (2010); McIntyre et al. (2009); IPCC (2007); McMichael et al. (2007).

8 Some valuable sources that consider the energy budget, climate impacts, and other air pollution burdens of industrial livestock production include: Goodland and Anhang (2009); Garnett (2009); Stehfest et al. (2009); Jarosz (2009); Fiala (2008); Weber and Matthews (2008); Pew Commission (2008); Motavalli (2008); McMichael et al. (2007); Halweil and Nierenberg (2008);

Steinfeld et al. (2006); Eshel and Martin (2006); Sainz (2003); Ervin et al. (2003).

9 Pimentel and Pimentel (2003).

10 Popkin (2009: 543); Campbell and Campbell (2006).

11 As noted in Chapter 3, this war metaphor had a very literal dimension, as reconstituted munitions plants were major sites of agro-chemical manufacturing after the Second World War. Carson's ecological critique was grounded in a far more radical political economic interpretation than is typically recognized within the mainstream environmental movement. It is also notable that she wrote the preface to Ruth Harrison's pioneering *Animal Factories*, in which she drew parallels between industrial monocultures and industrial livestock production. Foster (2009); Harrison (1964); Carson (1962).

12 Steingraber (2010 [1997]).

13 Pollan (2008).

14 Dona and Arvanitoyannis (2009); Shiva (2007); Altieri (2004).

15 Davis (2005).

16 Lyman (2001).

17 Nestle (2008); Eisnitz (2006 [1997]).

18 Kirby (2010); Eisnitz (2006); Stull and Broadway (2004); Johnsen (2003); Fink (1998).

19 Ellis (2007: 95).

20 The statistics in this paragraph are derived from FAOSTATS (2013).

21 Masson (2003: 221).

22 Singer (2002 [1975]).

23 Mason and Singer (1990 [1980]).

24 Foer (2009); Eisnitz (2006 [1997]).

25 Francione (2010); Foer (2009); Torres (2007); Williams (2004).

26 Torres (2007: 58); Francione (2010).

27 Singer (2003).

28 Torres (2007: 11).

29 Helpful accounts for this section include: Conover (2013); Kirby (2010); Foer (2009); Eisnitz (2006 [1997]);

Human Rights Watch (2005); Stull and Broadway (2004); Schlosser (2001); Fink (1998); Stull et al. (1995); Ufkes (1995).

30 Eisnitz (2006).

31 Fitzgerald et al. (2009); Sinclair (2003 [1906]).

32 Foer (2009: 256).

33 McIntyre et al. (2009); Shiva (2008); Altieri (1995, 1999); Gleissman (1997); Jackson (1985 [1980]).

34 De Schutter (2010b); Altieri and Toledo (2011); Snapp et al. (2010); Badgley et al. (2007).

35 Ploeg (2008) provides many valuable insights here.

36 Emel and Hawkins (2010).

37 Fairlie (2010).

38 Pollan (2008: 162; 2006) The message of Pollan's best-selling book *The Omnivore's Dilemma* might just as well have been conveyed with something like *The Herbivorous Challenge* (though it may not have been a best-seller if expressed in those terms!). Indeed, such imagery might, on a superficial level, detract from the intense criticism of industrial livestock production that the book contains. Similarly, Fairlie's imagery of blissful meat consumption might belie the nature of his argument, which is very far from a defense of the dominant system of meat production in industrialized countries.

39 Lyman (2001: 122); Motavalli (2009).

40 Foer (2009).

41 Torres (2007); Marcus (1998, 2005).

42 Koohafkan et al. (2012).

43 Guthman (2007).

44 Boyle (2012); Lappé (2010); Singer and Mason (2006); White (2000); Goodland (1997).

45 Lappé (1991 [1971]: 8).

46 This heading is borrowed from a famous line near the end of *The Jungle*. Sinclair (2003 [1906]: 338).

47 Moore (2010a, 2011).

48 Sanbonmatsu (2004: 203, 209, 222).

REFERENCES

Ackerman, F. (2009) *Can We Afford the Future? The Economics of a Warming World*, London: Zed Books.

Adams, C. (2000 [1990]) *The Sexual Politics of Meat: A Feminist-Vegetarian Critical Theory*, 2nd edn, New York: Continuum.

Allan, T. (2011) *Virtual Water: Tackling the Threat to Our Planet's Most Precious Resource*, London: I. B. Tauris.

Altieri, M. A. (1995) *Agroecology: The Science of Sustainable Agriculture*, Boulder, CO: Westview Press.

— (1999) 'The ecological role of biodiversity in agroecosystems,' *Agriculture, Ecosystems, and Environment*, 74(1–3): 19–31.

— (2004) *Genetic Engineering in Agriculture: The Myths, Environmental Risks, and Alternatives*, 2nd edn, Oakland, CA: Food First Books.

Altieri, M. A. and V. M. Toledo (2011) 'The agroecological revolution in Latin America: rescuing nature, ensuring food sovereignty and empowering peasants,' *Journal of Peasant Studies*, 38(3): 587–612.

Angus, I. and S. Butler (2011) *Too Many People? Population, Immigration, and the Environmental Crisis*, Chicago, IL: Haymarket Books.

Athanasiou, T. (1996) *Divided Planet: The Ecology of Rich and Poor*, New York: Little, Brown.

Austin, K. (2010) 'The "hamburger connection" as ecologically unequal exchange: a cross-national investigation of beef exports and deforestation in less-developed countries,' *Rural Sociology*, 75(2): 270–99.

Badgley, C., J. Moghtader, E. Quintero, E. Zakem, M. J. Chappell, K. Avilés-Vásquez, A. Samulon, and I. Perfecto (2007) 'Organic agriculture and the global food supply,' *Renewable Agriculture and Food Systems*, 22(2): 86–108.

Barnard, N. D. (1993) *Food for Life: How the New Four Food Groups Can Save Your Life*, New York: Harmony.

Barreto, P., C. Souza, R. Nogueron, A. Anderson, R. Salomao (2006) *Human Pressure on the Brazilian Amazon Forests*, Belem: World Resources Institute.

Beder, S. (1998) *Global Spin: The Corporate Assault on Environmentalism*, White River Junction, VT: Chelsea Green Publishing.

Bello, W. (2009) *The Food Wars*, London: Verso.

Berlan, J.-P. (1991) 'The historical roots of the present agricultural crisis,' in W. H. Friedland, L. Busch, F. H. Buttel and A. P. Rudy (eds), *Towards a New Political Economy of Agriculture*, Boulder, CO: Westview Press, pp. 115–36.

Black, R. (2008) 'Shun meat, says UN climate chief,' *BBC News*, 7 September, news.bbc.co.uk/2/hi/7600005.stm.

Bookchin, M. (1994) *Which Way for the Ecology Movement*, San Francisco, CA: AK Press.

Boulding, K. E. (1964) *The Meaning of the 20th Century: The Great Transition*, New York: Harper and Row.

Boyd, W. (2001) 'Making meat: science, technology, and American poultry production,' *Technology and Culture*, 42(4): 631–64.

Boyd, W. and M. Watts (1997) 'Agro-industrial just-in-time: the chicken industry and postwar American capitalism,' in D. Goodman and M. Watts (eds), *Globalising Food: Agrarian Questions and Global Restructuring*, New York: Routledge, pp. 192–224.

Boyle, E. (2012) *High Steaks: Why and How to Eat Less Meat*, Gabriola Island, BC: New Society Publishers.

Braudel, F. (1981) *The Structures of Everyday Life: Civilization and Capitalism, 15th–18th Century*, vol. 1, New York: Harper and Row.

Brockington, D., R. Duffy and J. Igoe (2008) *Nature Unbound: Conservation, Capitalism, and the Future of Protected Areas*, London: Earthscan.

Broomfield, M. (2012) 'Support to the identification of potential risks for the environment and human health arising from hydrocarbons operations involving hydraulic fracturing in Europe,' Report for the European Commission DG Environment.

Brown, D. (1970) *Bury My Heart at Wounded Knee: An Indian History of the American West*, New York: Holt, Rinehart & Winston.

Brown, L. R. (2011) 'The new geopolitics of food,' *Foreign Policy*, 186: 54–63.

Brown, O. (2008) *Migration and Climate Change*, Geneva: International Organization for Migration.

Campbell, T. C. and T. M. Campbell (2006) *The China Study: The Most Comprehensive Study of Nutrition Ever Conducted and the Startling Implications for Diet, Weight Loss and Long-term Health*, Dallas, TX: BenBella Books Inc.

Carson, R. (1962) *Silent Spring*, New York: Houghton Mifflin.

Catton, W. R. (1980) *Overshoot: The Ecological Basis of Revolutionary Change*, Champaign: University of Illinois Press.

Chen, C., J. K. Hill, R. Ohlemüller, D. B. Roy and C. D. Thomas (2011) 'Rapid range shifts of species associated with high levels of climate warming,' *Science*, 333(6045): 1024–6.

Chen, J., T. C. Campbell, J. Li and R. Peto (1990) *Diet, Lifestyle, and Mortality in China: A Study of the Characteristics of 65 Countries*, New York: Oxford University Press.

CIWF (Compassion in World Farming) (2009) *Beyond Factory Farming: Sustainable Solutions for Animals, People, and the Planet*, Godalming: Compassion in World Farming.

Clark, J. (2012) Ecological biopower, environmental violence against animals, and the "greening" of the factory farm,' *Journal for Critical Animal Studies*, 10(4): 109–29.

Cline, W. R. (2007) *Global Warming and Agriculture: Impact Estimates by Country*, Washington, DC: Center for Global Development.

Cochrane, W. W. (2003) *The Curse of American Agricultural Abundance: A Sustainable Solution*, Lincoln: University of Nebraska Press.

Cockburn, A. (1996) 'A short meat-oriented history of the world: from Eden to the Mattole,' *New Left Review*, 215: 16–42.

Colborn, T., C. Kwiatkowski, K. Schultz and M. Bachran (2011) 'Natural gas operations from a public health perspective,' *Human and Ecological Risk Assessment*, 17(5): 1039–56.

Conover, T. (2013) 'The way of all flesh: undercover in an industrial slaughterhouse,' *Harper's Magazine*, 326(1956): 31–49.

Cordell, D. and S. White (2011) 'Peak phosphorus: clarifying the key issues of a vigorous debate about long-term phosphorus security,' *Sustainability*, 3(10): 2027–49.

Cordell, D., J. Dangert and S. White (2009) 'The story of phosphorus: global food security and food for thought,' *Global Environmental Change*, 19: 292–305.

Costanza, R. and S. Farber (2002) 'Special issue: The dynamics and value of ecosystem services: integrating economic and ecological perspectives,' *Ecological Economics*, 41(3).

Costanza, R., R. d'Arge, R. S. de Groot, S. Farber, M. Grasso, B. Hannon, K. Limburg, S. Naeem, R. V. O'Neill, J. Paruelo, R. G. Raskin, P. Sutton and M. van den Belt (1997) 'The value of the world's ecosystem services and natural capital,' *Nature*, 387(6630): 253–60.

Cox-Foster, D. and D. van Engelsdorp (2009) 'Solving the mystery of the vanishing bees,' *Scientific American*, 300(4): 40–7.

Cronon, W. (1991) *Nature's Metropolis: Chicago and the Great West*, New York: W. W. Norton.

Crosby, A. W. (1972) *The Columbian Exchange: Biological and Cultural Consequences of 1492*, Westport, CT: Greenwood.

— (1986) *Ecological Imperialism: The Biological Expansion of Europe, 900–1900*, Cambridge: Cambridge University Press.

Davis, K. (2009 [1996]) *Prisoned Chickens, Poisoned Eggs: An Inside Look at the Modern Poultry Industry*, 2nd edn, Summertown, TN: Book Publishing Co.

Davis, M. (2001) *Late Victorian Holocausts: El Niño Famines and the Making of the Third World*, London: Verso.

— (2005) *The Monster at Our Door: The Global Threat of Avian Flu*, New York: New Press.

Davis, W. (2007) *Light at the End of the World: A Journey through the Realm of Vanishing Cultures*, Vancouver: Douglas & McIntyre.

De Schutter, O. (2010a) 'It's time to tackle climate change and agricultural development in tandem,' *Guardian*, 16 October, www.guardian.co.uk/global-development/poverty-matters/2010/oct/16/climate-change-agricultural-development-policymakers.

— (2010b) Report submitted by the Special Rapporteur on the right to food, to the Human Rights Council of the United Nations, Sixteenth session, Agenda item 3, www.srfood.org/images/stories/pdf/officialreports/20110308_a-hrc-16-49_agroecology_en.pdf.

Delgado, C. L., M. Rosegrant, H. Steinfeld, S. Ehui and C. Courbois (1999) 'Livestock to 2020 – the next food revolution,' Food, Agriculture, and Environment Discussion Paper 28, Washington, DC: International Food Policy Research Institute.

Dona, A. and I. S. Arvanitoyannis (2009) 'Health risks of genetically modified foods,' *Critical Reviews in Food Science and Nutrition*, 49(2): 164–75.

Dregne, H. E. (2002) 'Land degradation in the drylands,' *Arid Land Research and Management*, 16(2): 99–132.

D'Silva, J. and J. Webster (eds) (2010) *The Meat Crisis: Developing More Sustainable Production and Consumption*, London: Earthscan.

Duncan, C. (1996) *The Centrality of Agriculture: Between Humankind and the Rest of Nature*, Montreal and Kingston: McGill-Queen's University Press.

Ehrlich, P. (1971 [1968]) *The Population Bomb*, 2nd edn, New York: Ballantine.

Ehrlich, P. and A. Ehrlich (1989) 'Too many rich folks,' *Populi*, 16: 21–9.

Eisnitz, G. (2006 [1997]) *Slaughterhouse: The Shocking Story of Greed, Neglect, and Inhuman Treatment Inside the US Meat Industry*, 2nd edn, Amherst, NY: Prometheus.

Ellis, E. C. and S. M. Wang (1997) 'Sustainable traditional agriculture in the Tai Lake Region of China,' *Agriculture, Ecosystems, and Environment*, 61(2/3): 177–93.

Ellis, H. (2007) *Planet Chicken: The Shameful Story of the Bird on Your Plate*, London: Hodder and Stoughton.

Emel, J. and R. Hawkins (2010) 'Is it really easier to imagine the end of the world than the end of industrial meat?' *Human Geography*, 3(2): 35–48.

Emel, J. and H. Neo (2011) 'Killing for profit: global livestock industries and their socio-ecological implications,' in R. Peet, P. Robbins and M. Watts (eds), *Global Political Ecology*, London: Routledge, pp. 67–83.

Ervin, A. M., C. Holtslander and R. Sawa (eds) (2003) *Beyond Factory Farming: Corporate Hog Barns and the Threat to Public Health, the Environment, and Rural Communities*, Saskatoon: Canadian Centre for Policy Alternatives-Saskatchewan.

Eshel, G. and P. A. Martin (2006) 'Diet, energy, and global warming,' *Earth Interactions*, 10-009.

Fairlie, S. (2010): *Meat: A Benign Extravagance*, White River Junction, VT: Chelsea Green.

FAO (Food and Agriculture Organization) (2005) 'Pollution from industrialized livestock production,' Livestock Policy Brief #2, Rome: FAO.

— (2006a) 'World agriculture: towards 2030/2050,' Interim report, Rome: FAO.

— (2006b) 'Water monitoring: mapping existing global systems and initiatives,' UN Water Task Force on Monitoring, Rome: FAO.

— (2007) 'FAO sounds alarm on loss of livestock breeds,' FAO Newsroom, Rome: FAO, 4 September, www.fao.org/newsroom/en/news/2007/1000650/index.html.

— (2009a) *The State of Food and Agriculture – Livestock in the Balance*, Rome: FAO.

— (2009b) *The State of Food Insecurity in the World 2009: Economic Crises – Impacts and Lessons Learned*, Rome: FAO.

— (2011a) *Looking Ahead in World Food and Agriculture: Perspectives to 2050*, Rome: FAO.

— (2011b) *World Livestock 2011 – Livestock in Food Security*, Rome: FAO.

— (2011c) 'Climate change and food security in the context of the Cancun Agreements,' Submission by the FAO to the 14th session of the AWG-LCA, in accordance with paragraph 1 of the Bali Action Plan, Rome: FAO, unfccc.int/resource/docs/2011/smsn/igo/121.pdf.

— (2011d) *Climate Change, Water, and Food Security*, Rome: FAO.

FAOSTATS (Food and Agriculture Organization Statistics Division) (2013) *Production and Resource STAT Calculators*, Rome: FAO, faostat3.fao.org/home/index.html.

Fiala, N. (2008) 'Meeting the demand: an estimation of potential greenhouse gas emissions from meat production,' *Ecological Economics*, 67(3): 412–19.

Fiddes, N. (1992) *Meat as a Natural Symbol*, London: Routledge.

Figueres, C. (2010) 'Opening address,' Speech given to the Ad Hoc Working Groups on Further Commitments for Annex I Parties under the Kyoto Protocol and on Long-term Cooperative Action under the Convention AWG-LCA, UNFCCC, Bonn, Germany, 2 August, unfccc.int/files/press/statements/application/pdf/100802_speech_christiana.pdf.

Fink, D. (1998) *Cutting into the Meatpacking Line: Workers and Change in the Rural Midwest*, Chapel Hill, NC: UNC Press.

Fitzgerald, A., L. Kalof and T. Dietz (2009) 'Slaughterhouses and increased crime rates: an empirical analysis of the spillover from "the jungle" into the surrounding community,' *Organization and Environment*, 24(3): 99–101.

Flannery, T. (2001) *The Eternal Frontier: An Ecological History of North America*, New York: Grove Press.

— (2006) *The Weather Makers: How We Are Changing the Climate and What It Means for Life on Earth*, Toronto: HarperCollins.

— (2009) *Now or Never: Why We Need to Act Now to Achieve a Sustainable Future*, Toronto: HarperCollins.

Foer, J. S. (2009) *Eating Animals*, New York: Little, Brown.

Foley, J. A., C. Monfreda, N. Ramankutty and D. Zaks (2007) 'Our share of the planetary pie,' *Proceedings of the National Academy of Sciences*, 104(31): 12585–6.

Foley, J. A., N. Ramankutty, K. A. Brauman, E. S. Cassidy, J. S. Gerber, M. Johnston, N. D. Mueller, C. O'Connell, D. K. Ray, P. C. West, C. Balzer, E. M. Bennett, S. R. Carpenter, J. Hill, C. Monfreda, S. Polansky, J. Rockström, J. Sheehan, S. Siebert, D. Tilman and D. P. M. Zaks (2011) 'Solutions for a cultivated planet,' *Nature*, 478(7369): 337–42.

Foster, J. B. (2002) *Ecology against Capitalism*, New York: Monthly Review Press.

— (2009) *The Ecological Revolution: Making Peace with the Planet*, New York: Monthly Review Press.

Foster, J. B., B. Clark and R. York (2010) *The Ecological Rift: Capitalism's War on the Earth*, New York: Monthly Review Press.

Francione, G. L. (2010) *Animals as Persons: Essays on the Abolition of Animal Exploitation*, New York: Columbia University Press.

Friedmann, H. (1990) 'The origins of Third World food dependence,' in H. Bernstein, B. Crow, M. Mackintosh and C. Martin (eds), *The Food Question: Profits versus People*, New York: Monthly Review Press, pp. 13–31.

— (1993) 'The political economy of food: a global crisis,' *New Left Review*, 197: 29–57.

— (2005) 'Feeding the empire: the pathologies of globalized agriculture,' in L. Panitch and C. Leys (eds), *The Empire Reloaded: Socialist Register*, New York: Monthly Review Press, pp. 124–43.

Friedmann, H. and P. McMichael (1989) 'Agriculture and the state system,' *Sociologia Ruralis*, 29(2): 93–117.

Galloway, J. N., M. Burke, G. E. Bradford, R. Naylor, W. Falcon, A. K. Chapagain, J. C. Gaskell, E. McCullough, H. A. Mooney, K. L. L. Oleson, H. Stenning, T. Wassenaar and V. Smil (2007) 'International trade in meat: the tip of the pork chop,' *Ambio*, 36(8): 622–9.

Garnett, T. (2009) 'Livestock-related greenhouse gas emissions: impacts and options for policy-makers,' *Environmental Science and Policy*, 12: 491–503.

Geist, H. J. and E. F. Lambin (2004) 'Dynamic causal patterns of desertification,' *BioScience*, 54(9): 817–29.

Gerben-Leenes, P. W. and S. Nonhebel (2002) 'Consumption patterns and their effects on land required for food,' *Ecological Economics*, 42(1/2): 185–99.

Giampietro, M. and K. Mayumi (2009) *The Biofuel Delusion: The Fallacy of Large Scale Agro-Biofuels Production*, London: Earthscan.

Gilland, B. (2002) 'World population and food supply: can food production keep pace with population growth in the next half-century?' *Food Policy*, 27(1): 47–63.

Gleick, P. H. (ed.) (2012) *The World's Water*, vol. 7: *The Biennial Report on Freshwater Resources*, Washington, DC: Island Press.

Gleissman, S. R. (1997) *Agroecology: Ecological Processes in Agriculture*, Ann Arbor: University of Michigan Press.

Godfray, H. C. J., J. R. Beddington, I. R. Crute, L. Haddad, D. Lawrence, J. F. Muir, J. Pretty, S. Robinson, S. M. Thomas and C. Toulmin (2010) 'Food security: the challenge of feeding nine billion people,' *Science*, 327(5967): 812–18.

Goodland, R. (1997) 'Environmental sustainability in agriculture: diet matters,' *Ecological Economics*, 23(3): 189–200.

Goodland, R. and J. Anhang (2009) 'Livestock and climate change: what if the key actors in climate change are cows, pigs, and chickens?' *World Watch Magazine*, 22(6): 10–19.

Greenpeace (2006) *Eating up the Amazon*, Amsterdam: Greenpeace International.

Guthman, J. (2007) 'Commentary on teaching food: why I am fed up with Michael Pollan et al.,' *Agriculture and Human Values*, 24(2): 261–4.

Haberl, H., K. H. Erb, F. Krausmann, V. Gaube, A. Bondeau, C. Plutzar, S. Gingrich, W. Lucht and M. Fischer-Kowalski (2007) 'Quantifying and mapping the human appropriation of net primary production in earth's terrestrial ecosystems,' *Proceedings of the National Academy of Sciences*, 104(31): 12942–7.

Hall, D. (2011) 'Land grabs, land control, and Southeast Asian crop booms,' *Journal of Peasant Studies*, 38(4): 837–57.

Halweil, B. and D. Nierenberg (2008) 'Meat and seafood: the global diet's most costly ingredients,' in L. Starke (ed.), *State of the World 2008: Innovations for a Sustainable Economy*, New York: W. W. Norton, pp. 61–74.

Hansen, J. (2009) *Storms of My Grandchildren: The Truth about the Coming Climate Catastrophe and Our Last Chance to Save Humanity*, New York: Bloomsbury.

Hardin, G. (1968) 'The tragedy of the commons,' *Science*, 162 (3859): 1243–8.

— (1974) 'Living on a lifeboat,' *Bioscience*, 24(10): 561–8.

Harrison, R. (1964) *Animal Machines: The New Factory Farming History*, London: Vincent Stuart.

Hecht, S. B. (2005) 'Soybeans, development and conservation on the Amazon frontier,' *Development and Change*, 36(2): 375–404.

Hecht, S. B. and A. Cockburn (1989) *The Fate of the Forest: Developers, Destroyers, and Defenders of the Amazon*, London: Verso.

Heederik, D., T. Sigsgaard, P. S. Thorne, J. N. Kline, R. Avery, J. H. Bønløkke, E. A. Chrischilles, J. A. Dosman, C. Duchaine, S. R. Kirkhorn, K. Kulhankova and J. A. Merchant (2007) 'Health effects of airborne exposures from concentrated animal feed operations,' *Environmental Health Perspectives*, 115(2): 298–302.

Heinberg, R. (2005) *The Party's Over: Oil, War, and the Fate of Industrial Societies*, 2nd edn, Gabriola Island, BC: New Society Publishers.

— (2007) *Peak Everything: Waking up to the Century of Declines*, Gabriola Island, BC: New Society Publishers.

— (2009) *Blackout: Coal, Climate, and the Last Energy Crisis*, Gabriola Island, BC: New Society Publishers.

Hertel, T. W., M. B. Burke and D. B. Lobell (2010) 'The poverty implications of climate-induced crop yield changes by 2030,' *Global Environmental Change*, 20(4): 577–85.

Hertwich, E. G. and G. P. Peters (2009) 'Carbon footprint of nations: a global, trade-linked analysis,' *Environmental Science and Technology*, 43(16): 6414–20.

Hoegh-Guldberg, O., P. J. Mumby, A. J.

Hooten, R. S. Steneck, E. G. P. Greenfield, C. D. Harvell, P. F. Sale, A. J. Edwards, K. Caldeira, N. Knowlton, C. M. Eakin, R. Iglesias-Prieto, N. Muthiga, R. H. Bradbury, A. Dubi, M. E. Hatziolos (2007) 'Coral reefs under rapid climate change and ocean acidification,' *Science*, 318: 1737–42.

Hoekstra, A. Y. (2012) 'The hidden water resource use behind meat and dairy,' *Animal Frontiers*, 2(2): 3–8.

Hoekstra, A. Y. and M. M. Mekonnen (2012) 'The water footprint of humanity,' *Proceedings of the National Academy of Sciences*, 109(9): 3232–7.

Holt-Giménez, E. and R. Patel (2009) *Food Rebellions: Crisis and the Hunger for Justice*, San Francisco, CA: Food First Books.

Hooda, P. S., A. C. Edwards, H. A. Anderson and A. Miller (2000) 'A review of water quality concerns in livestock farming areas,' *Science of the Total Environment*, 250(1–3): 143–87.

Houtart, F. (2010) *Agrofuels: Big Profits, Ruined Lives and Ecological Destruction*, London: Pluto.

Human Rights Watch (2005) *Blood, Sweat, and Fear: Workers' Rights in US Meat and Poultry Plants*, New York: Human Rights Watch.

IEA (International Energy Agency) (2010) *World Energy Outlook 2010*, Paris: OECD/IEA.

— (2012): *World Energy Outlook 2012*, Paris: OECD/IEA.

IFPRI (International Food Policy Research Institute) (2010) *Global Hunger Index 2010: The Challenge of Hunger: Focus on the Crisis of Child Undernutrition*, Washington, DC: IFPRI.

Imhoff, D. (ed.) (2011) *The CAFO Reader: The Tragedy of Industrial Animal Factories*, Berkeley: University of California Press.

IPCC (Intergovernmental Panel on Climate Change) (2007) *Climate Change 2007: The Physical Science Basis, Contribution of Working Group I to the Fourth Assessment Report of the Intergovernmental Panel on Climate Change*, Cambridge: Cambridge University Press.

IUCN (International Union for Conservation of Nature) (2012) *The IUCN Red List of Threatened Species. Version 2012.1*, www.iucnredlist.org.

Jackson, W. (1985 [1980]) *New Roots for Agriculture*, 2nd edn, Lincoln: University of Nebraska Press.

Jarosz, L. (2009) 'Energy, climate change, meat and markets: mapping the coordinates of the current world food crisis,' *Geography Compass*, 3(6): 2065–83.

Jensen, D. (2006) *Endgame*, vol. 1: *The Problem of Civilization*; vol. 2: *Resistance*, New York: Seven Stories Press.

Johnsen, C. (2003) *Raising a Stink: The Struggle over Factory Farms in Nebraska*, Lincoln: University of Nebraska Press.

Johnson, A. (1991) *Factory Farming*, Oxford: Basil Blackwell.

Jorgenson, A. K. and B. Clark (2011) 'Societies consuming nature: a panel study of the ecological footprints of nations, 1960–2003,' *Social Science Research*, 40(1): 226–44.

Joshi, M., E. Hawkins, R. Sutton, J. Lowe and D. Frame (2011) 'Projections of when temperature change will exceed 2°c above pre-industrial levels,' *Nature Climate Change*, 1(8): 407–12.

Kaimowitz, D., B. Mertens, S. Wunder and P. Pacheco (2004) *Hamburger Connection Fuels Amazon Destruction*, Jakarta: Center for International Forestry Research.

Kanter, J. (2007) 'UN issues "final wake-up call" on population and environment,' *New York Times*, 25 October, www.nytimes.com/2007/10/25/world/europe/25iht-environ.4.8056185.html.

Keyzer, M. A., M. D. Merbis, I. F. P. W. Pavel and C. F. A van Wesenbeeck (2005) 'Diet shifts towards meat and the effects on cereal use: can we feed the animals in 2030?' *Ecological Economics*, 55(2): 187–202.

Kimbrell, A. (ed.) (2002) *The Fatal Harvest Reader: The Tragedy of Industrial Agriculture*, Washington, DC: Island Press.

Kirby, D. (2010) *Animal Factory: The Looming Threat of Industrial Pig, Dairy, and Poultry Farms to Humans and the Environment*, New York: St Martin's Press.

Kloppenburg, J. R. (2004) *First the Seed: The Political Economy of Plant Biotechnology*, 2nd edn, Madison: University of Wisconsin Press.

Kolpin, D. W., E. T. Furlong, M. T. Meyer, E. M. Thurman, S. D. Zaugg, L. B. Barber and H. T. Buxton (2002) 'Pharmaceuticals, hormones, and other organic wastewater contaminants in US streams, 1999–2000: a national reconnaissance,' *Environmental Science and Technology*, 36(6): 1202–11.

Koohafkan, P., M. A. Altieri and E. Holt-Giménez (2012) 'Green agriculture: foundations for biodiverse, resilient and productive agricultural systems,' *International Journal of Agricultural Sustainability*, 10(1): 61–75.

Lappé, A. (2010) *Diet for a Hot Planet: The Climate Crisis at the End of Your Fork and What You Can Do about It*, London: Bloomsbury.

Lappé, F. M. (1991 [1971]) *Diet for a Small Planet*, 3rd edn, New York: Ballantine.

Leakey, R. and R. Lewin (1995) *The Sixth Extinction: Patterns of Life and the Future of Humankind*, New York: Doubleday.

Leiztmann, C. (2003) 'Nutrition ecology: the contribution of vegetarian diets,' *American Journal of Clinical Nutrition*, 78(3S): S657–9.

Livingston, J. (1994) *Rogue Primate: An Exploration of Human Domestication*, Toronto: Key Porter Books.

Lovelock, J. (2007) *The Revenge of Gaia*, London: Penguin.

Lyman, H. (2001) *Mad Cowboy: Plain Truth from the Cattle Rancher Who Won't Eat Meat*, New York: Scribner.

Mackey, R. (2009) *The Atlas of Endangered Species*, Berkeley: University of California Press.

Mallin, M. and L. B. Cahoon (2003) 'Industrialized animal production – a major source of nutrient and microbial pollution to aquatic ecosystems,' *Population and Environment*, 24(5): 369–85.

Manning, R. (2004) 'The oil we eat: following the food chain back to Iraq,' *Harper's Magazine*, 308(1845): 37–45.

Mansfield, B. (2011) 'Modern industrial fisheries and the crisis of overfishing,' in R. Peet, P. Robbins and M. Watts (eds), *Global Political Ecology*, London: Routledge, pp. 51–66.

Marcus, E. (1998) *Vegan: The New Ethics of Eating*, Ithaca, NY: McBooks Press.

— (2005) *Meat Market: Animals, Ethics, and Money*, Boston, MA: Brio Press.

Marks, R. (2001) *Cesspools of Shame: How Factory Farm Lagoons and Sprayfields Threaten Environmental and Public Health*, Washington, DC: Natural Resources Defense Council and the Clean Water Network.

Mason, J. and P. Singer (1990 [1980]) *Animal Factories: What Agribusiness Is Doing to the Family Farm, the Environment and Your Health*, 2nd edn, New York: Harmony Books.

Masson, J. M. (2003) *The Pig Who Sang to the Moon: The Emotional World of Farm Animals*, New York: Ballantine.

— (2008) *The Face on Your Plate: The Truth About Food*, New York: W. W. Norton.

McCully, P. (2001) *Silenced Rivers: The Ecology and Politics of Large Dams*, 2nd edn, London: Zed Books.

McIntyre, B. D., H. R. Herren, J. Wakhungu and R. T. Watson (eds) (2009) *International Assessment of Agricultural Knowledge, Science and Technology for Development: Synthesis Report*, Washington, DC: Island Press.

McLaren, D. (2003) 'Environmental space, equity and the ecological debt,' in J. Agyeman, R. D. Bullard and B. Evans (eds), *Just Sustainabilities: Development in an Unequal World*, London: Earthscan, pp. 19–37.

McMichael, A. J., J. W. Powles, C. D. Butler and R. Uauy (2007) 'Food, livestock production, energy, climate change, and health,' *The Lancet*, 370: 1253–63.

McMichael, P. (2012) *Development and Social Change*, 5th edn, Thousand Oaks, CA: Sage.

MEA (Millennium Ecosystem Assessment) (2005) *Ecosystems and Human Well-being: Biodiversity Synthesis*, Washington, DC: Island Press.

Meadows, D. H., D. L. Meadows, J. Randers and W. W. Behrens (1972) *The Limits to Growth: A Report for the Club of Rome's Project on the Predicament of Mankind*, New York: Universe.

Mekonnen, M. M. and A. Y. Hoekstra (2012) 'A global assessment of the water footprint of farm animal products,' *Ecosystems*, 15(3): 401–15.

Melville, E. (1994) *A Plague of Sheep: Environmental Consequences of the Conquest of Mexico*, Cambridge: Cambridge University Press.

Merrifield, A. (2008) *The Wisdom of Donkeys: Finding Tranquillity in a Chaotic World*, Vancouver: Greystone.

Midkiff, K. (2004) *The Meat You Eat: How Corporate Farming Has Endangered America's Food Supply*, New York: St Martin's Press.

Monbiot, G. (2006) *Heat: How to Stop the Planet from Burning*, Toronto: Doubleday.

Monfreda, C., N. Ramankutty and J. A. Foley (2008) 'Farming the planet: 2. Geographic distribution of global agricultural lands in the year 2000,' *Global Biogeochemical Cycles*, 22(1): GB1003.

Montgomery, D. R. (2003) *King of Fish: The Thousand-year Run of Salmon*, Cambridge, MA: Westview.

— (2007) *Dirt: The Erosion of Civilizations*, Berkeley: University of California Press.

Moore, J. W. (2003): 'Nature and the transition from feudalism to capitalism,' *Review*, 26(2): 97–172.

— (2010a) 'The end of the road? Agricultural revolutions in the capitalist world-ecology, 1450–2010,' *Journal of Agrarian Change*, 10(3): 389–413.

— (2010b) 'Cheap food and bad money: food, frontiers, and financialization in the rise and demise of neoliberalism,' *Review*, 33(2/3): 225–61.

— (2011) 'Transcending the metabolic rift: a theory of crises in the capitalist world-ecology,' *Journal of Peasant Studies*, 38(1): 1–46.

— (forthcoming) *Ecology and the Accumulation of Capital*, London: Verso.

Motavalli, J. (2008) 'The meat of the matter: our livestock industry creates more greenhouse gas than transportation does,' *E Magazine*, July/Aug, pp. 27–32.

— (2009) 'Meat: the slavery of our time: how the coming vegetarian revolution will arrive by force,' *Foreign Policy*, 3 June, experts.foreignpolicy.com/posts/2009/06/03/meat_the_slavery_of_our_time.

Myers, N. (2002) 'Environmental refugees: a growing phenomenon of the 21st century,' *Philosophical Transactions of the Royal Society B*, 357(1420): 609–13.

Nally, D. (2011) *Human Encumbrances:*

Political Violence and the Great Irish Famine, South Bend, IN: University of Notre Dame Press.

Nash, R. (2001 [1967]) *Wilderness and the American Mind*, 4th edn, New Haven, CT: Yale University Press.

Nellemann, C., M. MacDevette, T. Manders, B. Eickhout, B. Svihus, A. G. Prins and B. P. Kaltenborn (eds) (2009) *The Environmental Food Crisis – the Environment's Role in Averting Future Food Crises*, UNEP, GRID-Arendal, Norway: Birkeland Trykkeri AS.

Nepstad, D. C. (2007) *The Amazon's Vicious Cycles: Drought and Fire in the Greenhouse*, Gland, Switzerland: WWF International.

Nepstad, D. C., C. M. Stickler, B. Soares-Filho and F. Merry (2008) 'Interactions among Amazon land use, forests and climate: prospects for a near-term forest tipping point,' *Philosophical Transactions of the Royal Society B*, 363: 1737–46.

Nestle, M. (2002) *Food Politics: How the Food Industry Influences Nutrition and Health*, Berkeley: University of California Press.

— (2008) *Pet Food Politics: The Chihuahua in the Coal Mine*, Berkeley: University of California Press.

Neumann, K., P. H. Verburg, E. Stehfest and C. Muller (2010) 'The yield gap of global grain production: a spatial analysis,' *Agricultural Systems*, 103(5), 316–26.

Nierenberg, D. (2005) *Happier Meals: Rethinking the Global Meat Industry*, Washington, DC: WorldWatch Paper #171.

NOAA/ESRL (National Oceanic and Atmospheric Administration/Earth System Research Laboratory) (2013) *Earth System Research Laboratory, Global Monitoring Division*, www.esrl.noaa.gov/gmd/ccgg/trends/.

Noble, D. F. (1999) *The Religion of Technology: The Divinity of Man and the Spirit of Invention*, New York: Penguin.

Opie, J. (2000 [1993]) *Ogallala: Water for a Dry Land*, 2nd edn, Lincoln: University of Nebraska Press.

Oreskes, N. and E. M. Conway (2010) *Merchants of Doubt: How a Handful of Scientists Obscured the Truth on Issues from Tobacco Smoke to Global Warming*, New York: Bloomsbury.

Pepper, D. (1984) *The Roots of Modern Environmentalism*, London: Croom Helm.

Pew Commission on Industrial Farm Animal Production (2008) *Putting Meat on the Table: Industrial Farm Animal Production in America*, Washington, DC: Pew Charitable Trusts and John Hopkins Bloomberg School of Public Health.

Pfeiffer, D. A. (2006) *Eating Fossil Fuels: Oil, Food and the Coming Crisis in Agriculture*, Gabriola Island, BC: New Society Publishers.

Pimentel, D. (2004) 'Ethical issues of global corporatization: agriculture and beyond,' *Poultry Science*, 83(3): 321–9.

— (2006) 'Soil erosion: a food and environmental threat,' *Environment, Development and Sustainability*, 8(1): 119–37.

Pimentel, D. and M. H. Pimentel (2003) 'Sustainability of meat-based and plant-based diets and the environment,' *American Journal of Clinical Nutrition*, 78(3S): S605–33.

— (2008 [1979]) *Food, Energy, and Society*, 3rd edn, Boca Raton, FL: CRC Press.

Ploeg, J. D. van der (2008) *The New Peasantries. Struggles for Autonomy and Sustainability in an Era of Empire and Globalization*, London: Earthscan.

— (2013) *Peasants and the Art of Farming*, Black Point, NS: Fernwood.

Pollan, M. (2006) *The Omnivore's*

Dilemma: A Natural History of Four Meals, New York: Penguin.

— (2008) *In Defence of Food: An Eater's Manifesto*, New York: Penguin.

Popkin, B. (2003) 'The nutrition transition in the developing world,' *Development Policy Review*, 21(5/6): 581–97.

— (2009) 'Reducing meat consumption has multiple benefits for the world's health,' *Archives of Internal Medicine*, 169(6): 543–5.

Postel, S. (1999) *Pillar of Sand: Can the Irrigation Miracle Last?*, New York: W. W. Norton.

Preece, R. (2002) *Awe for the Tiger, Love for the Lamb: A Chronicle of Sensibility to Animals*, Vancouver: UBC Press.

Pretty, J. (2008) 'Agricultural sustainability: concepts, principles and evidence,' *Philosophical Transactions of the Royal Society B*, 363(1491): 447–65.

Reisner, M. (1993) *Cadillac Desert: The American West and Its Disappearing Water*, 2nd edn, New York: Penguin.

Rifkin, J. (1992) *Beyond Beef: The Rise and Fall of the Cattle Culture*, New York: Dutton.

Ritzer, G. (2010 [1993]) *The McDonaldization of Society*, 6th edn, Thousand Oaks, CA: Sage.

Robbins, J. (1987) *Diet for a New America: How Your Food Choices Affect Your Health, Happiness and the Future of Life on Earth*, Walpole, NH: Stillpoint.

Robbins, P. (2003) *Stolen Fruit: The Tropical Commodities Disaster*, London: Zed Books.

Robin, M.-M. (2010) *The World According to Monsanto*, New York: New Press.

Rogelj, J., W. Hare, J. Lowe, D. P. van Vuuren, K. Riahi, B. Matthews, T. Hanaoka, K. Jiang and M. Meinshausen (2011) 'Emission pathways consistent with a 2°C global temperature limit,' *Nature Climate Change*, 1(8): 413–18.

Rosenzweig, C., D. Karoly, M. Vicarelli, P. Neofotis, Q. Wu, G. Casassa, A. Menzel, T. L. Root, N. Estrella, B. Seguin, P. Tryjanowski, C. Liu, S. Rawlins and A. Imeson (2008) 'Attributing physical and biological impacts to anthropogenic climate change,' *Nature*, 453(7193): 353–7.

Rostow, W. W. (1990 [1960]) *The Stages of Economic Growth: A Non-Communist Manifesto*, 3rd edn, Cambridge: Cambridge University Press.

Sabate, J. (2003) 'The contribution of vegetarian diets to health and disease: a paradigm shift,' *American Journal of Clinical Nutrition*, 78(3S): S502–7.

Sachs, W. (1999) *Planet Dialectics: Explorations in Environment and Development*, London: Zed Books.

Sage, C. (2012) *Environment and Food*, London: Routledge.

Sainz, R. D. (2003) 'Framework for calculating fossil fuel use in livestock systems,' *Livestock-Environment Initiative: Fossil Fuels Component*, Rome: FAO.

Sale, P. (2011) *Our Dying Planet: An Ecologist's View of the Crisis We Face*, Berkeley: University of California Press.

Sanbonmatsu, J. (2004) *The Postmodern Prince: Critical Theory, Left Strategy, and the Making of a New Political Subject*, New York: Monthly Review Press.

Sassen, S. (2013) 'Land grabs today: feeding the disassembling of national territory,' *Globalizations*, 10(1): 25–46.

Sauer, C. O. (1972 [1952]) *Seeds, Spades, Hearths, and Herds: The Domestication of Animals and Foodstuffs*, 3rd edn, Cambridge, MA: MIT Press.

Schindler, D. W. and J. R. Vallentyne (2008) *The Algal Bowl: Overfertilization of the World's Freshwaters and Estuaries*, Edmonton: University of Alberta Press.

Schlosser, E. (2001) *Fast Food Nation: The*

Dark Side of the All-American Meal, New York: Perennial.

Schmidhuber, J. and F. N. Tubiello (2007) 'Global food security under climate change,' *Proceedings of the National Academy of Sciences of the United States*, 104(50): 19703–8.

Schneider, M. (2011) *Feeding China's Pigs: Implications for the Environment, China's Smallholder Farmers and Food Security*, Minneapolis, MN: Institute for Agriculture and Trade Policy.

Shiva, V. (ed.) (2007) *Manifestos on the Future of Food and Seed*, Boston, MA: South End Press.

— (2008) *Soil Not Oil. Environmental Justice in an Age of Climate Crisis*, Boston, MA: South End Press.

Simon, J. (1981) *The Ultimate Resource*, Princeton, NJ: Princeton University Press.

Sinclair, U. (2003 [1906]) *The Jungle*, New York: Bantam.

Singer, P. (2002 [1975]) *Animal Liberation*, 3rd edn, New York: HarperCollins.

— (2003) 'Animal liberation at 30,' *New York Review of Books*, 50(8).

Singer, P. and J. Mason (2006) *The Way We Eat: Why Our Food Choices Matter*, Emmaus, PA: Rodale Press.

Smil, V. (2001) *Enriching the Earth: Fritz Haber, Carl Bosch, and the Transformation of Food Production*, Cambridge, MA: MIT Press.

Snapp, S. S., M. J. Blackie, R. A. Gilbert, R. Bezner-Kerr and G. Y. Kanyama-Phiri (2010) 'Biodiversity can support a greener revolution in Africa,' *Proceedings of the National Academy of Sciences*, 107(48): 20840–5.

Soulé, M. E. (1985) 'What is conservation biology?' *BioScience*, 35(11): 727–34.

Spiegel, M. (1996 [1988]) *The Dreaded Comparison: Human and Animal Slavery*, 2nd edn, New York: Mirror Books.

Standing Bear, L. (2006 [1933]) *Land of the Spotted Eagle*, Lincoln: University of Nebraska Press.

Stehfest, E., L. Bouwman, D. P. van Vuuren, M. G. J. den Elzen, B. Eickhout and P. Kabat (2009) 'Climate benefits of changing diet,' *Journal of Climate Change*, 95: 83–102.

Steinfeld, H., P. Gerber, T. Wassenaar, V. Castel, M. Rosales and C. de Haan (2006) *Livestock's Long Shadow: Environmental Issues and Options*, Rome: FAO.

Steingraber, S. (2010 [1997]) *Living Downstream: An Ecologist's Personal Investigation of Cancer and the Environment*, 2nd edn, Cambridge, MA: Da Capo Press.

Stull, D. and M. Broadway (2004) *Slaughterhouse Blues: The Meat and Poultry Industry in North America*, Belmont, CA: Thomas Wadsworth.

Stull, D., M. Broadway and D. Griffith (eds) (1995) *Any Way You Cut It: Meat Processing and Small-town America*, Lawrence: University of Kansas Press.

Tansey, G. and J. D'Silva (eds) (1999) *The Meat Business: Devouring a Hungry Planet*, New York: St Martin's Press.

Tilman, D., C. Balzer, J. Hill and B. L. Befort (2011) 'Global food demand and the sustainable intensification of agriculture,' *Proceedings of the National Academy of Sciences*, 108(50): 20260–4.

Tokar, B. (1997) *Earth for Sale: Reclaiming Ecology in the Age of Corporate Greenwash*, Boston, MA: South End Press.

— (2010) *Toward Climate Justice: Perspectives on the Climate Crisis and Social Change*, Porsgrunn, Norway: Communalism.

Torres, B. (2007) *Making a Killing: The Political Economy of Animal Rights*, Oakland, CA: AK Press.

Turner, G. (2008) 'A comparison of limits to growth with thirty years of reality,' *Global Environmental Change*, 18(3): 397–411.

Turzi, M. (2011) 'The Soybean Republic,' *Yale Journal of International Affairs*, 6(2): 59–67.

Ufkes, F. (1995) 'Lean and mean: US meat-packing in an age of agro-industrial restructuring,' *Environment and Planning D*, 13(6): 683–705.

UN (United Nations) (2009) *World Economic Situation and Prospects 2009*, New York: United Nations.

UN Water (2007) *Coping with Water Scarcity: Challenge of the twenty-first century*, New York: UN-Water, www.unwater.org/wwdo7/downloads/documents/escarcity.pdf.

UNDP (United Nations Development Programme) (1999) *Human Development Report 1998: Consumption for Human Development*, New York: Palgrave Macmillan.

— (2007) *Human Development Report 2007–8: Fighting climate change: Human solidarity in a divided world*, New York: Palgrave Macmillan.

UNEP (United Nations Environmental Programme) (1999) *Global Environment Outlook 2000: Overview*, Nairobi: UNEP.

— (2007) *Global Environment Outlook – 4: Environment for Development*, Valetta, Malta: Progress Press.

UNFCCC (United Nations Framework Convention on Climate Change) (2007) *Impacts, Vulnerabilities and Adaptation in Developing Countries*, Bonn, Germany: UNFCCC.

UNFPA (United Nations Population Fund) (2011) *The State of World Population: People and Possibilities in a World of 7 Billion*, New York: UNFPA.

USDA NASS (US Department of Agriculture, National Agricultural Statistics Service) (2008) *The Census of Agriculture, National Agricultural Statistics Service*, www.agcensus.usda.gov/Publications/2007/Full_Report/usv1.pdf, accessed 20 April 2011.

Vidal, J. (2010) 'Soil erosion threatens to leave Earth hungry,' *Guardian*, 14 December, www.guardian.co.uk/environment/2010/dec/14/soil-erosion-environment-review-vidal.

Vitousek, P., P. Ehrlich, A. Ehrlich and P. Matson (1986) 'Human appropriation of the products of photosynthesis,' *Bioscience*, 36(6): 368–73.

Wackernagel, M. and W. E. Rees (1996) *Our Ecological Footprint: Reducing Human Impact on the Earth*, Gabriola Island, BC: New Society Publishers.

Wackernagel, M., N. B. Schulz, D. Deumling, A. C. Linares, M. Jenkins, V. Kapos, C. Monfreda, J. Loh, N. Myers, R. Norgaard and J. Randers (2002) 'Tracking the ecological overshoot of the human economy,' *Proceedings of the National Academy of Sciences*, 99(14): 9266–71.

WCED (World Commission on Environment and Development) (1987) *Our Common Future*, New York: Oxford University Press.

Weber, C. L. and H. S. Matthews (2008) 'Food-miles and the relative climate impacts of food choices in the US,' *Environmental Science and Technology*, 42(10): 3508–13.

Weis, T. (2007) *The Global Food Economy: The Battle for the Future of Farming*, London: Zed Books.

— (2010a) 'The ecological hoofprint and the population bomb of reverse protein factories,' *Review*, 33(2/3): 131–52.

— (2010b) 'The accelerating biophysical contradictions of industrial capitalist agriculture,' *Journal of Agrarian Change*, 10(3): 315–41.

— (2013) 'The meat of the global food crisis,' *Journal of Peasant Studies*, 40(1): 65–85.

White, T. (2000) 'Diet and the distribution of environmental impact,' *Ecological Economics*, 34(1): 145–53.

Williams, A. (2004) 'Disciplining animals: sentience, production, and critique,'

International Journal of Sociology and Social Policy, 24(9): 45–57.

Williams, M. (2006) *Deforesting the Earth: From Prehistory to Global Crisis*, Chicago, IL: University of Chicago Press.

Wilson, E. O. (2002) *The Future of Life*, New York: Vintage.

Winders, B. (2009) *The Politics of Food Supply: US Agricultural Policy in the World Economy*, New Haven, CT: Yale University Press.

Winders, B. and D. Nibert (2004) 'Consuming the surplus: expanding "meat" consumption and animal oppression,' *International Journal of Sociology and Social Policy*, 24(9): 76–96.

Wright, R. (2004) *A Short History of Progress*, Toronto: Anansi.

WSPA–Canada (World Society for the Protection of Animals–Canada) (2012) *What's on Your Plate? The Hidden Costs of Industrial Animal Agriculture in Canada*, Toronto: WSPA.

WWAP (World Water Assessment Programme) (2009) *The United Nations World Water Development Report 3: Water in a Changing World*, Paris/London: UNESCO/Earthscan.

York, R. and M. H. Gossard (2004) 'Cross-national meat and fish consumption: exploring the effects of modernization and ecological context,' *Ecological Economics*, 48(3): 293–303.

York, R., E. A. Rosa and T. Dietz (2003) 'Footprints on the earth,' *American Sociological Review*, 68(2): 279–300.

INDEX

About Zed Books

Zed Books is a critical and dynamic publisher, committed to increasing awareness of important international issues and to promoting diversity, alternative voices and progressive social change. We publish on politics, development, gender, the environment and economics for a global audience of students, academics, activists and general readers. Run as a co-operative, Zed Books aims to operate
in an ethical and environmentally sustainable way.

Find out more at:

www.zedbooks.co.uk

For up-to-date news, articles, reviews and events information visit:

http://zed-books.blogspot.com

To subscribe to the monthly Zed Books e-newsletter, send an email headed 'subscribe' to:

marketing@zedbooks.net

We can also be found on **Facebook**, **ZNet**, **Twitter** and **Library Thing**.